PRAISE FOR SAVING ADAM SMITH

"Someone once said that you get knowledge from non-fiction, but you get wisdom from fiction. Jonathan Wight demonstrates this beautifully. Wight uses an entertaining and profound story to show how we can live a better life, have a better society, and serve the best in everyone by taking a broader view—one of both virtue and practicality. People of all ages, but particularly students, will have this book available to give them a deeper, more integrated view of what our world can be. This is a remarkable achievement and a fun read."

—Michael Ray
Professor, Stanford Graduate School of Business,
co-author, *Creativity in Business* and *The New Paradigm in Business*
and author, *Two Questions* (2002)

"*Saving Adam Smith* provides us an everyday look at traditional economic theory put into real-time business decision making ... a socially responsible approach to globalization. Anyone who talks about the 'invisible hand' and doesn't understand the moral context in which it operates has probably never read this book, nor ever had the pleasure of a campfire conversation with Adam Smith!"

—Daniel J. Gertsacov
CEO, Forum on Business and Social Responsibility in the Americas
(Forum EMPRESA)

"We all live in Adam Smith's economic world, but as Jonathan Wight's wise and witty story show us, it's not exactly the world that Smith had in mind. In his lively tale, Wight brings Smith back to remind economics students and readers of all stripe that we are not here to serve the economy, the economy is here to serve the needs of everyone in our society."

—Joanne B. Ciulla
Professor and Coston Family Chair in Leadership and Ethics,
University of Richmond and author of *The Working Life:
The Promise and Betrayal of Modern Work*

"Terrific.... [T]he book will make the ideas of Adam Smith much more accessible to high school and college students.... Adam Smith's philosophy emphasizing the virtue, morality, and trust that are needed for a market economy is right on the money for today. *Saving Adam Smith* [is] an outstanding addition to the economic theory novel genre."

—John Morton
Vice President, National Council on Economic Education

"Wight's tale of adventure presents Smith's insights about self-interest in the wider context of his social philosophy. The book challenges students—and economists—to follow Smith in making room for justice and conscience in economic choices."

—David C. Smith
President, Council for Ethics in Economics

"The story is engaging at several levels. I was drawn to keep reading it... This manuscript makes a real contribution."

—James Halteman
Carl R. Hendrickson Professor of Business and Economics,
Wheaton College

Saving Adam Smith

ISBN 0-13-065904-5

90000

9 780130 659040

FINANCIAL TIMES
Prentice Hall

In an increasingly competitive world, it is quality
of thinking that gives an edge—an idea that opens new
doors, a technique that solves a problem, or an insight
that simply helps make sense of it all.

We work with leading authors in the various arenas
of business and finance to bring cutting-edge thinking
and best learning practice to a global market.

It is our goal to create world-class print publications
and electronic products that give readers
knowledge and understanding which can then be
applied, whether studying or at work.

To find out more about our business
products, you can visit us at www.ft-ph.com

FINANCIAL TIMES PRENTICE HALL BOOKS

For more information, please go to www.ft-ph.com

JONATHAN B. WIGHT

Saving Adam Smith

A Tale of Wealth,

Transformation,

and Virtue

A CIP catalog record for this book can be obtained from the Library of Congress

Editorial/Production Supervision: *MetroVoice Publishing Services*
Acquisitions Editor: *Tim Moore*
Marketing Manager: *Debby van Dijk*
Manufacturing Manager: *Maura Zaldivar*
Cover Design Director: *Jerry Votta*
Cover Design: *Anthony Gemmellaro*
Interior Design: *Gail Cocker-Bogusz*
Project Coordinator: *Anne R. Garcia*

 © 2002 Prentice Hall PTR
Prentice-Hall, Inc.
Upper Saddle River, NJ 07458

Prentice Hall books are widely used by corporations and government agencies for training, marketing, and resale.

The publisher offers discounts on this book when ordered in bulk quantities.
For more information, contact: Corporate Sales Department, Phone: 800-382-3419;
Fax: 201-236-7141; Email: corpsales@prenhall.com; or write: Prentice Hall PTR,
Corp. Sales Dept., One Lake Street, Upper Saddle River, NJ 07458.

Printed in the United States of America

10   9   8   7   6   5   4   3   2   1

ISBN 0-13-065904-5

Pearson Education Ltd.
Pearson Education Australia PTY Ltd.
Pearson Education Singapore, Pte. Ltd.
Pearson Education North Asia Ltd.
Pearson Education Canada, Ltd.
Pearson Educación de Mexico, S.A. de C.V.
Pearson Education—Japan
Pearson Education Malaysia, Pte. Ltd.
Pearson Education, Upper Saddle River, New Jersey

CONTENTS

PREFACE

As one of the greatest minds of the Enlightenment, Adam Smith wrote with sharpness and wit across a spectrum of disciplines—the arts, natural sciences, law, politics, and economics (the latter subject firmly part and parcel of moral philosophy). Smith worked to develop a system of thought that would unify the branches of "human" science, specifically in the realm of markets and morals. This unifying moral vision is a long-neglected area for economists—and has become increasingly important with the intensifying debate about globalization. As emerging market economies throw off old structures, they are discovering they may not have in place the balancing social and institutional structures that developed democracies take for granted. Put simply, Adam Smith would not be pleased if wealth were uncoupled from its moral foundations. What are the practical implications of Smith's ideas, one wonders, for the world of business today?

Saving Adam Smith tackles this issue as a fanciful work of "academic" fiction. In it, the "father" of economics introduces readers to the global economy and to the moral roots that sustain it. International trade and specialization are the cornerstones through which businesses create wealth, but Smith gives a powerful warning: free society and markets are threatened by a disregard for fundamentals—principally, a concern for justice and the cultivation of virtue. These are essential elements if a commercial system is to be made sustainable over the generations with a minimum of government intrusion.

In the midst of plenty there are also those who face profound psychological and spiritual challenges. Smith notes that the unbridled pursuit of riches "corrupts," robbing us of the very things that can provide meaning and ultimate happiness: the development of a moral conscience based on genuine feeling for other human beings. Smith thus anticipates the rise of a values-based business model that in Smith's words unites, "the best head to the best heart." Economic efficiency and virtue are mutually reinforcing.

Adam Smith speaks to us with an urgency that is as real today as it was at the dawn of the Industrial Revolution. Smith's own words are used throughout this novel, although his sentences are at times shortened or paraphrased to maintain the flow of dialogue. Interested readers will find the sources of Smith's writings in the annotated notes. The Appendices also provide a guide to course instructors, a timeline of Smith's life, and suggestions for further reading.

As to whether the sublime Adam Smith would approve of using his words in a fanciful work of fiction, he has this to say:

> *It is only the teller of Ridiculous Stories that can be at all tollerable in conversation, as we know his design is harmless so we are readily inclined to grant him some licence* (Lectures on Rhetoric and Belles Letters, p. 119).

In that spirit, let us listen to the "father"—and perhaps also the wise "mother"—of modern economics and business.

—J.B.W.

DISCLAIMER

Except where otherwise noted, all characters in this book are purely fictitious, and bear no intended resemblance to any real persons, living or dead. Hearst College of Fredericksburg, the World Chemical and Material Supply Corporation (WorldChemm) of San Francisco, People Over Profit (POP), Mammoth Oil Company, and the Workplace Fair Conduct Association (WFCA), are all fictitious creations, and bear no intended resemblance to any real organizations, past or present.

WEALTH

"Every economic act, being the action of a human being, is necessarily also a moral act."

—WILLIAM LETWIN,
THE ORIGINS OF SCIENTIFIC ECONOMICS (1964)

1 ADAM RISING

The man arrived with the downpour. It was a distinctive Virginia thunderstorm, dark bulbous clouds rising and swirling in the early evening. Gusts of spring air tore at the patio umbrella and rain began to flow like a wide-open faucet, hitting the ground and splashing up the glass door to the deck. Rex, my eight-year-old collie, raced from room to room barking at thunder. I went upstairs to close windows, then heard a banging that sounded like a loose shutter. Through the glass I spied a dilapidated car resting at the curb. A figure huddled on my stoop, drawing on the butt of a cigarette. He rapped again impatiently—a knock that would turn my orderly and solitary life upside down, lead me on a barnstorming flight across America, and very nearly cost me my life.

None of this I suspected as I examined the silhouette on the front porch. I flipped a light switch and the figure materialized into an elderly man about six feet tall. Short white hair ringed the sides of his bald pate. He leaned into the inadequate shelter, glancing about awkwardly. I pulled Rex aside, and opened the door. The man sighed, showing large teeth.

"Dr. Burns? I came to see D—Dr. Richard Burns?" he stuttered.

"I'm *Mr.* Burns," I said, keeping the screen door latched.

The man tried to smile, but the lips turned into a frown. He spoke as if in a slumber. "Julia Brooks gave me your name. From church."

I raised an eyebrow.

"She said you teach at the college."

I nodded.

His brown eyes appraised me and could not contain their disappointment. "You're so young..." He began to turn away, then apparently changed his mind. "Ahh. Maybe you can help. I need to talk to someone ... someone who knows an older economist."

The man had a curious, old-world accent, muffled by the hammering rain. He raised his voice. "He's not old, I mean— he's from a long time ago. Some guy called 'Adam Smith.' You ever hear of him?"

My face flushed. "Some guy" called Adam Smith? Some guy? The rain bore down. Rex pawed the carpet behind me, which was odd. Normally he'd weasel past to greet any guest.

"Adam Smith—the 'father' of economics?" I asked.

"Yeah, that must be him."

I hesitated a moment then opened the screen door. He shook off a spray of water and stepped inside. The living room lamp betrayed an older gentleman, his face flushed and heavily lined, bearing a prominent nose. A damp white mustache hung over his thin, pressed lips. The man melted into the couch and I perched at the other end. I glanced at my watch: Five minutes to my favorite television show.

"Been a rough couple of weeks," the man said weakly. His black work boots oozed rainwater onto my rug.

I examined the man with a mixture of curiosity and impatience. Despite his disheveled appearance, there was an incongruous dignity to his bearing. Had it not been Julia who'd sent him, though, he probably wouldn't have made it inside the door. But Julia had said, some time ago, that moral posturing without action was just talk. Whether the words were her own, or she'd quoted someone, didn't matter. They stung, and busy as I was, I forced myself to show patience.

He cleared his throat. "Where to begin? Might as well go back to April, I guess, three or four weeks ago, when I started having strange dreams. I call them dreams because the voice started at night when I was asleep. But it went on after I woke up." His voice cracked. "Scares me to death! Sounds like a sermon, ringing in my ears. Ahh!"

He dropped his head and his shoulders began to shake.

Rex whined under me. He wasn't barking, and that was to the credit of my damp visitor. But he showed wariness, and I echoed that and reached down to give him a rub behind the ears.

"Been a rough couple weeks," the man sobbed, wiping an eye. "This babbling in my mind, night and day, this voice going non-stop in my head." He rummaged in his grease-stained jacket. "Mind if I smoke?" He changed his mind and stuffed the cigarettes back. "I think I'm going crazy."

Where did Julia Brooks find these people? I went to the kitchen and brought out a saucer for an ashtray. He lit up, flicking the spark on a dented Zippo lighter. He drew deeply. "This voice ... it does not make sense, not to me anyhow. Something about 'setting the world straight.' What does that mean? Dr. Burns, I'm a truck mechanic, I fix diesel engines. What do I know about fixing the world? This voice keeps going on and on and on. That's when I told myself, 'Harold, get some help.'"

"Harold?"

"My name—Harold Timms." He offered a hand. His accent sounded vaguely European, but his name gave no clues; I'm an economist, not a linguist.

"Where're you from?" I asked.

"Romania, many years ago," he replied, squeezing my hand.

At the end of my second year of teaching at Hearst College, in Fredericksburg, I was completely spent—exhausted by stacks of grading, drained by interminable faculty meetings, and frayed by an endless struggle to finish my doctoral thesis. My side table held a pile of unanswered Christmas cards. My laundry basket overflowed. The aroma of my microwave chicken dinner wafted in from the kitchen, and my stomach growled.

Harold Timms drew on the cigarette again and looked off into a corner at nothing. Apparently, there would be no short version to his story. Somehow he mistook me for a medical doctor, and letting him continue would be dishonest, not to mention take up time to no purpose. Julia or not, I made a decision.

"Interesting," I said, rising to my feet. I used his clinging hand to help him up. "You know, there are good medicines for what ails you, Mr. Timms, all kinds of things these days." I steered him to the front hall. "But I'm afraid there's a big mistake; I'm not a doctor that could prescribe any of them for you."

He looked stunned. "But you've got to help me!"

"I'm sure Julia can recommend a good physician. I'd be wasting your time."

I opened the door and he lumbered out. He stood with his feet spread, round eyes gaping at me like an abandoned pet. Canned laughter emanated from the television set and rain blew in the entryway.

"Good luck!" I waved my hand and shut the door slowly.

Something nagged at me. I reopened the door. The forlorn figure hadn't budged.

"What does this have to do with Adam Smith?" I asked.

"It's *him*," he said. "He's taken over my mind! Wants the whole world to hear him out … or *else!*"

Shaking my head, I closed the door on the madman.

2 HIGHER AND DEEPER

Professor Robert Allen Lattimer, holder of the Adam Smith Chair in Economics, sat across the table from me at the Old Ebbett Grill in downtown Washington, D.C. Lattimer carried himself with the dignity of his exalted position, reaching six feet two inches toward the ceiling, with erect posture and closely cropped gray hair. The buzz cut gave him the rugged bearing of a military man, and his extreme devotion to punctuality and schedules fit the image.

As he often did, Lattimer hopped the shuttle from his academic post in Boston to consult with movers-and-shakers in the nation's capital. This time it was across the street at the Treasury Department, where the Indonesian default crisis was the topic *du jour*. Since Hearst College was only fifty miles away in Fredericksburg, it was my custom and Lattimer's expectation that I fill-in spare time: a sandwich grabbed on the run or a drink at the airport. Today I got lucky and we actually sat at a restaurant table for lunch.

"You won't believe what happened yesterday," I said, after ordering a club sandwich and a beer. "This old man shows up at my door in the pouring rain…"

He cut me short. "Look, Burns, save the chitchat for later. What have you got for WorldChemm?"

Lattimer, blunt as usual, reserved social pleasantries for his equals. There was little evidence of that here. He held the power of God over me, which is to say, he directed my doctoral dissertation. I'd been his teaching and research assistant since my second year of graduate school. It was an exhilarating honor to be selected by the great Lattimer, a dark horse for the Nobel, but it meant I had no life of my own. Everything revolved around his schedule, his needs, his agenda. Today his agenda was WorldChemm, the World Chemical and Material Supply Corporation. WorldChemm got its start as a small lab in San Francisco making chemicals for the Second World War, then grew into a diversified manufacturing and raw materials conglomerate, with operations in thirty-five countries. Lattimer's renown in international economics made him a prize catch for their board.

Lattimer fancied himself the architect of the post-Cold War global economy. As a phenomenally creative researcher, he had more government grants, consulting opportunities, and publishing requests than time to fulfill them. The collapse of the Soviet Union produced worldwide domino effects, and theorists like Lattimer helped fill the inevitable void in power and ideas. His now-famous reform slogan "S–L–P" ("Stabilize! Liberalize! Privatize!") played a highly visible role in government retrenchments and deregulations around the world. S–L–P called for slashing budget deficits, eliminating subsidies, and opening markets to competition and free trade. Socialist industries were dismantled and privatized, with global multinational companies providing the greater part of the capital and technology to rebuild transition economies.

These policy prescriptions made Lattimer a celebrity at international conferences, Cabinet dinners in Georgetown, and weekend retreats on Long Island with Wall Street financiers. All the while, Lattimer was burned in effigy in the despairing barrios of Rio de Janeiro, Lagos, and Jakarta. Indeed, this morning's newspaper, at Lattimer's elbow, blared in front page headline that rioters were looting the Indonesian capital in reaction to price controls being lifted from food. A photo of Lattimer carried the caption, "Foreign Advisor Stands Firm on Restructuring." A quote attributed to him was typically unsympathetic: "The former president fleeced the country for decades, and now the man on the street blames the IMF? Hey, there's no such thing as a free lunch. Gotta be pain before you see gain." Whether true or not, Lattimer's unvarnished blasts did little to win sympathy outside the audience of central bankers and finance ministers.

One day after class I'd shared with Lattimer the hunch that now formed the basis of my dissertation, namely, that it was possible to construct a dynamic model of stock market valuation in a country undergoing rapid restructuring, and even in a country so recently socialist as Russia. Lattimer seized on the idea, and before a month was out, he'd lined up summer support from the economics department, and I was officially one of his protégés.

Through Lattimer, quite a few multinational companies took interest in my progress, WorldChemm among them. Of course, my work was theoretical; I spoke no Russian, had never been to Russia, and knew only a smattering of its history. But I did know enough theoretical finance and mathematics to wow WorldChemm's project leaders on the implications for privatized asset values. At least on paper.

The gas lights at the Old Ebbett Grill were dimmed, even at lunch, to create the illusion of privacy in a city of rampant egos and a pestilent press. Even in this gloom my eyes were drawn to a fortyish-looking man two tables over, nursing a beer. He focused intently on our table, seemingly trying to lip-read our conversation. Our eyes locked for an instant before his darted away.

"Are you listening, Burns?"

"That fellow over there. Do you know him?"

Lattimer swiveled, and quickly turned back. "Max Hess," he grimaced. "One of my biggest mistakes. A helluva way to ruin the day."

Max Hess rose and approached our table. He was short and wiry like a pent-up spring. Blonde hair cascaded over his open shirt collar.

"Ah, the great Doctor Lattimer," he said.

Lattimer ignored the man. Undeterred, Hess stood by our table bearing down. "How is he today, the God of free markets?" he asked.

"I'm in a meeting," Lattimer said. "Do you mind?"

"You have a roof on your head and something good to eat," Hess said. "What do you say to the billion children without these?"

Lattimer said nothing, seeking the eye of the house manager.

The man went on, scorn in his tone. "S—L—P." He spit out the syllables. "The poor people starve with unemployment and that you call *stabilization*! The price of milk and bread go too high and that you call *liberalization*! The elite steal the money of the nation and that you call *privatization*!"

Lattimer's eyes were slits. Given his Marine background, I didn't think it would be much longer before Hess got an earful of Lattimer's unusual and colorful phraseology.

"The Third World is raped for the export profit," Hess continued. "And why is that? Just to repay the fat foreign banker?"

The house manager arrived and Hess edged away. "You are an evil man, Doctor Lattimer." Hess's cold gray eyes met mine. "And who is he, your new minion?" A shiver went down my spine as he departed.

Lattimer shook his head. "GRE scores couldn't have predicted that one. His were solid 800s."

"A student of yours?" I asked.

He nodded. "Twenty years ago. A German boy, perfectly normal. Then he spent a summer doing field work in Bolivia and came back spouting Che Guevarra."

"And his dissertation?"

Lattimer pursed his lips. "Mumbo jumbo about class warfare. Not one equation in the whole damn thing. I couldn't let it get through."

"And now?"

"He shows up here and there, always insulting. I don't think he's ever found a job." Lattimer shrugged. "Hazards of the profession, I guess. Anyway, back to business." He stirred his coffee. "WorldChemm liked the last section, Burns. Quite good stuff. When do I see the final chapter?"

"It's almost done," I lied, averting his eyes. The stuffed walrus head over the bar glared down at me ominously.

Lattimer looked like he was going to snap. "Hell, I'm not telling you anything the market isn't whispering anyway, Burns, even that fool Hess probably knows." He leaned toward me, lowering his voice to a whisper. "WorldChemm's gonna bid on the Russian aluminum industry! It'll be the biggest goddamn privatization the world's ever seen."

I let out a whistle. "So that's their interest in my dissertation."

"Bingo." Lattimer was about to continue then stopped. "You enjoy doing things your own way, Burns," he finally said, "you always have, like you've got some goddamned chip on your shoulder." He smiled grimly. "Except there's a helluva lot of anchovies riding on this one. Your model would give World-Chemm a huge edge in negotiating." He leaned back into the green velour seat. "Could be worth a billion dollars to World-Chemm on a deal this big."

I swallowed.

"They can't wait forever, Burns. Besides, you think Craig Mansfield and his team in Palo Alto are twiddling their thumbs? You've got a head start, Burns, and I'll be damned if Stanford beats us to publishing this."

Lattimer downed his drink. "With everything else you've done, it'll be a hell of an impressive dissertation. One of my best."

Like many professors, Lattimer treated the output of his doctoral students as proprietary. Woe to the Ph.D. candidate who didn't add Lattimer's name to published papers. Lattimer's legacy was his cadre of doctoral students; without them, who would pass on the torch of his greatness? Who would do the work for which he received credit?

"It's goddamn hard recruiting top students these days," Lattimer went on to say. "There're few good Americans anymore: they'd all rather chase ambulances as class-action lawyers. Our supply in Latin America's drying up, and the West Coast gobbles up most of the Asian market."

He exhaled. "That reminds me, Burns, I've passed your early chapters to the Samuelson Committee." I froze. He smiled slyly as though my discomfort was a joke. "They'll send them out for review, of course, but on first pass, they were damn impressed. Congratulations."

I was nominated for the Samuelson Prize, the most prestigious award given to any economics graduate student! My mind swirled, and what Lattimer said next flew over my head. I caught the tail end of a sentence.

"…on September 8. Can you make it?"

My mind was blank.

"Wake up, Burns! Can you make it or not?"

"Uhh, sure."

"Good. Edda will send you the details. Don't screw up on this, Burns," he said. "It's my ass on the line."

It amazed me that someone who spoke so crudely could be an endowed chair at a distinguished university. Then I remembered President Nixon's secret White House tapes, filled with expletives that would shock a sailor. America's social structure is so fluid that success never guarantees social graces.

As the waiter prepared our bill, I suddenly remembered my visitor from the evening before. "By the way, the strangest thing happened last night," I said.

Lattimer raised an eyebrow.

"A man shows up at my door in the pouring rain, says he's having hallucinations, that a 'voice' has taken over his mind! Get this, you'll find this ironic," I chuckled, "he says it's the voice of Adam Smith!"

"Look, Burns, I'd love to chat." Lattimer glanced at his watch and withdrew a cell phone from his coat. "My flight leaves in a couple hours. I've got some calls." Lattimer was already talking elsewhere as I rose, feeling like a servant dismissed. Fishing money from my wallet I over-tipped, sure beyond doubt that Lattimer would err in the opposite direction.

✳   ✳   ✳

The train ride back to Fredericksburg gave me time to ponder my long-running relationship with Lattimer. As much as I owed him for his sponsorship, it grated that he took this sudden interest in my finishing. I was an "ABD" (all but dissertation)—someone who had finished the course requirements for a Ph.D. but not the doctoral thesis. This made me dead in the job market, forced to accept slave wages. It worked out splendidly for Lattimer and the handful of other professors who treated graduate students as indentured servants.

I'd met many professors who were the very opposite of Lattimer, but it was my luck to get the odd one like him. Blinded by his wide reputation, I'd thought about little else. I made my choice of advisor after weighing the costs and benefits, forgetting one of the first lessons of economics: the true cost of something is often hidden. I realized, only after my fifth year, that I'd never finish being wedded to Lattimer. So, I bucked the system and abandoned the ivied halls of Cambridge, in the academic heart of Boston, for the brick halls of Hearst College, in Virginia, a place where I could focus on students and work alone. At least that was the plan. Lattimer fought my decision and never let up. Once his man, always his man; and as long as he directed my dissertation, he had me over the gunwale of his ship, sailing in his direction. The project for WorldChemm was presented as an unspoken ultimatum: accept it or Lattimer would drop out as my dissertation advisor. Finding another chair, this late in my graduate studies, was virtually unthinkable.

The train slowed and the air horn wailed as we ambled through the town of Quantico. In the distance I saw Marines in shorts and T-shirts jogging along a tree-lined avenue. In a moment the train increased speed as it paralleled the Potomac River. Through the trees were sandy beaches punctuated by massive sandstone boulders. Soon, the train clung to the edge of the bank, and the river broadened into a wide body of water. The afternoon sun shimmered, and a brisk wind whipped whitecaps. On the right, a stately colonial home stood alone in a field, looking as if it withstood the British fleet's incursion up the Potomac in 1776.

My thoughts rambled with the train, and I admitted to myself that I'd simply gone along with Lattimer today. I'd lied. I'd been "economical" with the truth, telling him what he wanted to hear. Truth is, I was nowhere close to finishing the last chapter of my dissertation. Three times I'd written it, and shelved each draft. I had the ingredients but they didn't coalesce. Something was missing. Maybe what I had was good enough to get by, and maybe Lattimer wanted to appease WorldChemm enough that it didn't matter. Certainly I couldn't win the Samuelson Prize unless I finished.

Back in my office in Fredericksburg I phoned Lattimer's number in Cambridge. Edda McCory answered on the first ring. While the epitome of secretarial efficiency, Edda was also the heart of the economics department. She remembered birthdays, sent flowers to the ill, and proffered a gentle shoulder and sympathetic ear. After exchanging warm greetings, Edda asked about my life. For the second time that day I lied, assuring her everything was fine, then inquired about the mystery meeting in September.

"September 8?" Edda paused, and I could hear pages turning. "That's WorldChemm's annual meeting, at their headquarters in San Francisco. Dr. Lattimer asked me to make reservations for you. You're giving a presentation to the Board."

I whistled under my breath. The date was set, my final chapter due. I stared in exasperation at the mass of papers on my desk. It was high time to finish, yet I wallowed.

*   *   *

At my town house a few hours later I fixed a nightcap of Drambuie, sitting back with Rex spread over my lap. The black highlights of his honey-colored fur gave his eyes a streak of mascara. A solid white collar was likewise interrupted by patches of dark, picked up again in the tail; each paw was a white snowball: he was no show dog.

Scratching Rex's ears relaxed me as much as it did him. My lunch with Lattimer was enough to get my stomach churning. On top of that was the run-in with Max Hess, the ex-graduate student with a venomous stare. And last night's visitor was in his own way intimidating—Harold Timms, insisting that Adam Smith had taken over his nutty mind. What odd characters invaded my world these last twenty-four hours.

Rex yawned, looking up at me with brown eyes. I could almost call them innocent eyes were it not for the mischief I knew Rex was capable of inventing. This time I wondered if I saw a glimmer of reproach in his eyes for how I'd handled Harold Timms last night. I took a sip of Drambuie. All in the past, I mused.

3 A DANGEROUS BUSINESS

Two weeks later, Julia Brooks and I met at the church library that served as a lounge. Our handshake was friendly, almost affectionate. Somewhere in the genuine glitter of her smile was a hint of that time, a year ago, when we'd shared a few dinners. I'd seen little of her since, except at church. Julia was my age, nearing thirty, but the sort of woman who could appear child-like or sophisticated by a quick upsweep of her long brown hair. Her petite build gave a hint of curves. I'd always found her disarmingly attractive.

"Thanks for coming," she said, her green eyes somewhere between apologetic and reproachful.

I'd been thinking over what I might say at this meeting, but having her in front of me made me a little less certain. I poured a cup of coffee, she a cup of tea with milk, and we settled onto a worn couch.

"Sorry to involve you in this," she said, traces of her ties to England slipping through in her accent. "The Reverend and I are at a loss. You're the only economist we know."

I gave her a tentative smile. "I can't help this Harold Timms fellow."

"The poor man's going absolutely looney. It's been almost two months since this voice started in his mind." She shook her head. "Channeling isn't his choice, by the way, it's an obsession. Awfully dangerous." She looked at me squarely. "He needs to talk to you."

"Perhaps he should see an exorcist?" I winked, hoping for a laugh. Her lips pinched tighter, and I realized that her opinion of me mattered.

She took a breath and expelled it as a sigh. "Believe me, Rich, this isn't demonic possession. It's not madness, either."

I mumbled "Hmm" and sipped my coffee. Her eyes were pools of liquid sorrow, stirred for a moment. "How do you know?" I asked.

"I've been through it all before," she said, her voice thickening. "You may remember, my mum and dad were missionaries. We lived in Nigeria among the Yoruba. I came to appreciate, if not accept for myself, their worldview that ancestors inhabit the earth, in a spiritual form. They contact spirits for healing and guidance. In America the practice became vilified as 'voodoo'—quite misunderstood."

"How'd you get involved?"

"Before art, I dabbled in anthropology. I even wrote my master's thesis on *candomblé*. Ever hear of it?"

I shook my head.

"African slaves taken to the New World were stripped of their religions. Banning these spiritual practices didn't make them go away, they just went underground. Drums were used to call the spirits, and that's where Brazilian *samba* comes from. In America, you've got the blues."

"Interesting," I said, "but out of my academic realm."

"This isn't academic to me, it's personal." She crossed her arms. "Harold went to the Reverend for help, and the Reverend asked for mine. Harold's channeling someone good and kind, with a terrible urgency to be heard."

"So it seems."

"His wife died a year ago. He's been unhappy and bitter, with outbursts of anger—revealing, I think, loneliness and fear. He has no family near, and he's lost his friends. Along comes this voice jabbering in his head twenty-four hours a day. He can't sleep. He can't work."

"Maybe he's speaking in tongues," I said, making sure Julia saw my grin.

"Speaking in tongues?" echoed a deep voice from behind me. I turned. It was the Reverend. He had his head cocked and his hands on his hips a few yards away. He was a broad-shouldered man with silver hair and steel-rimmed wire glasses. His short-sleeved black shirt was set off by a white clerical collar.

"It's Harold Timms," Julia said, "he's speaking in tongues, babbling economics."

"Speaking in tongues is a gift of the Holy Spirit." The Reverend had a resonating baritone, developed in a Chicago slum. "I've heard of American Indians—shamans—talking to spirits. Does it strike you as odd, Rich?" He greeted me with a pat on the shoulder.

"Very odd."

"Well, I just got a phone message from Harold. Bad news, I'm afraid. He's lost his job at the garage."

Julia slapped the arm of the couch. "Oh no!"

"You can't fight change," the Reverend said, "you've got to face it." He turned to leave. "I'd better go see him."

"I don't see why Harold needs *me*," I said to Julia.

"You've got the background to understand what this voice is saying. Harold can't possibly do that, nor could a doctor who would just drug him into silence. If he resolves this Harold will be free to reclaim his life. Rich, promise me you'll help? Besides, it's summer. You've got free time now, don't you?"

Time is money, I thought, but instead I said, "I'm really busy."

"Who isn't?" She gave me a look from those sparkling eyes, and I found myself regretting my flip words.

I was not an extrovert, and sharing my life's problems was not something I did naturally. It made me feel vulnerable, especially with a beautiful woman whom I'd once dated. I pulled a crumpled letter from my pocket. It was from the Provost at Hearst College.

"Listen," I said, imitating the stilted cadence of the Provost, "Renewal of your fall contract is contingent upon satisfactory completion of a terminal degree."

"I understand the words," she said quietly, "but what does it mean?"

"I need to finish my dissertation or I'm canned." I stood, not waiting for her response, but mumbling mostly to myself, "It's mid-June and I need two papers accepted, in good journals, or I'll never win the Samuelson Prize. Can't you see? I don't have time."

She was impassive. Then she said, "Perhaps you've more time than you think." Her response was penetrating because it revealed how well she knew me. Harold, my research papers, the Provost—they were not excuses, but fears. More important, she seemed to know the secret to them.

*   *   *

Julia's quaint federal house, across the Rappahannock River in Falmouth, was one of the few surviving from colonial times. Its wood siding was freshly whitened, the red tin roof neatly painted. Her few pieces of furniture were an eclectic mix of antique and modern, blended to create a warm environment despite the sparseness.

Julia, Harold, and I sat in the living room. It was already a hot morning. How I ended up there was not entirely clear to me. I knew I didn't understand Julia, not very well, even as I was drawn to her once again. I loved the control she seemed to have over her life, so unlike my own. That realization both shamed and encouraged me. A few days ago I had felt like water rushing into a vortex, and today I was doing what she wanted, and not just for her sake.

On the coffee table was a small tape recorder placed between Harold Timms and me. We were an unlikely pair: blood vessels lined his curved nose, descending from outsized brown eyes. His portly jowls bore long sideburns. By contrast, my black beard hid childish cheeks, and my hair lapped the back of my collar. Tortoise shell glasses perched on my nose. Unlike Harold's paunch, my stomach was lean and tight, much of that from stress.

Julia sat across the room. She watched me as I strained to be obliging to Harold Timms: "What should I call you then … Dr. Smith? Or, Professor Smith?"

Harold Timms covered a cough and closed his eyes. When the eyes re-opened a new voice became eerily apparent, strong but hoarse. A crisp British inflection obliterated his stutter.

"Call me … Smith. Plain Smith will do."

I sat upright, startled by the stark change. I searched Julia's reaction, but she was looking down, listening intently.

"Where do we start?" I said. "I've never done this before." My embarrassment showed.

"Leave it to me," he said with authority. "The record needs setting straight, and I'm the one to do it. People have such an abominable view of me. I've become a caricature! Oh, it's not my pride talking, I tell you our very liberty hangs in the balance!"

The Free World about to collapse? I kept a straight face.

Harold curled his hand into a fist and brought it to his mouth. His teeth clenched the knuckle of his forefinger. I waited for him to speak. He said nothing, nothing at all. I used the silence to peruse the room. Every wall was covered with panels of Julia's framed art, each one a bright pastel of over-sized flowers, with giant and beautiful insects on them. In one a black widow spider perched on a leaf, its belly glistening. I nodded at the canvas, then at Julia. She nodded back, smiling.

The voice continued intensely. "Our system of commerce is under attack, and people are scurrying around like ants on a pot of honey, no one attending to the big questions. The *fundamentals*. Oh, you may laugh, but without that, civilized society is lost, adrift." He rapped the arm of the chair. "I address this in particular to my fellow economists!"

"Like hell," I muttered.

"What did you say?" The man's eyes narrowed.

"Economists idolize Adam Smith," I said. "If we were a Catholic order, Smith would be our patron saint."

He shook his head. "Economists may honor me with their lips, but not with their hearts. In vain do they worship me, teaching their own precepts as my doctrines."

Julia inclined her head. "That's the Gospel of Mark, isn't it?"

"Economists stoke the flame of free markets and promote the workings of the 'invisible hand,'" I said. "I'm afraid you're woefully unaware of events in Asia, Africa, and elsewhere. Even in Russia, of all places, they're privatizing industry."

"You've got half of it." He lumbered to his feet, towering over me. He shuffled to the window and turned back, his large hands on his hips. "You've got wick and you've got wax, but a candle won't burn without oxygen."

"Meaning?"

"I'm delighted with the move to free markets, don't misunderstand. The reason I've come back, and by God, it wasn't easy—you try getting through the mind of Harold!—is because you've all missed the essence of what makes a market work in society. In *society*, do you see?"

I was about to ask what in blazes sociology had to do with modern economics when Julia walked over to this "Smith" and sat tentatively on the edge of the couch.

"You know, there's one thing ... one thing that doesn't seem to fit," she said. "Your accent is English, not Scottish."

I raised my eyebrows, "Ah-hah."

The figure stared back impassively.

Julia continued, "That's easy for a Yank to miss, but I'm English, you know. And Rich told me the real Adam Smith was Scottish."

Julia glanced at me, then back at Harold.

He worked his mouth around like he was chewing a wad of tobacco, which he wasn't. At last he said, "If yew like, I kin imitate a pearrfect brogue. Would that warm yer hearts? Wood yew like to heer a Highlands tune? Am I to dew a jig? Wear a kilt and blow the pipes? Wood that be yir proof?"

Julia and I were speechless.

"Ah doot a fellah," he continued, "kin nai mair forgit 'is past than divine 'is future."

"But how—"

"There's no mystery," he said, reverting to highbrow English. "All my Scottish mentors had superior English accents and so do I. After all, I could scarcely have survived my studies in England rolling my R's. Anyone sounding like a Scot was liable to be bludgeoned for it. There was a Civil War, you know! The Jacobites rose up against the English in—oh, the year means little to you—1745."

He slapped the palm of his hand against the arm rest. "I'm a pragmatist, not a fool, so I adapted. I became inconspicuous by speaking the mother tongue that ruled, and why not? The Scottish of my day was a corrupted language. How could there be scientific progress in that mishmash of idioms?"

Smith mused for a moment, then said, "You might even like to know, I got my start in life as a teacher of rhetoric—yes, and even literature. That's when I was unemployed, a few years out of graduate school, and living at home with my mother. A friend suggested I go to Edinburgh and give public classes. It didn't hurt my fees, having that Oxbridge accent, quite the opposite. Those lectures helped me earn a faculty position at Glasgow a few years later."

I looked at Julia.

"'Oxbridge' is short for Oxford and Cambridge," she said. "It's the caviar of education, an intellectual gentleman's posh polish."

I scrunched my eyebrows. This was hardly what I imagined channeling to be. If Harold found this voice and these words by some sort of lunacy, he was pulling off a pretty good trick. Yet I thought the real Adam Smith, if he were to channel anything at all, would commiserate with me about high taxes and the intrusion of government in our lives. Instead, I felt I was being interrogated on a graduate school oral exam.

"If I may say so," he went on, "a key problem in rhetorical communication is that the listener may hear something different from what the speaker intended. Alas that is the very problem I face today: modern economists, even when they listen, don't understand me."

"Can we go back to your point, something about wick and wax?" I asked. "What have economists missed about society?"

He raised a finger for emphasis: "The vital interplay *betwixt* human beings that makes it a society, the 'fellow-feeling' that is the foundation for moral conduct."

"Betwixt?" I winked at Julia. "*Dr.* Smith," I said, stressing the title, "in this day and age clinical psychologists deal with emotions, sociologists worry about society, and philosophers debate morality; economists stay away from all that by studying markets. It's called 'division of labor', something you endorsed, unless I'm mistaken."

He pointed at me. "I also said too much division of labor could make one stupid—and the nobler parts of a man's character obliterated and extinguished. Don't be cute, young man. I know what I wrote a trifle better than you."

I surrendered. "What's your point?"

Smith glowered: "A market can't exist in isolation from people. People are the glue and the reason. An impersonal market force does not mean we become impersonal people!"

"What are you talking about?"

"The big picture is that feelings matter. Even if the market mechanism is disinterested, I as a person cannot be, must not be."

"What does this have to do with business, for God's sake?"

"You're an impatient fellow, aren't you?" Smith said.

Julia interrupted. "Take a break you two."

"And if you're Adam Smith," I said, rising, "why channel through Harold? What do you want from me?"

"Enough! We're taking a time out," Julia insisted.

Julia and I marched to the back yard. "What do you think?" she asked.

"Is he nuts?" I threw my hands up in the air. "I don't know what to think. He's got a plausible explanation for that English accent; that's a feat considering Harold's twisted Romanian. Still, I can't really see what this has to do with the Adam Smith I know."

"Can you stop attacking, and start listening—really listening? It's risky enough for Harold as it is."

"Riskier for me; I might lose my sanity."

"I'm serious," she said. "Edgar Cayce healed thousands of patients with psychic readings, just down the road in Virginia Beach. The exertion killed him. Channelers can't rest, can't sleep, can't think until the message is delivered. Harold is bursting."

"Then take him to a shrink. Get him a real doctor."

Julia glared. "Harold's not psychotic or schizophrenic, he's channeling. You can tell the difference."

"If he's a mechanic," I said, "why isn't he spouting Henry Ford? Look, I'm trained to be skeptical. This isn't exactly science."

Julia was annoyed. "Is that so?" She ran her fingers through her hair, not worried about how the strands fell back into place. "What about *A Course in Miracles*, channeled by two psych professors at Columbia. Is that acceptable pedigree?"

"I hope they had tenure."

Julia lifted her hair into a bun, a charmingly unconscious gesture that suddenly stirred memories of our brief relationship.

"They spent seven years transcribing that voice," she said. "Their books sold a million copies and changed thousands of lives."

"Then why isn't Smith channeling through me?"

"Rich, you can't choose these things. It's possible Harold and this spirit share an alignment, a meeting of spirits. You'll never know if it's the real Adam Smith. But surely you can tell something by what he says, can't you?"

It was at that moment, her back pressed against the door with the sun shining on her face, a slight shadow cast by her nose and eyebrows, that the thought flashed in my mind a second time in as many days: Julia was every bit as lovely as I'd remembered. It was not just surface beauty, but an inner quality. Her spirit seemed to bubble and disarm my objections.

She seemed to read my mind. "Rich, I'm here for Harold. Promise me you'll help him?"

*   *   *

The voice filled the room as we entered.

"Let me answer your query: why did I pick Harold? You might as well ask, why did Harold pick me?

Julia and I looked at each other.

"You think this is the first time I've channeled through someone? Pfff!—not at all. I've whispered in many young minds, trying to awaken the consciousness of my teaching. I've had successes, here and there. It takes more than a few." He smiled at me. "I succeeded with you, for awhile."

"Me?"

"In high school, early college, you listened. But by graduate school you began denying your intuitions. You began parroting your professors, assuming they must know everything. It's a tragedy, young minds set so quickly, and older minds are like rusted iron fortresses."

I rose. No words came out, and he put a hand to my shoulder. "Sorry to upset you."

I drew away and he said softly, "You'll admit to being happier in those care-free days, before abandoning your values?"

"I abandoned nothing."

"Where is your heart?"

"In my own body at least."

The man rose and went to the kitchen counter. He picked up a lime and rolled it pensively. "Why did I choose Harold? Because we share a resonance, not in an intellectual sense, of course. He's a good man, a simple man. But he's troubled and melancholy. It's easier when we need each other."

"Apparently he doesn't agree," I said.

"Wait 'til you have the facts."

"Why do you need me?"

He shrugged. "You may need me, more than I do you. You must promise to write down what I say. See that it's published."

"No promises," I said. "For Julia's sake I'll listen, that's all."

✵   ✵   ✵

Down by the river is a modest French bistro where Julia and I met for dinner that night, at my suggestion. The linguine with clam à la Bordelaise and bottle of light Frescati was beyond my budget, but the occasion demanded it. I felt in a groove of time and moment, and I didn't want it to stop. Was I trying to impress Julia? Of course!

We kept the conversation light. Her laughter was infectious as she recounted experiences from her graduate school days in anthropology. She'd eventually decided to abandon academic work: too much pretentious writing, she said. Painting was more gratifying, and the public response was quicker, more rewarding.

"Buyers aren't shy about what they like," she said. "I know what sells, and doing a few of those gives me the time to do what I love." Fortunately, the public was learning, Julia said, to appreciate her better works. Her paintings rarely hung for long at the gallery.

The mood of the evening snapped when Julia beat me to the check, "It's my treat."

"I invited you," I said.

"It's a well-deserved thank you for your help with Harold," she said softly. She wanted to keep it strictly business, and I felt my cheeks flush.

Together we walked back to the parking lot. I helped her to her car and she turned to look up at me, a sweet smile on her face. Then she was gone.

I aimlessly put my boot into a clump of gravel, spreading it where it should have been, feeling satisfaction from having controlled some small part of my world.

4 WILL THE REAL ADAM SMITH PLEASE STAND UP?

"So, Dr. Smith," I asked, "what is this urgent message for the world? You want people to know the secrets of wealth? The gains from trade?"

"Of course, of course. Quite essential."

Harold was breathing deeply, emoting now this richer voice of "Smith." The sunlight coming through the half-drawn shades of Julia's living room cast his face in partial shadow.

"But perhaps that's rushing the cart," he continued. "Perhaps people worry about wealth, when they should ask whether wealth is the final goal? Eh?"

"We can assume that most people want wealth."

"Yes, we can assume that," he sighed, "but use logic. If something happens to be an important goal, does that make it the most important?"

"A heavy stone in the garden isn't necessarily the heaviest."

"So, we can stipulate that increasing wealth is highly desirable, even as something else could be more desirable, something even … intangible?"

"Intangibles can't be measured or counted," I said.

"Ah—you like to count. Then how do you measure a successful life? Bear with me, if you can. How would you determine that?"

I shrugged, "Happiness?"

"Yes. And happiness is the consequence of?" He waited expectantly.

"Dying with the most toys?" I joked.

He rapped his cheek with his knuckles. "No, no, no, think! Something basic."

I thought of my faded eight-year-old station wagon, its sticky transmission needing overhaul. If I had the money, I'd trade it in for a new Saab turbo. Wasn't that basic to my happiness? Then there's the vacation cottage on the Rappahannock River I coveted. The down payment was out of reach, but that cottage would bring real joy: kayaking the river by day and rocking on the porch at night with a cold beer. But getting real basic, winning the Samuelson Prize would provide the career boost I needed, to catapult me to a research university with untold consulting opportunities. I'd have to move, but that was a small price for recognition and status.

Smith threw up his hands. "It's *peace of mind*."

"Huh?" I woke from my reverie.

"Tranquility of being! That's the basis for happiness."

"It's hardly the driving desire for me or anyone else," I shot back.

"Ah, but it must be cultivated! Humans need to acquire skills in moral development as well as in material development."

I rolled my eyes. "We spout peace and love on Sundays. What does this have to do with economics?"

A welcomed breeze billowed the lace curtains and delivered the scent of magnolias that shaded the neighborhood. I caught the moment and thought how long it's been since I appreciated this wonderful time of year. Now, everything came with a deadline, and here I was at Julia's wasting time when I should have been … well, almost anywhere else.

Smith paced a patch of rug. After a minute he slowed and drew up in front of one of Julia's paintings: a bumblebee, drawn to huge scale, hovered over a field of clover. Smith raised a hand as if to stroke the tiger belly.

He turned suddenly. "Answer this, are you happy?"

"What's the relevance? Why drag economics over a philosophical abyss?"

He winced and started breathing with difficulty. The thought flashed in my mind that Harold was a weak old man. The lines in his face were a mass of tributaries. Blood vessels bristled, and dark patches of perspiration grew under the armpits of his sweatshirt. He slumped in a chair.

Smith's voice came out a whisper. "How can I justify, in a sentence, ideas I labored over for forty years? My masterwork explains all this."

I was startled. "*The Wealth of Nations*?" Smith's masterpiece was the cornerstone of my discipline. Although I'd never read it, we all knew this was Smith's epistle to laissez faire economics, to hands-off government. Economics without Smith's "invisible hand" of the market seemed unthinkable.

Smith shook his head. "No, no, no. My *Theory of Moral Sentiments*. It's the foundation."

I'd never heard of it.

He raised a finger, addressing an imaginary audience. "The danger to freedom is forgetting moral meaning. Before it's too late, I must awaken people to it in this day and age."

"Are you saying," I asked, "that Adam Smith thinks—*you* think—his most important accomplishment was in moral development, not economic development?"

"Quite. Every man is rich or poor according to the degree to which he can afford the necessities, conveniences, and amusements of life. But that same richness, that same poverty, has no essential corollary with his happiness." He sat back relaxed, as if he thought I finally understood.

In my two years of front-line teaching, it had been a constant struggle to harden the romantic hearts of students to the real-world, to the truth that businesses inexorably pursue profits to the last marginal dollar, that countries relentlessly boost Gross Domestic Product, even to the possible detriment of the environment and future generations. I thought about the Adam Smith I imagined who was the guide and cheerleader for this joyously avaricious, free market scramble for material wealth. It crystallized in my mind that my dissertation sat untended while I listened to the drivel of this untutored, quixotic fossil.

Irritated, I blurted: "You expect me to believe that Adam Smith cared more about morality than markets?"

Julia rose and stood with her arms crossed. "Rich…"

The Smith fellow opened his mouth but I'd worked myself into a warm flush. "Why for a minute should I believe you're the real Adam Smith!"

I picked up my tape recorder and headed for the door. Julia didn't stop me.

"You're supposed to be the academic," he yelled after me, his voice carrying through the open door. "Do your homework! Doesn't anybody *read* anymore?"

❊   ❊   ❊

With agitated steps I walked back to my office at Waller Hall, a Georgian brick building overlooking the town's historic hill. The site was a bloody battlefield during the siege of Fredericksburg in the fall of 1862. General Ambrose Burnside and the Union Blues charged up this hill, and the Confederate Grays under Robert E. Lee mowed them down from behind an impregnable stone wall. Thousands were slaughtered under Burnside's inept command. He wasn't able to react to the day's events, to think on his feet. The Army of the Potomac was crushed for that year, and Burnside's job handed to Fighting Joe Hooker. I felt like one of those Blues, slogging my way up the rise, unable to respond to events.

Walking relaxed me, but not today. I resented the shifting of positions that made me the focus of inquiry. Of course I wasn't content with my life. I assumed that finishing my dissertation and later receiving tenure at a prominent university would bring that feeling, sometime in the future. Having those milestones would bring me money, prestige, even fame. After that, I could worry about other things.

Back at my office I checked my voicemail and downloaded email messages. It was the usual post-graduation surge of students needing advice and letters of recommendation. One student wanted to discuss his final grade. I slipped into the faculty lounge, hoping to avoid colleagues. Fortunately, the room was empty. My mailbox was typically stuffed with paper, the flow slowed only slightly since school let out. There was the dean's report on curriculum reform, a publisher's request to review a textbook, and the registrar's reminder that catalogue revisions had been due a week ago.

A bulky eight by eleven manila envelope jolted me. It had an imprint of the prominent journal where I had sent an article six months ago. I sat on the lounge couch, feeling my breath accelerate. Every publishing opportunity counted, especially now. I ripped open the flap. The referees' comments were extensive and caustic, but the editor's cover letter was encouraging. The paper needed substantial revision, she wrote, but she was willing to accept a resubmission. Thank God! Yes! At a journal that published only one of every ten submissions, a "revise-and-resubmit" was the best news an unknown could expect.

"Yee-haa! Yee-haa!" I yelled to no one but the pigeons, who flapped away from the building eaves at my outburst. I hurried to my office and dialed Julia's number. Before the line connected I cradled the mouthpiece. I rose and stared out the window onto the quadrangle, where summer students in shorts threw Frisbees. Others sauntered by with ice cream cones. My gaze returned to the mass of papers heaped on my desk—my final chapter on privatization. How indeed could anyone find the time to read anymore?

I filed the referees' comments and leaned back in my chair. My encounter with this channeled Smith-voice still troubled me. I could hear his parting words: my *supposing* to be an academic! Well, it's true I didn't have a Ph.D. yet, making me touchy on the subject of my qualifications. I'd no intention of seeing Harold again, but I wanted to tell Julia what a farce the whole exercise was. What *did* I know of Smith's writings? I rose wearily before my bookcase.

Where had I put it? There, used as a bookend for my research folders, was Adam Smith's, *An Inquiry into the Nature and Causes of The Wealth of Nations,* published in 1776. I'd found it at a yard sale, and strange as it sounds, I never cracked it in school. Why should I have? History of economic thought was a dying field during my graduate school days, populated by those who couldn't stomach calculus and matrix algebra. Older historians of thought died off or retired, and their replacements were scholars in the modern fields of game theory, econometrics, and macroeconomic dynamics. With the proliferation of knowledge in the present, who had time to deal with antiques from the past? No, the pithy Adam Smith quoted in textbook blurbs was all the Smith anyone needed today.

I turned to the editor's introduction:

Before proceeding to the economics it may therefore be useful to review the main elements of the other branches of Smith's work, and to elucidate some of their interconnections.... Smith himself taught the elements of economics against a philosophical and historical background ... concerned with much more than economics as that term is now commonly understood....

What this meant was soon apparent: Smith's questions focused on, *"Wherein does virtue consist?"* and *"How is this character of mind recommended to us?"*

"Damn." I slammed the book shut. I wanted easy, quantifiable answers, not complicated intangible ones. An eighteenth century discourse on virtue sounded like a dreary waste of time. But how did Harold Timms know of Smith's interest in moral philosophy? A vague conclusion loomed in my mind. Could this alleged channeling be part of an elaborate joke? There were serious pranksters on campus who wasted their time on such deeds. They concocted satirical, intricate high jinks. Associate Professor "Burgy" Burgess, in my own department, led the pack of jokers; his sharp ears and eyes missed little of notice. These harassers had one thing in common: frustrated in their own careers, they turned on anyone appearing to make progress. Their antics, not limited to paper, could be brutal. One weekend, a few years ago, they stealthily bricked-over the departing dean's door before movers arrived on Monday. Another time they disassembled a colleague's Volkswagen Beetle and reassembled it on the floor of the gymnasium the day of his promotion to full professor. Such fraternity pranks indicated these people had empty time on their hands. Could Harold's channeling be one of their elaborate jokes, a final hazing to ensure I joined the ranks of the academically immobile?

The caper would test their wits against my gullibility. I could hear Burgy's voice reverberating in the faculty lounge. "He bought it! He ... he ... gets stuck on his dissertation, and the first thing he does is have a *séance* with Adam Smith!" Howls and guffaws would follow. Burgy would elaborate with a louder bray, "Channeling my garage mechanic!" The room would explode with belly laughs.

The tale would spread to the faculty locker room, from where it would amplify in allegorical fashion on email, finding its way inevitably to the provost, the president, and the world beyond. The student newspaper might run a derisive piece. Even faculty spouses would know, and social events would become painful ordeals of heads nodding my way, stifled giggles, and not-so-gentle ribbing by these self-appointed keepers of humility.

It could get worse. What if the Samuelson Committee heard of this? The award was the most prestigious given to young scholars. The recipient earned a $10,000 check and the honor to address the five thousand conference members at the American Economic Association's annual meeting. The paper would be printed in the "bible" of journals, *The American Economic Review*. It was the opportunity I needed to leapfrog to a better school, with teaching assistants and Ph.D. students writing under me for a change. The award was a guaranteed career boost, if this Smith business didn't dismount me first.

I was wasting time in mental gymnastics when action was needed. I picked up my knapsack and hurried out the door.

*   *   *

Crossing the central quadrangle I barely avoided colliding with a group of prospective students and their parents on a college tour. I mounted the steps to Lee Library, last remodeled in 1985. A large glass and steel addition now assaulted its Georgian façade. The new wing was hermetically sealed, offering stale re-circulated air, heavy with the fumes of carpets, drapes, and printer's ink. The metal chairs were spindly with ninety-degree angled backs. No architect or college administrator would put up with this sterile, depressing place, yet somehow they imagined students and faculty would.

Entering the marbled foyer of the older structure, I passed the security check area and stopped at a bank of computers. A few clicks of the keyboard and the answer to my search popped up on the screen. Descending circular stairs, I entered the underground collections. The second basement was a mere seven feet high, and books were perched on metal shelves floor-to-ceiling. It was as oppressively claustrophobic as a submarine. Fluorescent lights stuttered; the antiquated ventilation system droned, pinged, and hiccuped, adding to the dreamlike, underwater illusion.

I meandered through this murky confine, looking at call numbers. At the "BJ 1000s" I turned right, down a narrow row. A few moments later my forefinger rested on a thick volume. This was it! *The Theory of Moral Sentiments*. Its brown leather cover was faded and cracked. I lifted it gently, wiping dust from its binding.

I moved to a library carrel and sat down. Cautiously, I lifted the cover. The lending card showed it had been checked out only once. But the spine was stiff, the pages uncut. This book had never been read by anyone. I fished a penknife from my pocket and began freeing pages. The frontispiece instantly caught my eye. The subtitle was an eighteenth century teaser, *"An essay towards an analysis of the principles by which men naturally judge the conduct and character, first of their neighbour, and afterwards of themselves."*

I turned to the first chapter, and soon was reading, blinking, and murmuring. My expectation had been of a dull, irrelevant treatise on moral philosophy. I was having trouble reconciling that view with the effervescent insights and sparkling writing that jumped from the pages. I was mesmerized. Unlike the colorless prose and methodological rigidity of my graduate training in economics, this was new and invigorating. After a half hour I set the book aside.

"Haaaa!" My discovery brought equal parts unease and chagrin. I re-read the passage that had so upset my equilibrium:

> *Happiness consists in tranquillity ... What can be added to the happiness of the man who is in health, who is out of debt, and has a clear conscience? To one in this situation, all accessions of fortune may properly be said to be superfluous ... Do they imagine that their stomach is better, or their sleep sounder in a palace than in a cottage? The contrary has been so often observed, and, indeed, is so very obvious ...*

Distinguished looking or not, how in blazes had Harold Timms—a wrench-turning, belt-tightening, Romanian mechanic—known the slightest thing about an obscure treatise by Adam

Smith? How had he come to fathom that the world's most revered economist was also a closet anti-materialist, sounding every bit like a romantic, anti-growth zealot? Why had I never heard of this aspect of Smith's reasoning? Did it refute *The Wealth of Nations*? The laws of economics? More importantly, was any of it relevant for business and society today?

If I could be ignorant of this work, what of my colleagues? Did they know of Smith's *Moral Sentiments*? If Harold Timms were part of some elaborate hoax, I would have to unmask him. I rose from the carrel and returned to the stacks. There must be a way of distinguishing the real Scotsman—if this voice was his—from some prankster, imposter, or nut. It wasn't long before I found what I needed and wound my way through the labyrinth to the check out counter.

"Mr. Burns," the librarian smiled, "you just missed one of your admirers. Your ears must be burning!"

"Oh?"

"He said he was a former student … very nice. He asked all about you, what you were researching. I told him about your work on Russia."

I dislike idle gossip. "What did he look like?"

She pondered, lifting a hand to her mouth. "L … Like most students. You know, sunglasses, blue jeans, blonde hair. Looked a little older than most, though. Said he graduated five years ago."

"Mrs. Peabody, I wasn't teaching here five years ago. How could I possibly have had him as a student?"

She looked flustered. "I'm sorry, I haven't seen you all summer."

"I don't come in much," I replied. I wanted to add that libraries were becoming an anachronism, that on-line databases accessible from my home and office now gave me far more information than the printed tomes stuck in some inaccessible library basement. Aside from being a cruel thing to say, it wouldn't even be true, since I now clutched under my arm Smith's *Moral Sentiments*, two biographies of Smith, and three history of thought surveys. But my patience was almost to its limit.

Instead, I said, "Thanks for thinking of me, Mrs. Peabody. I've found some jewels here."

＊　　　＊　　　＊

An hour later I phoned Harold. He answered on the fourth ring.

"Sorry I ran out on you this morning, Harold. At the time, nothing you said made sense to me."

He cleared his voice with a lumbering cough.

I went on. "I still don't know who you are. But what you said checks out."

"It's not what *I* said." Harold drew heavily on a cigarette. "I don't know what you and this Smith talked about, but my shirt was soaked with sweat like I'd p—pulled the motor off a rig. Slept the rest of the morning. You know that voice, going like a radio in the background? Don't bother me as much since you started talking to it."

"Can you turn the voice on now?" I asked.

"Lemme sit down." He grunted and all I heard was nasal breathing. Then, "Hello? Hello?" It wasn't Harold's voice.

"Professor 'Smith'?"

"The same. Still here, ready to proceed. I recall I was in the process of..."

"Excuse me," I interrupted.

"...elaborating the theory of moral sentiments..."

"Excuse me," I repeated louder.

"...without which society..."

"Will you please be quiet!" I shouted.

The other end of the phone fell silent.

"I have a list of ten questions," I said. "You have five seconds to answer each one. Otherwise, I'll mark you a fraud."

"What on earth—questions? You mean a test?"

"A simple test. Pass it and I'll take you seriously. Otherwise, this ruse is history."

"Outlandish!" the voice cried. "Do you know who you're talking to?"

"I know who you claim to be. Now you have a chance to prove it. Decide now." Part of me hoped he would refuse, and the prank would end. I could tell Julia I'd exposed an elaborate, if convincing, hoax.

I silently counted to eight before the voice replied. "Pfff! Waste our precious time with this foolishness. Go ahead then."

I pulled a list of questions from my pocket.

"One. Date and place of your birth."

"Seventeen twenty-three, in Kirkcaldy." The last word was mangled, to my untrained ear, coming out as "Kir-kaw-dee." He continued, "A small fishing village in Scotland, just across the firth—the bay—from Edinburgh."

"Two. Your mother's name and birthplace?"

"My dear mother was Margaret. Of Strathenry Estate."

"Maiden name, I mean."

"Douglas. She was Margaret Douglas." His voice trailed off.

"Three. Your father's name and birthplace?"

"Adam Smith, of Seaton."

"How old was he when he died?"

"How old? Well, I never knew him; he died before I was born. Mother was an expectant widow. Let me see."

"Time," I said.

"He was born in sixteen seventy-nine, so that would have made him…"

"Your time's up."

"He was forty-three!"

"Let's go on. Four: did you have siblings?" I asked.

"That's question five!"

"All right, five then. Answer it."

"A half-brother, Hugh. From my father's first marriage. He was sickly like me, I'm afraid. He passed on when I was a boy."

"Doesn't matter," I said. "Six. Where did you study?"

"My grammar school was on Hill Street. Then on to Glasgow University. My advanced degree was from Balliol College, at Oxford. What a miserably calcified place that was!"

I made the seventh question appear innocuous. "When did you marry?"

"Trick question! You know perfectly well I'm a bachelor." The voice sounded wounded and slightly wistful, but I didn't slow down to ponder this. I was getting to the make-or-break questions.

"Eight. Who called you 'ugly as the devil' and the most 'absent-minded creature' she'd ever met?"

"Ah, that would be ... that would be Madame Riccoboni." His voice softened. "I was her pet in Paris. How she adored me. I'm no Casanova, mind you, a little too bookish I've been told, but that's not to say I didn't have my moments."

"Never mind. Nine. Whose paranoia caused an international incident, aligning you with Turgot, the French economic reformer?"

He didn't hesitate. "You're referring to that rascal Jean Jacques Rousseau! He set into my dearest friend, David Hume, quite unprovoked. We tried to keep it out of the press. Spilled over eventually, nothing Turgot or I could do about it. An all-around unpleasant affair."

I'd saved the stickler for last. "Ten. What do you know of gypsies?"

"Gypsies?" There was silence, then a youthful exclamation. "The Romany wanderers? Ha! Of course, my kidnapping! I was three, playing in the field behind Strathendry Castle—"

"That's good enough."

"I was fooling around, throwing rocks, catching crickets, studying the clouds. A band of migrants was encamped on a hill nearby. I was intrigued and probably made a pest of myself. The next morning they came in their troupe past the castle, and before I knew it an old hag scooped me up and threw me in a wagon. A heavy wool blanket landed on top. I howled, but there wasn't enough air under there to make much noise. They scampered off with me up the north road."

He sucked in more air, and I let him finish.

"It was a good three hours before I heard galloping and shouting from behind. I found myself flung onto the side of the road. Smacked my head on a rock, but good, I did. The gypsies fled into the woods, the old woman hurling insults and threats back at my uncle who came to rescue me. Quite an adventure, I should say, quite an adventure."

There was an awkward silence as I sat musing, a silence which he finally broke.

"Well, did I pass? Did I pass? Oh, confound it, why would I even ask!"

*   *   *

I pondered these bits of trivia as I sipped a Drambuie that evening on my porch. What if those gypsies had gotten away with their theft? If, in place of his doting, scholarly mum, Adam Smith had been raised by a band of illiterate wanderers, his pens and books replaced with rocks and rags? Would the pragmatic world of business have evolved differently without Smith's injunctions against government meddling, his admonitions about the unanticipated consequences of do-goodism, his railings against special interests and monopolies?

I was woefully lost in thought, for my collie, Rex, licked my hand to remind me my job was to scratch his ears. I yawned and did so. My mind, however, continued toying with the day's discoveries. Among these was the cruel irony that Adam Smith and John Maynard Keynes shared the same birthday, June 5, which just happened to be tomorrow. Keynes, the brilliant architect of government intervention to pull the economy out of the Great Depression, proposed policies diametrically opposed to Smith's ideal for limited government. Later in life, Keynes even abandoned support for free trade.

It was Keynes' conviction that, "Practical men, who believe themselves to be quite exempt from any intellectual influences, are usually the slaves of some defunct economist." I considered myself a practical man, and I wondered if I was now slipping into the role of eavesdropper on some defunct economist from the eighteenth century. I slumped in my chair. What indeed would this Adam Smith think of my dissertation?

The jangle of the phone startled me.

It was Julia, inviting me to dinner the following evening.

5 CONTRABAND

Julia cooked stuffed pork chops with mashed potatoes and gravy, green beans, and apple-sauce. I brought a bottle of California Chardonnay, inexpensive but at least barrel fermented. Her little house lacked a formal dining room so we ate on the patio, where she set up a card table with a red-checked tablecloth and candle. The June air was crisp.

"Harold called," Julia said, after we sat. "You've been spending time with him and I'm so grateful."

Her genuine gratitude made me a little uneasy: my time with Harold had a dual motive.

I told Julia about my research at the library and about the test I'd given Smith. Today was Adam Smith's birthday, I added.

Julia thanked me, then frowned. "I worry about the toll on Harold." She looked at me. "And you, too. I know this interrupts your work."

I veiled my guilt with a smile and shook my head. "I'd like to blame my inertia on Harold, but I can't. I've got my own dissertation demons."

She looked at me silently. I couldn't tell whether it was approval or hesitation that I read there.

"Does your anthropology," I asked, changing the subject, "help your art? What about that *candomblé* business?"

"It's part of both professions to observe and discern," she replied. "*Candomblé* helps me focus on essence, not form."

"Helps you see the inner person?"

She studied me. "Inside you, for example?"

"Well, sure." I nodded, embarrassed.

She held my palm and pretended to examine lines. She was playing with me. "Let's see," she mused, "I'd say you're an attractive man. An intelligent over-achiever. Hmm ... likely never pleased with yourself. Your work's a refuge: you're so focused there's little room for, well, anything..." Her voice trailed off.

This was interesting. "What else do you see?"

Color rose in her cheeks. "Oh, I don't see anything, Rich," she said, releasing my hand. "Let's talk about something else. A toast—to Adam Smith!"

After dinner I asked to see her garden, and we strolled to a pair of apple trees she'd planted. The light was dim and I wanted to embrace her, or, at least reach for her hand. I stopped myself.

We'd been this close once before. Then I'd run from it. Just a year ago, near this very spot, I was drawn to Julia's warmth and beauty, her intelligence, her art. It was our fourth date, and we'd seen a movie and returned for a glass of wine and to laugh about the comedy. We knew each other pretty well, at least on the surface, and well enough that the strong draw between us needed some resolution. One of us had to give a sign, make a commitment—leap forward toward something deep and rich in promise—or fall backward to security and control. For most people, I suppose the choice would be easy. There seemed no doubt in her mind. But for me, uncertainty reigned. If such a thing is possible, I was liking Julia too much, drawn into depths over my head. It wasn't being with a woman that frightened me—I'd joked my way into my share of happy, short term, romances. Rather, I felt claustrophobic, realizing that a deeper relationship was in store, one requiring far more emotional intimacy. I rationalized my hesitation by enumerating how attachment led to entanglement, and how I liked my freedom to do as I pleased, especially if the alternative risked pain.

So, I'd pulled back, with the ready excuse of a dissertation hanging over my head; it provided a face-saving obstacle. Still, I felt every bit the fool I was. My insides tonight were once again twisted in a knot. But this time … I resolved to keep to the first path. Julia had her back to me, lifting her hand to examine a spider that floated onto an apple leaf. I put my hand on her shoulder. She surprised me, turning to face me. She took my hand and held it. Then she gently placed it by my side.

She turned away. Somewhere I heard the soft lift and fall of night wings, an owl swooping. Finally, she said, "I didn't invite you here to stir up the past. I just wanted to thank you for helping Harold, that's all. I'm sorry, Rich."

She struggled with this answer, and after another silence, she turned back, and for a second I was encouraged. Then she said, "You know, maybe this wasn't such a good idea—my asking you to help Harold, given our past. I don't want to be the reason you're seeing him. But you're the only economist I know." She looked past my shoulder, at the sliver of a moon, or the stars. I don't know. I was caught by the reflection of light in Julia's eyes; she wasn't looking at me because I'd been measured and fallen short.

The breeze was cool and should've been a comfort. I wrestled with a dozen things to say, but found nothing that didn't sound like a glib defense.

She laughed. "Come on. Let's enjoy the wine."

*   *   *

"Lunch at the Faculty Club, all right?" I asked Harold on the phone a week later. It had been a month since his last paycheck and he was a charity-case now. Julia and others made him casseroles, and the Reverend helped him apply for temporary disability. The Faculty Club was convenient, subsidized, and half-empty this time of year.

"I asked a couple of colleagues to join us," I said vaguely, not wanting to tell him the whole truth, that I was embarrassed to introduce this Smith-spirit to fellow economists. Instead, I'd substituted two left-leaners from related disciplines, holdovers from Cold War battles fought in developing nations. With their classical Marxist training they could smell a rat. Would this Smith-monologue hold-up under harsher scrutiny?

"One other thing," I emphasized, "I'll introduce you as Dr. Smythe, a retired professor. Today you're Dr. Smythe."

At noon I pulled up to Harold's small, box of a house. Undisciplined stalks of grass waved in the breeze. His old car was lifted onto blocks and three rolled newspapers were scattered about the lawn. I picked them up and deposited them on the porch. Harold was wiping his hands on a rag when he got to the screen door, a cigarette hanging from his lips. His bloodshot eyes squinted into the sunlight. Julia warned me that channeling was draining him, but I wasn't quite prepared: Harold looked depressingly shabby, his shirt missing a button, exposing a ragged tee shirt, and his pants smeared with grass stains. Dropping the cigarette to the ground, Harold slid into the car. Lunacy or not, I couldn't help but feel sorry for the man.

After a few blocks I looked over again. His eyes were open and he was sitting up straight.

"Richard, have you an apology to make?" The voice was not Harold's, but Smith's.

The quick change of characters unnerved me, and I almost ran a light as I peered over at him. Passing over the leather-bound volume of *The Theory of Moral Sentiments*, I recounted my vain search to disprove him. "Looks like the second time the book's been checked out," I said. "Last time was 1923."

He grinned. "Bicentennial of my birth!"

I didn't mention the uncut pages; no author needs to know the worst.

The campus bustled with landscapers, painters, and carpenters on several construction sites, but I had no trouble finding a parking spot in front of the Faculty Club. Joining us inside were Dr. Carol Norton, a sociologist, and Dr. Wayne Brown, a professor of International Relations. Neither of them found Harold's casual, and not terribly clean, attire remarkable: a professor's other-worldliness is simply taken for granted. After introductions and a few pleasantries, we made our way to a table. It was summer, with no classes, so we ordered drinks with the meal: wine for Carol and Wayne, beer for me, and scotch for Smith.

"Didn't know you touched the stuff," I said.

"My dear mother was a devout Presbyterian," Smith responded. "Nonetheless, I've always supported free markets in spirits. I myself acquired a fondness for French wine, some might say too great a fondness." He laughed. "But I feel curiously like having something from home today."

We smiled politely and in that moment I glimpsed a nightmarish vision: Susan Mitchell, of the Samuelson Prize Committee, was entering the Faculty Club with Burgy Burgess! The Samuelson Committee interviewed the colleagues of finalists, but God help me—not Burgy—the prankster himself, the nemesis of anyone with ambition. This was an improbable encounter, and I wanted to dissolve into my seat. Too late! I was spotted. We waved and exchanged smiles. Unsettled, I turned back to my guests.

Wayne sipped his wine, then said to Smith: "Rich tells us you left academia to become a government bureaucrat."

Smith nodded. "True, I was a Commissioner of Customs."

"Rather a step-down, wasn't it," Carol said. "I mean, Rich warned us you were libertarian—laissez faire and all that—

and then you became a tax collector. How perfectly ironic. I imagine pensions don't cover much these days."

"Good heavens, I didn't do it for the money! I gave away most of what I made." Smith sipped his single malt. He looked down at the clothes he wore and seemed to notice them for the first time. "Pshaw!" he gasped in surprise. "My dress today is as shabby as the day I became Customs Commissioner!" He let out a belly laugh. "You see, I owned a closet-full of fancy clothes, but they were smuggled imports. I didn't know it until I saw the official list. I had to burn my contraband to set an example. Goes to show how futile trade prohibitions are in practice."

"Don't we know it," Carol agreed. "We've tried to keep out drugs without success."

"There was nothing shameful about customs work, mind you," Smith explained, "we desperately need good civil servants. Truth is, the job was interesting, and even challenging. Every government needs the revenue from modest duties."

Smith glanced at me reprovingly. "Contrary to the impression our Richard might have given you, I never aligned myself with any utopian fantasy like laissez faire. I'm far too practical for such extremes. For Heaven's sake, I never once even used the term."

I gave a nervous start, though neither Carol nor Wayne were equipped to grasp what he'd said the way I could. "But your ideas on government weren't that far from that, were they?"

"It's true," Smith said, "no government promotes the happiness of mankind as much as the general wisdom and virtue in society itself." He lifted his tumbler, then went on, "All government is but an imperfect remedy for the deficiency of these. But having said that—a system of commerce can't work its best without some limited government, just as it can't work its best without moral foundations in society. I've been trying to explain that to Richard for several weeks now."

I glanced over my shoulder to the far table where Mitchell and Burgy were deep in conversation. Burgy had drops of bread crumbs on his beard. Good. I hoped he was making a fool of himself.

"I didn't think capitalism *had* a moral element," Carol was saying, grinning to let us know she had little regard for capitalism or its high priests—economists.

Wayne chimed in. "You don't have to be Marxist to wonder about that. The IMF bail-out in Asia shows once again the system is rigged." He looked around to make sure he held our attention. "Big business expects a government rescue package whenever things go wrong, but listen how they scream if you ask them to give up some of their gains when things go right! We socialize the risks, they privatize the benefits!"

Smith sipped his drink, then said patiently, "I've always said people would try to abuse the market system for their personal gain. After all, I spent most of my life pointing out the consequences of governments granting absurd monopolies and privileges to the favored few. All the more reason for me to say," he eyed each of us in turn, "economic freedom cannot well survive without morals, especially at the top."

Wayne nodded. "Communists and fascists agree on the need for strict morals. Mao Zedung attacked the moral evils in China: during the Cultural Revolution children even turned in their parents."

Smith took a long look at Wayne. "Surely you miss my point," he said. "Society needs an *internalized* base of morality."

"Come on," Carol said harshly, "the Berlin Wall is down, communism is dead, and you're worried about the survival of free markets?" Carol looked around the table incredulously. "Except for the Red Brigades, the Shining Path, and a few other wacko terrorists, like those ... those ... 'People Over Profit.'"

I looked at her, a line tightening on my forehead.

"Haven't you read the papers?" Carol pulled a newspaper from her briefcase and spread it on the table. The headline blared: "Assassination Foiled: Russian Envoy to U.N. Targeted." The subheading read: "POP group claims responsibility for bombing."

"POP?"

Wayne raised an eyebrow. "Where've you been the last year, Rich?"

I smiled wanly. "Trying to get this dissertation monkey off my back."

A glow came onto Wayne's face. "Well, everyone else has heard of 'People Over Profit.' They came on the radar three years ago in Germany, protesting the IMF's neoliberal economic policies the way Greenpeace protests whaling." Wayne glared at Carol. "They're no wackier than others fighting for justice—after all, most American colonists didn't support our Revolution until after it'd been won. Same's true here."

Carol continued: "Anyway, six months ago POP escalated from passive resistance to acts of destruction. Now they've upped the ante to murder."

The main course arrived and Smith seemed relieved to cut into his lamb chops and chew pensively. Then he put down his fork. "I *am* worried about the endurance of liberty," he said. "It's not a long-lived concept, not in historical terms. The violence and injustice of the rulers of mankind is an ancient evil, no less than the monopolizing spirit of merchants and manufacturers. Neither are, nor ought to be, the rulers of mankind—but do you expect them to stop trying?"

"You're giving new weight to the phrase 'dismal science,'" I said, drawing a laugh from Wayne and Carol.

"See here," Smith went on, "institutions don't survive simply because they work, and even work well! Institutions reflect the circumstances of society, and they survive because they're defended by an underlying fabric of moral support. America may allegedly be structured upon Montesquieu's separation of powers, but Montesquieu cautioned that the spirit of a republic is *virtue*."

"Civic consciousness," Carol interjected.

"Isn't it logical," Smith said, picking up his fork, "that both democracy and free markets arose in the eighteenth century when leaders were infused with Enlightenment ideals? The concept of the "individual" was layered with notions of mutual rights, responsibilities, and duties. Moral precepts acknowledged not only the dignity of individuals, but their social interconnectedness. Society would crumble into nothing if mankind were not generally impressed with a reverence for moral rules."

"Markets and democracy have never been stronger," I said.

A bead of perspiration formed on Smith's forehead. Fatigue made him forceful, as if every breath counted. "Markets are spurred by the base elements of human nature," he said. "You balance these with benevolence and justice to form a civilized society." Smith raised his voice. "But what if the moral checks to conduct are cast aside? Will people support the institution of free markets if greed runs rampant? If impersonal logic and rationality become shields to justify every unjust outcome?"

"How can logic undercut anything but superstition?" I steamed.

Two shadows fell over our table and I groaned inside.

"Is this a good time to say hello?" Susan Mitchell's voice rang out from behind. I rose to make introductions, faltering when I got to the "retired professor, Dr. Smythe."

Burgy, my colleague in name but never in spirit, did a double-take, started to say something, then stopped. He inspected Smith as if with x-rays. In that awkward silence, Susan Mitchell beamed, "Dr. Smythe, we're all impressed with Rich—a Samuelson Prize finalist. Are you familiar with his work?"

Smith worked his mouth around, hesitating. "Since you're here, I'm sure it must be good."

Burgy pressed him. "You've no opinion of your own?"

Smith glanced at me hard. He shrugged. "Like much modern work, his writing fails to address the big picture. He spins intricate theories from his own insides, elegant and logical equations from absurd and untested assumptions. Some might say it's just blackboard scribbling, little to do with the world."

"I've always said economists navel-gaze," Wayne said.

I sunk my head while the others' mouths fell open. Smith seemed oblivious, going on, "Oh, I dare say there are a few economists today who read, fewer still who read history. Francis Bacon, the father of science, said it best, he did: Be like bees, go to nature for your raw materials. Study the human animal in his natural environment—in society, I say."

"Here here," Carol nodded. "Sociologists have said that all along."

"Exactly why economics and sociology parted company a hundred years ago," I muttered. "Too much buzzing and no theory."

6

SELF INTEREST IS NOT SELFISHNESS

Smith prattled on through the rest of our main course and I wanted to choke him. All that babble to Susan Mitchell! With disappointment on her face, and unrestrained glee on Burgy's, the two retreated from the table. If guilt were by association, I was ruined. Prestigious economic prizes were given for deducing theories, complex mathematical ones! Assumptions didn't matter as long as the prediction worked: Nobel laureate Milton Friedman showed us that. Smith's silly jabber about bees would do me little good with the Samuelson Committee.

"All for themselves and nothing for other people," Smith intoned as we sat with our desserts, twenty minutes later into this unmitigated disaster of a lunch. "That has been the vile maxim of our rulers in every age."

"You sound like a comrade," Wayne said, digging his spoon into a chocolate mousse.

Smith seemed pleased with the attention. "How strange it is, really. You know that Karl Marx took Adam Smith to heart—those angry passages in *Wealth of Nations* where Smith denounces the deceitful traders, manufacturers, and landlords as exploiters and oppressors of workers. By Jupiter, landlords are the worst of the lot, completely indolent, and ignorant to boot, their sole motive to gratify the most childish vanities."

Carol chimed in, "Still true in Central America. Coffee and banana plantations exploit the indigenous workers, after stealing their lands. The Spanish *conquistadors* were bloodsuckers and their descendants haven't changed in five hundred years."

Smith grew despondant. "It's a terrible injustice that no institution protected the sanctity of their property."

The arrival of coffee and tea filled-in for a reply. After the waiter left, Smith continued, "It's well known that the *search* for profit puts into motion the greater part of the useful labor of every society. But it's astonishing to discover that whilst wages and rents rise with prosperity, profits rise with *poverty*—yes, the highest profits are in those countries going rapidly to ruin."

Wayne nodded vigorously.

"Seems backwards," I said. "Profits rising with poverty?"

"It's simple, really, poor countries have monopolies and guilds which restrain trade." Smith looked around, leaning into the table to bring his head closer to ours. He whispered, as if imparting a state secret. "You know, people of the same trade seldom meet, even for merriment and diversion—just as we do here—but the conversation ends in a conspiracy against the public! In some contrivance to raise prices!"

He leaned back, speaking louder. "And hear me. Do these exorbitant monopoly profits alleviate poverty or promote industry? Far from it!" He took a deep breath. "There is no order of society that suffers so cruelly from such a stagnant economy as labor, who live by wages which often are barely enough to bring up a family, and in decline they fall even below this. And whoever imagines that employers don't contrive to sink the wages of workers is as ignorant of the world as of the subject itself."

"My research bears that out," Carol agreed.

Smith became moody. He spoke softly. "No society can be flourishing and happy when the greater part of the members are poor and miserable." He lifted a spoon, gesturing at the busboys gathering dishes. "Besides, is it not equitable that the whole body of people should share in the produce of their own labor? So they are at least tolerably well fed, clothed, and lodged?"

Raising a finger, Wayne said, "I must get you a copy of my latest book, *The State and World Society*. It shows how the corrupt rulers in Third World countries are mere puppets of transnational corporations." His face flushed with pride. "Only when profits and capital are expropriated—and private property abolished—can a society of virtue flourish. Mao and Fidel both showed what a single man could accomplish in that regard."

"Abolish private property?" Smith said, stunned, waking from a reverie. He looked around the table, grasping for words, as if his life depended on it. "That ... that Karl Marx was Adam Smith's demonic disciple! Went off on a dead wrong course. Good gracious, trying to create 'Utopia' here on earth!"

Wayne's mouth dropped; his eyes became small black disks.

Smith didn't notice. He rapped on the table. "The solution to oppression is not more oppression; the solution to oppression is competition! Wages rising with growth, growth resulting from the natural tendency of people to truck and barter—if they're given the freedom. Free exchange gives workers an alternative place to sell their labor. Workers who have *options* is what slays the arrogant landlord!"

Smith swept his arms out. "As for morality, you can't impose it! It must be cultivated. A free society is better able to do this than the man of system roosting on his high throne. A *man of system...*"

Smith caught himself, and for the first time noticed the slow burn on Wayne's face. "Oh, my." He reached out a hand. "Forgive me, I'm not wholly myself. Not myself at all. Normally, I'm well mannered. But I've had to borrow the mind, the persona, you see, of someone else."

My foot pressing under the table caught his shin, and he choked on his words.

Smith examined Wayne's face. "My temper was greatly provoked," he said, "at the thought of letting any man on his high throne, a so-called 'benign dictator,' establish all the rules of morality and commerce. Such a man, a man who constructs his own 'perfect' system, is apt to be very wise in his own conceit! So enamored with his own ideal plan that he cannot suffer the smallest deviation from it!"

Smith picked up a salt and pepper shaker in each hand and began methodically placing them on different squares of the checkerboard tablecloth. "Mao, in the past—or the communist ruler of China today—imagines he can arrange the different members of the great Chinese society with as much ease as my hand arranges the pieces on a chess board. But in the great chess board of human society, every single piece has a principle of motion of its own, altogether different from that which the man of system might wish to impose upon it."

The condiments shuffled about the table under Smith's big paws. "For the man of system to make his judgment the supreme standard of right and wrong requires the highest degree of arrogance, and surely leads to the greatest misery of that society!" With this conclusion Smith swept his arm across the table, sending both shakers sailing. Salt and pepper sprayed the floor, attracting the attention of other diners. Mitchell and Burgy interrupted their meal to look in our direction. Mitchell shook her head slowly; Burgy wagged his index finger and grinned. He was enjoying himself thoroughly.

✻   ✻   ✻

Eager to escape this fiasco, I suggested we finish our coffee on the outside patio overlooking the campus. It was empty, and we found shade under an umbrella. Wayne sat mutely, fuming, while Smith picked his teeth unobtrusively. I searched for a way to relieve us of Smith's monopolizing conversation. Just then an economics honor student appeared on the path.

"Hi Raj," I called out.

Raj approached shyly. "Hello, Mr. Burns. I finished the reading you gave me. When should we meet?"

I was about to answer when Smith interjected brightly, "Join us, young man! I've a question or two for you."

I cringed.

Raj pulled up a chair. "Yes?"

"What did you learn in your principles class about Adam Smith, author of *The Wealth of Nations*?"

Raj reflected a moment. "That greed is good. Selfish actions lead to the betterment of society, even if the action is not intended to."

"You see!" Smith was triumphant. "He thinks he learned *that* from *me*!"

Wayne and Carol exchanged glances. Raj searched for my reaction.

I had to think fast. "Professor Smythe tutored some of our students," I said. "It's hard for him to remember which ones."

"I mean from Adam Smith!" Smith corrected himself. "You think *The Wealth of Nations* promotes greed?"

"Doesn't it?" Raj asked. "Our teacher made us memorize this quote: 'It is not from the benevolence of the butcher, the brewer, or the baker, that we expect our dinner, but from their regard to their own interest.'"

"Oh blast it, that's a complete misinterpretation if you think it means *selfishness* is good!" Smith was turning a shade of purple. "How can you take one quote, out of the twelve hundred pages of Smith's two books, and construe any such thing?"

Raj looked dumbfounded and crestfallen at the same time.

I held up my hand to stop Smith. Like most teachers, I had almost memorized the quote from every principles textbook: "Surely," I exclaimed, "Smith did say that businesspeople employ their capital so as to promote their own greatest profit … and are thus 'led by an invisible hand' to advance the public's interest more effectually than if they really intended to promote it."

Smith shook his head. "It's a lovely quote, but you can't read *The Wealth of Nations* in isolation. Would the *New Testament* make sense without the *Old Testament*? Well, would it?"

Finally, it was Raj who said, "I guess not."

"So, why do people quote one passage from *The Wealth of Nations*, which is a sequel, and totally ignore its foundation?" he fumed. "*The Theory of Moral Sentiments* laid it out so clearly."

A worried Raj tried to get my eye. Smith hammered on, "You've all confused Adam Smith with *Mandeville,* for God's sake. He's the one who said, 'private vice makes public virtue.' Smith spent his life refuting that view."

Carol stifled a giggle, holding a hand over her mouth, and finally caught Wayne's eye. I shot them dirty looks: even if he were a crazy old man, couldn't their egos take a jostling? This entire lunch was humiliating.

Smith set down his cup and spoke imploringly. "Human society is like a great, immense machine, and virtue is the fine polish on its wheels. Vice is a vile rust that causes the wheels to jar and grate upon one another. Knowing what he wrote, how could anyone say Adam Smith thought *selfishness* was good?"

Smith sat back, peering at me through the corner of his eye. No one spoke, and finally he went on, with a satisfied air: "Smith did say, however, that 'self-love' was a natural, and within limits, even a desirable, virtue."

He looked triumphant, and we stared back blankly. My mind was overwhelmed. Smith navigated tighter intellectual waters than anyone I'd known.

Now Smith's argument took hold. He rapped on the table. "Self-*love*, don't you see? Didn't Jesus say, 'Love your neighbor as yourself'? By loving yourself, did anyone take that to mean he favored selfishness?"

"No," said Raj, "because it would clearly be out of character."

"Exactly!" Smith beamed. "And it would be out of character to think Adam Smith meant anything else either. Self-love is a means, in *Wealth of Nations*, to inspire effort and production. When we confound means with ends, that is what leads to selfishness."

"What difference does it make?" Wayne grumbled. "Capitalism's the same either way."

"On the contrary," Smith sniffed. "The sentiment of the heart from which any action proceeds—and upon which its whole virtue or vice depends—must first be understood in relation to the motive which gives rise to it."

"But in practice—"

"In practice," Smith interrupted, "self-love is quite different than greed."

"How different?"

"Self-love means you take prudent steps to provide for your own needs and security and not be a leech on society." Smith shifted in his chair. "After all, carelessness in economic matters is no virtue. Every person is first and principally recommended to his own care, and every man is certainly fitter and abler to take care of himself than of any other person."

"And that's not selfish?"

"Of course not. Selfishness is an egoistic attachment to your own needs when they conflict with the legitimate rights of others." Smith rose and began pacing. "Selfishness could lead to harm or neglect of another. Nobody likes a selfish person, least of all me." Smith shot a glance my way.

"The butcher and the baker—they're not selfish?" I asked.

"Not necessarily," he replied. "They're promoting their own interest without harming others. Church doctrine in my time said that *all* self-interest was a sin. I showed that in looking out for oneself, others could benefit, too. Self-interest is morally virtuous in that narrow sense." Smith looked around dreamily, his eyes glazed. "Surely no one wants to bake his own bread, or sew his own clothes. It is the maxim of every prudent master, never to make at home what it will cost him more to make than to buy."

Smith swayed, speaking in a chant, "And what is prudence in the conduct of every family can scarce be folly in that of a great nation. But prudence does not demand selfishness."

Smith seemed to freeze.

I asked, "Isn't it human nature to be selfish?"

"Yes, but it is also human nature to try to balance that feeling." He gasped for air. "A virtuous person must develop the habit, must cultivate the consciousness, of … of…"

His eyes focused on my forehead. Swaying, he slid sideways onto the table. We grabbed for him, but not soon enough. His legs collapsed, sending his heavy form crashing onto the deck.

7 ON THE ROAD WITH ADAM SMITH

"How's the patient?"

Julia spread her hands to encompass the living room. "Better. It's been three days getting there. He asked for you."

I listened for accusation in her tone but didn't hear any. She seemed glad I'd come at all. After Harold's collapse at the Faculty Club, Julia took him in and fixed up her guest room. She removed the footboard so his long feet could stretch over the end of the bed, installed blinds in place of frilly curtains, and set a small television within arm's reach.

Harold was half watching the television when we entered. His face was bloated, and his eyes appeared as small opaque buttons on a stuffed tiger. My borrowed pajamas were small for his large frame, their diamond pattern dizzying to the eye.

"Ahh … it's you! Why'd you try and kill me?" Harold said woozily.

"I didn't try to kill you."

"You gave that Smith a drink … you think I got these lines in my face rebuilding carburetors? I *was* on the wagon, fifteen years now."

"I didn't know."

"M—m—my liver sure did."

Harold must've been more than an average drinker in his day to react that way to a drink or two. Julia probably came to the same conclusion, because she looked at him with a knowing concern that made me feel incomplete, incompetent, or both.

"Doc gave me these." He held up a prescription bottle. "That and the TV keeps me from hearing that voice anymore. Last thing I need is for you two to get started again. Damn near killed me."

"Damn near killed my prize," I muttered, low to myself.

Harold turned back to the television show, the medicine keeping him half asleep. Julia and I eased out of his hearing. I filled her in on Smith's devastating comments to Susan Mitchell at the lunch.

"Will it cost you the prize?" she asked. "I'd feel terrible about that."

"Might have, but didn't turn out that way. Susan Mitchell was in the parking lot when we carried Harold to the car. Now I'm Mr. Nice Guy, trying to help a senile old man."

"He isn't senile." She lowered her eyes. I wanted to tell her how attractive she looked, but I left well enough alone. We were friends, she'd said, period.

"I'm sorry," I said. "I'm caught up revising that journal article. You know the pressure I'm under."

Her eyes lifted, and I was again amazed at and appreciative of her capacity for forgiveness. She worked up a smile, the kind I gave Rex when he knocked something over in his enthusiasm. "No, I should apologize. That was quite a risk, taking Harold to the Faculty Club."

She went on, "Worry makes me so insistent I forget my sense of humor. You deserve thanks, not my growls. What you did took a lot of courage." The way she said it, and the warm smile she flashed, gave a hint of something different. Subtle hints have a way of flying over my head, however. Perhaps she felt something also, because she quickly changed the subject. "What do you think of that channeled voice now?"

"It grew on me," I said. "Half the time I didn't know whether to feel sorry for it or strangle it. I'll miss it, though. I guess Harold's under a good doctor's care now ... hasn't heard the voice anymore."

"Uh-huh."

I looked at Julia, listening for clues in her response, and said, "I'm ... I'm heading for the West Coast in a few weeks."

"You're leaving?"

"I came by to tell you. I've rented a cabin near Yosemite, a working vacation. I do my best writing away from home."

Harold must have heard, because he looked up. "You're going away?" Panic crept into his voice.

I moved closer to Harold's bed. "I need to," I said. "I'll bike in the Sierras, camp on Half Dome, even see if I can make it up El Capitan. If that doesn't shake my dissertation loose, I don't know what will."

Julia pursed her lips, looking at Harold.

I put my hand on Harold's shoulder. "I began to enjoy that voice of yours, Harold. It wasn't as crazy as I thought. It had coherence, a vision."

"That's not what Wayne said when he helped carry him in," Julia said.

I laughed. "Wayne was upstaged by Harold's eloquence. You should have heard yourself, Harold!"

Julia walked me to my car.

"I do feel for Harold," I said, when I saw the earlier warmth now missing from her eyes. "The medicine is helping; he looks better already. You understand my needing to go, don't you?"

"Of course," she said flatly.

"Still friends?" I asked.

She crossed her arms and gave a smile. "Sure. Thanks for everything, Rich. And good luck."

I hesitated, then leaned forward to peck her cheek.

❋   ❋   ❋

I spent the next weeks preparing for my journey. By the last morning I'd put the finishing touches on my "revise and resubmit" journal article. I printed the requisite three copies, wrote a cover letter, and sent it off. Then I surveyed the calamity of my dining room, which served as a home office. Paper enveloped my world: old drafts of my dissertation and that irksome last chapter were piled in clumps. I picked them all up, added the contents of my trash bin, and carried them outside. The solid *thump* of paper landing in the recycling tub was a high-five slap to my mind, a door slamming on the past.

In late afternoon the camping store became my home as I indulged myself with toys. I settled on a half-dome tent—easy to assemble. I threw in an assortment of other gear: ground cushion, sleeping bag, lantern, stove, first-aid kit, and an assortment of dehydrated meals. From the larder I added peanut butter, crackers, candy bars, soups, and my flask of Drambuie. I stuffed an ice cooler with cheese, eggs, and orange juice.

By the eve of departure my station wagon was crammed to the hilt. Four heavy boxes of books, journals, and research papers took up the far back, my laptop computer and briefcase wedged beside them. On the back seat was camping gear, food, and a suitcase. I'd left room for Rex, attaching a dog harness to the back seatbelt. On the passenger seat was the cooler, and on the floor below rested my shaving kit and a box of CDs. The odometer on my wagon had rolled past a hundred thousand miles, and being this loaded down, the wagon would struggle getting over the Rockies. The transmission had slipped recently, but I didn't want to spend several thousand dollars for a new one. I would set the cruise control for sixty-five, and keep my fingers crossed.

Rex barked non-stop from inside the house, probably upset at the upheaval. I stepped back to admire my handiwork and to stretch my aching shoulder blades. I anticipated the journey starting the next morning to be one of release and catharsis, and all the busy-work had kept me from thinking about Julia or Harold. Tiredness must be the culprit: for why else couldn't I feel a damn thing?

I went inside to make goodbye calls, holding the yapping Rex on my lap. I phoned my parents; there was no pick-up. I called Julia, and again—no answer. Getting out my address book I went down the list of friends and colleagues for whom my departure might mean something, and started dialing. My last call was to my retired neighbor, Frances, to ask her if there was anything she needed before I left.

"I'll be scared without you next door," she said. "We got rabid raccoons around here again. Look what they did to your trash, and it wasn't even dark yet!"

"My trash?"

"Dumped all over the alley," she said. "I must have scared 'em off when I drove in a half-hour ago."

I swore under my breath. "I'll pick it up, thanks."

I retrieved a flashlight and trotted to the back gate with Rex, who was now wagging his tail with "I-told-you-so" pride. The raccoons had indeed been there—the garbage was tipped over and the lid thrown to the side. But strangely, so too was my recycling bin, the contents strewn over the alleyway. Grumbling, I picked up a bottle here, a section of newspaper there. At least there was no wind to blow things about.

Why would raccoons get into the recycling? The bottles and cans were rinsed, and the newspapers inedible, even for a rabid animal. I put everything back that was lying on the ground, and stood with a hand on my hip, surveying the containers with the narrow beam of a flashlight. Something wasn't quite right. The recycling bin was only half-full. With dawning realization, my jaw clenched. My dissertation drafts were gone.

*   *   *

It was nine-thirty before I came back in, poured a jigger of Drambuie on ice, and dropped into the overstuffed recliner. I pulled my feet up, and turned off the light. This was a ritual after a hard day: sitting in the dark, Rex at my side, savoring the liqueur on my tongue and throat, letting go of the day's events.

The shock of violation I felt, that someone rummaged through my papers and made off with my manuscripts, was matched only by my self-flagellation at being so dim-witted as to leave them out. What an idiot! I'd heard of academic dishonesty, feuding professors stealing another's idea to publish it first. That sort of thing was folklore in the academic hotbeds of Cambridge and Palo Alto. But it seemed so remote from sleepy Fredericksburg that it never occurred to me to worry.

My mind chased possibilities. It could have been a random prank—juvenile delinquents rolling trash cans. I shook my head: whoever took the texts went deliberately for them. That meant someone watched the house when I deposited them this afternoon. Having several drafts meant they could follow the progression in my thinking. On the other hand, I was nowhere close to finishing. I had the pieces, but lacked a unifying theory, and those papers wouldn't help them. With the great Lattimer as witness to my proprietary rights, no respectable journal would publish anyone else using my material. What then could be the motive?

I suddenly recalled what Lattimer said at our lunch in Washington, "A deal this big could be worth a billion dollars to WorldChemm." My mind churned: was this industrial espionage? WorldChemm was not the only conglomerate interested in raking in Russian rubles—dozens of firms would love the chance of that. I ran my hand through my hair. I had set out to write a dissertation, and hadn't asked for life to get this complicated. I took a sip of liqueur and threw my head back. I slipped into an uneasy snooze.

When I drifted awake, a welcoming breeze wafted through the open window from the garden. With it came the fragrance of a flowering olive bush. In the distance I heard popping and cracking explosions, and saw flashes of fireworks. It suddenly dawned on me this was the fourth of July, and I'd gone nowhere to celebrate, and indeed, had no one besides Rex with whom to celebrate. No doubt, I was feeling sorry for myself.

I floated back to sleep, moonbeams angling over my torso. In a dream state a cumulous cloud called my name, its mist enfolding me. I heard a muted thudding, a silence, then brushing and rasping. I rearranged my body on the recliner, but the cloud came back, speaking to me; I couldn't understand.

My eyes bolted open. A giant figure peered at me from the window, its form framed by the mullions and back lit by the moon. For what seemed like an eternity I felt paralyzed in a dream state, staring at a monstrous danger. My so-called guard dog Rex had done nothing to warn me; he stood alert, ears perked, his tail wagging like a flag at an Independence Day parade.

"I'm going with you," the giant form said from the window.

"Who is it?" I stuttered. "Oh, you! Harold! Jeez!"

"Not him—me," the voice said hoarsely. "Smith."

I flung myself up. "You scared the daylights out of me."

"I'm going with you," Smith said. "I've got a satchel of his things with me."

"You're standing on my shrub, crushing my olive bush!"

Another voice came through the window. It was Julia's. "Rich, I couldn't stop him."

In a few moments we were positioned in my living room: Smith opposite me in his tan jacket, clutching a duffel bag, Julia between us. Rex sniffed with interest at the visitor's large feet.

"This is insane," I yelled. "You can't make decisions for Harold."

Julia was less-than-calm herself. "When I got back from my studio tonight he was sitting on the front porch with his bag."

"Harold seemed so well last time, so normal," I said, ignoring Smith.

"He insisted I bring him here," she said. "I didn't know what to do."

"Let's all calm down," Smith said. "So what if it is me? You'll do Harold a favor by taking me along. Those drugs are a wrecking ball to his body. He'll do better getting me heard."

"I can't do this," I said.

There was silence for a moment.

Then Julia sighed, and looked up at me. "This is asking an awful lot, Rich, but the more I think about it, the more sense it starts to make. If he doesn't go with you, Harold will have to find someone else to help channel Smith. You know how nearly impossible that is. This isn't going to go away."

"Not exactly my problem," I said, in a sleepy, cross tone.

Julia faced me, imploring. "Can you always walk away from others so easily?"

"I haven't room," I said. "See for yourself, the wagon's crammed."

"I don't need to," she shot back. "We make room in our lives for what's important."

Julia had a talent for direct hits.

As quickly as she said it, she blushed. "There goes my tongue again. I'm sorry, Rich, I shouldn't have said that. We're asking way too much of you." She took Smith's arm. "Come on, big fellow, let's go."

Smith raised his shoulders, looking at me. "I implore you then, if not on my behalf, then for Harold's sake. His only sister lives in a borough called Oakland, out where you're going."

Julia nodded her head slowly. "I'd forgotten that. He could certainly use his sister's help now. Did you know his health insurance ran out?"

None of these were my problems, and I had every right to say "no" to such an absurd imposition. The whole idea was crazy.

Rex sat calmly at Smith's feet as if he were waiting for a doggie treat. Smith obliged him with a caress of his ear. "A good sheep dog here," Smith said.

Julia snapped her fingers. "Hey, Harold's a mechanic! He'd be able to help if your old wagon breaks down." Her look at me softened. "Oh, Rich, say you'll take him?"

Rex chimed in with a bark, and all of them were looking at me.

And so that is how, at seven the next morning, I set off on a journey across America with a big-boned senior citizen, the tired Romanian from whose fading body arose a voice-spirit calling itself Adam Smith. I went along with this insanity, seduced and cajoled from being the driver of my own fate to a passenger on a journey I could not define. I could say I went along just for Julia's sake, or to have a mechanic along, but that wouldn't be all of it. The voice intrigued me—and some part of me hungered to hear more.

8 CREATING WEALTH

We set off at dawn, the dew still damp on the lawn and a clear sky brightening overhead. Julia was there to snap a picture and wave goodbye, doing so until we rounded the corner and disappeared from sight. My loose itinerary was to visit a college roommate in Chicago, see a few historical sites in the Rockies, and arrive at the summer cabin in the Sierras by early August. Despite my misgivings about having a passenger along, the trip would go quicker with someone to share the monotony. Once in California, I'd deposit Harold with his sister and enjoy the solitude of Yosemite by myself. I thought of little more than adding distance from my empty home.

I'd chosen a circuitous route to see rugged terrain, less encroached by man than the massive interstates. We left Fredericksburg on back roads, heading north and west, soon finding ourselves in rolling horse country. Colts and dams grazed against a backdrop of tidy white fences and pristine red barns. We had the road to ourselves and my companion and I spoke little.

At Manassas we turned west, gaining altitude. Within thirty miles we were swept into the Blue Ridge Mountains. Once over the summit we started a steep drop to the South fork of the Shenandoah River. An arid summer yellowed the fields and leaves clung limply to trees. Almost immediately the dinosaur's hump of the Massanutten Mountains rose out of the plain and again we climbed into cooler air before dropping to the broad Shenandoah Valley. Small, prosperous farms nestled the lowland for miles—a prodigious grocery of apple, corn, poultry, cattle, and dairy products. This was the breadbasket of the Confederacy, from which "Stonewall" Jackson conducted his diversionary raids in the early years of the Civil War. This same land Sheridan turned into desolation and destruction in its final years.

At New Market the North fork of the Shenandoah River descended from the mountains, and we had no choice but to turn off our quiet country road onto rushing I-81. Traffic grew heavy as the morning progressed. Eighteen wheelers whizzed by with Arizona, Florida, and Ohio license plates, their hefty loads a variety of sizes, shapes, and colors. We hit a patch of rain which made the road slippery, but that didn't seem to slow anyone.

"It's getting nasty," I said. "Everybody thinks they own the road, weather be damned."

"Marvelous!" Smith cried out like a little boy. He had a road map on his lap. "We cut through those mountains like they didn't exist. We passed into a new territory without even being stopped!"

The sign marker read, "Welcome to Maryland."

Smith gestured across the busy highway. "Remember the first day we spoke? You asked about wealth? This is the key! Astonishing roads like these expand your market size to almost three hundred million people!" His early reticence was broken, a levee breached after a flood. I turned on the tape recorder.

"It's no mystery how to create wealth," he went on. "You improve the skill, dexterity, and judgment of workers. But how can society do that? How did our friend Harold, a penniless immigrant from Romania—in whose body I now dwell—how did *he* raise his productive powers? Hmm?"

Smith eyed me with the alert look of a bull frog who's spied a fly on a lily-pad. "It is exchange!" he exclaimed. "Human nature has a natural propensity to truck and barter, to exchange one thing for another. Exchange allows for *specialization*. Differences between people's natural talents are limited, but differences do arise from habit, custom, and education. Our friend Harold took a liking to diesel motors, and over time—at least before his ... er, recent illness—Harold became especially good at that one thing. A specialist does things quicker and better than a generalist. The division of labor improves productivity not a little, but by a factor of ten or a hundred!"

Smith was on a roll. "Now then, what allows Harold to specialize? The secret is this: he carries out his trade within a large city. A wide market area allows him the luxury of directing his energies to repairing one thing, diesel engines. He knows all there is about glow-plugs, compression ratios, and the minutia of this narrow field. Special tools are laid out, everything at the ready for this one task. Harold tears through those motors, by Heavens! And what is true of Harold is true of every other worker in the wider market—farmers, doctors, teachers, and factory workers."

"How do you know anything about glow plugs?" I asked.

"What's in Harold's mind is mine for the borrowing," he said. "Now let me finish. When the division of labor is thoroughly established, a man supplies but a small part of his wants with his own labor. He more easily meets his other wants by exchanging his surplus for the produce of others. Every man thus lives by exchanging, and the society itself grows into what is called a commercial society."

I listened with half a mind, concentrating on a platoon of speeding tractor trailers in my rear view mirror. A semi hauling a herd of cattle loomed twenty feet behind my bumper and was still accelerating as I swerved over. Rex whined as our vehicle lurched.

Smith, oblivious to it, continued. "Contrast that with what happens if Harold's production is confined to a small village. To have enough customers he'd repair not just diesel motors but all motors, and not just motors but mufflers and brakes, even transmissions. How many more tools would he need, most of them sitting idle? How complicated and confusing that would be."

Smith fixed his eyes on the horizon. "No ... a limited market, whether resulting from political or geographical isolation, can't help but make a people poor." He turned to me. "That's why I despised the town corporations of my day. They restricted trade, insulating local producers from competition. Mercantilists they were, and I dare say, the poor pay dearly for this foolishness."

Another convoy of semis dieseled by, creating a wind blast that swayed us to the edge of the road. Rain and grime splattered the windshield. A blue sedan appeared from nowhere—a dented blight of a car. With no warning, it cut us off. I wrenched the wheel to avoid being side-swiped. "Idiot!" I yelled, flooring it and soon outdistancing him. When I looked back, the blue sedan had changed lanes and was again alongside us. Crazy driver! I lowered my window. The passenger window on the sedan was already down. From inside, a hand pointed a pistol at me.

I slammed the brakes as the gun exploded. We careened, the rear of our loaded wagon spinning leftwards across two lanes of traffic. I felt suspended in time, cars and landscape whirling by in slow-motion. A tractor-trailer bore down with its air horn blaring. Suddenly the nightmare ended and centrifugal forces flung us headlong off the road and rattling down an embankment. The wagon lurched to a rest in a field of chicory. Neither Smith nor I could move, frozen in place by our shoulder belts and shock.

Soon a burly truck driver scampered down the embankment, opened my door and helped me out. Then he lifted Smith onto the grass. Still shaking, I opened the back door and pushed aside the suitcases. Rex's nose was buried into the seat, paws pressed over his head. The harness held him. We were stunned, but unhurt.

Traffic slowed with rubberneckers. Another truck driver arrived at a trot. "Don't ch'all worry. I called 911."

As we waited for help, the two men examined the vehicle. "Took a lickin' here, but it doesn't seem too bad," the first one said. He pointed to the bullet hole in the front panel, and traced its exit on the other side. "Damn lucky it missed the fuel line."

The other man walked to the back of the station wagon and sighted down the side panel. "Frame's okay. You'll be able to drive away, once you get towed out."

"What about the other guy?" I asked.

"The coyote in the blue four-door? He didn't even slow down. Hey, here's the Smoky."

A state trooper in a clear plastic poncho waded toward us. He wrote quickly on his metal clip board, asking rapid questions of me and the truckers. He examined the bullet holes. Handing me a copy of his report he said, "I've seen more road rage this year than I did my first ten years combined." He shook his head. "Sure wish someone got his license, or even a good visual. There're hundreds of blue sedans on the road. Not much to go on."

Ten minutes later two tow trucks pulled up to the side of the highway.

"The hyenas have arrived," said one of the truckers.

The operators got out. From the arm waving and reddening faces it appeared that a dispute was underway. Finally, one of the drivers marched back to his cab, revved the engine, and took off. Within minutes we were pulled up the embankment by the other operator. The mechanic checked over the vehicle thoroughly, then cranked the engine. It coughed to life.

"You're good to go," he said.

I paid the tow driver and tried to press "beer" money on the two truckers who'd stopped to help. They adamantly refused, and I wondered if I'd broken a code of honor by offering. We waved goodbye and I eased into traffic, keeping below the speed limit. Still shaken, I pulled off at the next exit and checked us into a motel. Smith had little to say, as shocked as I by our brush with death. We watched mind-numbing television and dropped into a restless sleep.

*   *   *

"Not a lucky start to our trip," I said over breakfast the next day.

"Hardly auspicious," Smith said. "And yet, we've no injury, except of the memory. Very thankful for that."

By eight o'clock we were back on the highway, cautious and alert. I gripped the wheel, repeatedly scanning the rear view mirror. Eventually the monotony of the road took over, and yesterday's events began to fade. It would be an awful trip spent in agitation over a freak assault. Is that what it was? After the theft of my dissertation papers, the question wasn't preposterous. But I had no stomach for paranoia. I let it drop.

I finally relaxed enough to pick up the conversation with Smith from before the accident, using a line of attack my students habitually used on me.

"I'll grant you that specialization increases productivity," I said. "But haven't you forgotten something? It's monotonous repairing the same engines, day after day. Suppose Harold prefers variety and craftsmanship?"

"That's a bully point," he replied. "The division of labor, confining someone to a few simple operations, removes the need for the exercise of invention, of overcoming difficulties. A man's dexterity at his own trade is acquired at the expense of his intellectual and social virtues."

"Contradicting the argument for the division of labor," I said. "It lends credence to Marx's accusation that workers in a capitalist system are alienated."

Smith waited for a truck to pass, then raised a finger skyward. "Progress comes at a social cost, but there's a remedy—subsidized public education, for the poorest children."

"Subsidized, with vouchers?"

"I mean the teacher paid only partly by government. If the schoolmaster were paid wholly by government, he would soon learn to neglect his business."

I decided to play devil's advocate again: "Free trade may help the rich," I said, "but labor unions say tariffs and other import barriers help the poor keep their jobs."

Smith shot back, "Less trade means lower productivity, and that means fewer goods to go around. And it is goods, not monetary gold or silver, that are the true measure of wealth." He surveyed the landscape. "In my day the English fought unending wars with France. Hostilities kept cheap French wheat—what we call 'corn'—from the British market. That gave a monopoly to British growers. Wheat jobs in England rose with protection, I'll grant you that, but in the very commodity England was ill-suited to produce. Those of us who had to *buy* bread—which is everyone else—paid a stiff premium for those artificially-created jobs."

Now his speech raced. "As a corollary, there were fewer home jobs in manufacturing, the commodity England was well-suited to produce. We could hardly export when others mimicked our import restrictions. You must always ask which jobs will be *lost* through trade wars, not just count the ones saved."

He rubbed his eyes. "The natural advantages which one country has over another are sometimes so great that it is in vain to struggle with them. In Scotland, for example, we can make very good grapes in hotbeds, and produce a reasonable burgundy—at about *thirty times* the expense of importing. Should we prohibit the import of wine merely to encourage its production in Scotland? Compare the benefit with the cost! Such a restriction seems unlikely to pave the road to riches."

I was about to respond, but he went on, "And wine is hardly necessary for the nation's defense—one of the few reasons for subsidizing domestic industry."

"Food production would qualify, I assume?"

"Sailors and ships!" His eyes glistened. "We can always buy food if we have transport and trade—that's the *roundabout* way of consuming."

One of the greatest insights in economic thought, I reminded myself, was the roundabout way to consumption through trade. The topic is so central it's covered in virtually every introductory economics course. The case Adam Smith made for trade was surpassed by David Ricardo's theory of comparative advantage, a few decades after him. Yet I was continually impressed by Smith's easy, common sense manner of explaining wide-ranging issues. While my rational mind couldn't explain it, I no longer thought of him as a channeled charlatan, but as a real voice. I found myself embracing this pontificating personality: he wasn't "Smith" anymore, just plain and simple Smith, quotation marks removed.

We veered onto Route 68 at Hagerstown and followed a westward course parallel to the Potomac River and its dredged Chesapeake and Ohio Canal. Where the C&O ended in Cumberland, we picked up old Route 40, and shortly pulled into a rest area. I made cheese sandwiches with spicy mustard and we sat on the grass to eat. Rex, plenty of puppy left in him, played his favorite game of herding, circling us counter-clockwise at a gallop, barking for attention, and staying just out of reach. Eventually he tired and plopped next to Smith.

A faded historical marker caught Smith's attention. "It says here," he motioned to the sign, "that this Cumberland Highway follows an old Indian trail through the Appalachian Mountains ... that George Washington rode it during the French and Indian Wars! Hmm ... Then, as President, he made it into the first interstate, opening up commerce to the Ohio Valley." Smith's voice rose. "By Jupiter, don't you know that's what I was talking about? Roads to markets!"

"I remember a little history myself," I said, "and Washington didn't build it just for economics. Mountain farmers had trouble transporting heavy corn to market, so they fermented it into liquor. Then they refused to pay the federal tax on liquor, prompting the 'Whiskey Rebellion.' Washington built this road to keep those settlers loyal, and out of the French and Indian Alliance."

"I never said good politics didn't make good economics at times," Smith retorted. "Yes indeed, this was a wise use of public money."

We ate our sandwiches and watched a storm build to the South. Soon the sun went behind clouds and a slight chill reminded me that summer wouldn't last forever. In barely two months I would address WorldChemm's directors, and I couldn't delay work indefinitely while I lollygagged across America. I lay back, putting it from my mind. A nap was just the thing.

✳   ✳   ✳

Rex woke me with a soft growl. Nose to the ground, he circled the sleeping Smith. I tried to shush him, but Smith stirred.

"Ah ... you were talking about me?"

It was no longer Smith's lilt, but the curious Romanian of Harold Timms.

"Harold? You're back! My God!"

Harold looked around at the buzzing highway, the parked cars, and the two of us sprawled on a grassy knoll with a dog barking at him.

"Where are we?" he asked.

"Pennsylvania. Just across the border."

"Where are you taking me?"

"Harold, let me explain."

I replayed the events of the last few days—how Smith showed up at my house, and demanded I take him to Harold's sister in Oakland.

Harold worked his jaw but no sound came out.

"I'm sorry," I said. "I thought this was stupid from the start. It's kidnapping, and I have no excuse." I stood up and brushed grass from my knees. "Let's go. I'll drive you back to Virginia."

I tied Rex to his lead, and started toward the car.

Finally words came from Harold's mouth. "No ... I don't want to go back." Harold dropped back to the ground, a stalk of grass protruding from his lips. He said, "I'll miss Julia, but I need my sister. I thought about making this trip so often, and I couldn't bring myself to do it. Maybe that's why..." his voice trailed off.

As quickly as he arrived, Harold was gone and Smith's persona returned. After a puzzled moment, Rex whimpered and rolled on his back.

"You think I'm capable of kidnapping, eh?" Smith said icily. He patted Rex's tummy. "How little you must think of my character. Kidnapping!"

"What else could I assume?"

"That Harold has free will, for one thing," he said. "I'm channeling through his mind, but I've not become his mind. I couldn't do anything against his nature."

Harold's brief visit put a whole new twist to things. Smith pestered me to do what turned into the right thing for Harold. It advanced Smith's interest, but served a broader purpose. I wondered at my own behavior. Was I guided by puppet strings attached to some invisible hand?

✻   ✻   ✻

Basking in the sun, we stayed at the rest stop longer than planned. Smith was engrossed by the endless stream of big rigs dieseling by. I curled up with my *International Economy* magazine. An article on the Russian economic collapse caught my eye. Amidst all the financial reforms was the disturbing news that billions of dollars loaned by the IMF, World Bank, and other multilateral lenders, was smuggled out of the country, with destinations of New York, Bermuda, and other money-laundering locales. The country was in the grip of a powerful mafia, the *nomenclatura*. Corruption ruled daily life, fed by a determined bureaucracy.

Smith examined the backside of the story as I flipped pages.

"Not cross with me, are you?"

My grunt was non-committal.

"Good. Would you like me to summarize, then, the keys to wealth?"

I put down the magazine.

"To listen to some of your contemporaries," Smith said, "you would not think they understood me—not wholly." He pointed to the magazine article on Russia. "Creating wealth is more complicated than just allowing markets to exist. Before trade, before anything, society must maintain each individual in his perfect rights."

He paused to blow a blade of grass from his lips. "Society can't subsist among those who are at all times ready to injure one another. The first and chief design of government is to prevent one individual from encroaching against another: to protect the weak, to curb the violent, and to chastise the guilty." Smith rubbed his forehead. "Justice is the main pillar that upholds the edifice of society. If it stops working, if it is removed from the mix, the great fabric of human society must in a moment crumble into atoms."

His flowery rhetoric added to the weight of substance, and I knew that many countries fit such an agonizing description of anarchy. He seemed to intuit my thoughts. "Justice *is* the pre-condition for social order. Upon that foundation you will build commerce. To rush into it any other way is folly."

"I'm no lawyer or philosopher," I said. "Once we've got justice, tell me about wealth."

Smith gave me a hurt look, like I'd blown out the candles at his birthday party. "If you've met the preconditions for justice, the key to wealth is simple: expand the areas of market exchange, promoting specialization and competition."

"Through perfectly free trade?"

Smith shook his head. "I'm not an ideologue, remember? Governments need to raise revenues somehow. More than that," Smith turned on his side and thought a few moments, "a wealthy nation is of all nations most likely to be attacked. Unless the state takes measures for public defense, the natural habits of its citizens render them quite incapable of defending themselves."

"That's guarding wealth, not creating it."

"Wherever there is a great deal of property, there is great inequality. That's why a wealthy society is in far greater need of more government to protect every member from injustice or oppression."

"Otherwise, the poor will riot?"

He laughed. "No, the avarice and ambition of the rich man prompts him to injure others no less than the envy or resentment of the poor."

"You haven't proposed," I said, "any role for government that conflicts directly with the private sector."

"We're getting to that," he said. "Investments in public works and institutions may be in the highest degree advantageous to society, however they are of such a nature that the profit could never repay the expense directly to any one individual or small group. Therefore we could not always expect any individual or private group to erect or maintain enough of such investments."

"Such as?"

"Transportation—you can see how roads, bridges, and harbors expand markets and break down monopolies. And public education is also such an investment."

"To summarize," I suggested, "a nation's wealth hinges on this: society through government first establishes a system of justice, to protect the poor and the rich. Government invests in limited areas lacking immediate profit, but valuable for society as a whole and for business ultimately—such as infrastructure and education. Finally, government provides protection from external aggression. Beyond that, freedom?"

Smith nodded. "Every man, as long as he does not violate the laws of justice, should be free to pursue his own interest his own way. That means bringing both his industry and capital into competition with any other man. The *saving* and *accumulation* of that capital, over time, is what allows for continually greater progress."

He scanned the sky. "That being so, the natural effort of every individual to better his own condition is so powerful a principle that it alone is capable of carrying society to wealth and prosperity—of surmounting the hundred obstructions which the folly of human law encumbers!"

9 THE POOR MAN'S SON

"There's a paradox," I said to Smith as we pulled back on the highway. "You're animated about expanding wealth, yet the first time we spoke, you bit my head off for saying wealth was the objective."

"I'm an empiricist." Smith said, rapping the dashboard. "I like to record observable facts. As such, it's my obligation to examine whether material things make people happy. The issue is complicated, I'll admit, but are economists today so narrow-minded the issue doesn't seem important?"

I felt rebuked. "A growing national output or GDP is almost always considered a sign of a 'healthy' economy," I replied. "Oh, there are people on the fringes who talk about *Small is Beautiful* and the *Genuine Progress Indicator* (GPI)—which subtracts from GDP the negative impacts of pollution, crime, rising inequality, and such things—but most economists don't take time to consider these issues. Virtually all our models assume that higher output is the goal without a second thought."

"Let me lay out the broad picture," Smith said, "saving specifics for later?" He was covering a lot of ground, and I wasn't sure I had the patience, or he the stamina, to finish. Nevertheless, I nodded.

"It's clear to me," he said, "that one's material station in life isn't the ultimate factor explaining happiness. This is corroborated by numerous observations, naturally anecdotal ones, but enough surely to cloud the *unexamined* notion you so easily accept. No," he paused to punctuate his words, "happiness is fairly immune to economic fortune."

"You think peace of mind determines happiness?"

"Ultimately," he said.

"Doesn't wealth affect your peace of mind, your security for the future?"

"To a point. Man's existence requires many things that are external to him. Abject starvation isn't conducive to peace of mind; the utility of wealth can't be questioned in that regard. Eliminating such scourges is critical because it eases real, physical burdens. Perhaps a third of the earth's people still need to feel those benefits." Smith stroked his chin. "But for those who are beyond abject destitution, there's little real difference between the potential happiness of a rich person and a poor person."

"But there's a difference, holding all else constant?" I asked.

"Some, but not that great. And can you really hold all else constant?"

Smith looked at me. "May I tell you a story from my *Theory of Moral Sentiments*? One of my favorites."

I nodded.

"It's the 'Parable of the Poor Man's Son.'" He closed his eyes, and began to recite:

A poor man's son, whom heaven in its anger visited with ambition, begins to look around himself and admire the condition of the rich. He finds the cottage of his father too small for his accommodation, and fancies he should be lodged more at his ease in a palace. He is displeased with being obliged to walk a-foot, but sees his superiors carried about in carriages, and imagines that in one of these he could travel with greater convenience. He judges that a numerous retinue of servants would save him from a great deal of trouble. He thinks if he had attained these conveniences he would sit contentedly in the tranquillity of his situation. He is enchanted with the distant idea of this felicity.

Smith's voice became deeper and louder, and I found myself drawn in to this story as if it were my own unhappy fate.

To obtain these conveniences, he submits in the first year, nay in the first month of his application, to more fatigue of body and more uneasiness of mind than he could have suffered through the whole of his life from the want of them! He slaves to distinguish himself in some laborious profession which he hates, forces himself to be obsequious to people he despises, and, by so doing, finally acquires all the material riches he so long sought. But by now he's in the last dregs of life, his body wasted with toil and diseases, his mind galled and ruffled by the memory of a thousand injuries and disappointments, and he begins at last to realize that wealth and fame are mere trinkets of frivolous utility, no more adapted for procuring ease of body or tranquillity of mind than the tweezer-cases of the lover of toys.

"What's a tweezer-case?" I asked.

"A small box for tiny tools. Men of leisure carried them," Smith said. He waited for this to sink in. "Anyway, the poor man's son threw away the key to happiness which was with him all along. The stumbling block to happiness lay in his mind, not in his luxuries." Smith looked at me as if I should extract some particular meaning.

I didn't respond. It was a poignant parable, but I struggled to accept the claim that money couldn't buy peace of mind.

❈   ❈   ❈

We pulled up to "Sonny's Sports Bar" on the outskirts of Wheeling, West Virginia the next afternoon a little after one. We'd spent the night at a rundown motel with saggy mattresses and faded curtains. The motel owner allowed Rex to stay in her fenced yard while we went to lunch. The morning's sports pages inspired my choice of restaurant, as the baseball season was heating up. A sizzling rivalry between Pittsburgh and Cincinnati, in the National League Central Division, had caught my eye, and I'd had little time to watch the sport recently. A perusal of the Yellow Pages yielded a sketch of what now stood in front of us: a low-slung building with dirty wood siding and a V-roof providing the only architectural interest. A glowing neon "BAR OPEN" sign hung in the window.

The gravel parking lot was half-full of dreary, worn vehicles, mostly pick-ups. Their side panels proclaimed a variety of businesses: plumbing, roofing, landscaping. I parked beside a garish '80s Chevy with jacked wheels and shimmering lime green metallic paint; silver medallions hung from the rear-view mirror.

We walked out of the hot, bright day into a dark, air conditioned interior. It was a large open room, and we wandered toward the big screen.

"What'll you boys have?" asked a smiling waitress. She was a curvy brunette in her thirties, wearing blue jeans, a short-sleeved shirt, and sneakers.

"You got Coors?" I asked.

"Sure, hon."

"And for me, soda water," Smith said.

Heading back to the bar, she passed a man who reached out to pat her behind.

The waitress whirled.

"Jimmy, you quit that!" She gave his hand a hard slap. "Do that again and I'm calling your probation officer."

The waitress moved away to greet an incoming customer, "Lannette! You made it, darlin'! Where's Charlie?"

"Right behind, Millie."

As new customers entered, this scene was repeated, Millie's name called out, hugs passed around, and orders taken. With swift efficiency the waitress seemed to be everywhere, handing out endearments with bottles of beer. The man called Jimmy sat brooding, observing events behind his baseball cap.

Smith nodded toward the three couples seated in front of us. From the empty bottles in front of them, these Pittsburgh Pirate fans had started preparing for the game hours ago. Two of the men were in their forties, with huge bellies and arms like tree trunks. They were loud but friendly, sporting garish orange and black bandanas and eye patches, giving them courage and title to bellow wisecracks to anyone in the room. One of them turned our way and grinned. "You'all not from around here, are you?"

"No, just passing through," I said.

"You'll need some of these." He handed over some newspaper coupons illustrated with Pittsburgh Pirate symbols. "Saves twenty-five cents on each beer. Give 'em to Millie before you pay."

I thanked him.

"No big deal." The pirate took out a pack of cigarettes and thumped it on the table top. Smith eyed the pack and I wondered if the Harold inside that body was craving nicotine. The pirate withdrew a cigarette, felt in his pockets for a match, and came up empty-handed. He looked around.

Smith volunteered, "Need a light?" He fumbled through his pockets and pulled out Harold's dented Zippo lighter.

The pirate hesitated, then reached for it. He flicked the battered top and struck the flint, lighting the wick on the first try. "Pretty nice," he said, returning it.

"Perhaps you'd care to keep it?" Smith said. "I seem not to need it anymore."

"Really? You sure? Hey, thanks man."

Smith could see my chagrin and whispered, "Benevolence is part of Harold's nature as well as mine. I wouldn't be able to do anything to which he objected."

The pirates' wives, meanwhile, hovered over a stack of photographs, making exclamations. In contrast to their husbands, they'd spent time fixing themselves up: their hair was curled; one wore dangle earrings, the other costume pearls. The third couple at the table was younger, in their twenties. Their chairs were a few inches apart, their legs and arms intertwined. The young man was smartly dressed in cowboy hat and boots, pressed blue jeans, and a Madras shirt with rolled-up sleeves. The woman was thin, her hair bleached blonde, worn to the middle of her back. The couple was self-engrossed.

"Think they're newlyweds?" I asked Smith.

"They act like it," Smith nodded, in private reverie. "Takes me back. You see, in Edinburgh there was a Miss Campbell. She was lovely, and at one time I thought … well, it doesn't matter."

One of the pirates caught us observing the couple and said, "They've been engaged seven years. She won't marry him 'till they have a house of their own. He's twenty-seven, and still livin' at home." He chortled, "Who can save for a house when you got that boat payment of his?"

The National Anthem filled the bar and the big game was on the screen. No one expected it to be such a tough game for the Cincinnati Reds, at home against the Pittsburgh Pirates. Smith watched transfixed, interrupting to ask questions as the game unfolded. "Harold doesn't know a thing about baseball," he said, rolling his shoulders in a shrug of apology.

The sounds of the umpire's calls, the smack of the ball on bat, and the headlong catch by an outfielder brought the audience to its feet, hooting and hollering. Pirates' and Reds' fans were equally numbered in the bar, and good-natured ribbing flew back and forth. All eyes were glued to the screen, except for the outcast Jimmy, who sat alone against the far wall, nursing a beer and chain-smoking. His eyes lasered holes into the bottom of his glass.

There was another roar from the crowd. The third base umpire's hands flew up to call the runner safe, and a middle aged man in black plastic glasses stormed to the pirates' table in front of us. He made a production of pulling a dollar bill from his wallet and slapping it onto the table. "For paying off the umps," he said. A big grin showed off his missing teeth. Hoots and hollers rose from partisans in the crowd.

I looked back to the far wall; the morose Jimmy was gone.

"Chili's on!" Millie strode from the kitchen carrying a big iron kettle. We got in line and dished ourselves a steaming bowl, threw on a handful of dry crackers, and spread slabs of butter on cornbread. The meal came at just the right time in that overly air conditioned bar, and precipitated a splurge of beer orders as burning mouths sought relief. That woman Millie was nobody's fool.

The television camera panned the stadium of 50,000 fans. Behind glass partitions in luxurious sky-boxes, tuxedoed waiters served a few privileged guests.

"Hey, that's the Prattston Coal box," cried a burley man. "That's management spending your raise!" The crowd jeered at the screen.

"What do those fancy seats cost?" Smith asked.

"Five thousand, and up," I said. "Corporate money."

"Can it enhance someone's enjoyment of the game? Is there the same fellow-feeling as in here?"

I shrugged.

By the bottom of the ninth, tension filled the bar to a frenzy. Both teams performed superb fielding and hitting. More bills were slapped on the pirates' table in front of us, as part of a betting pool. The game appeared headed into extra innings with a 4–4 tie, two outs, and a lone runner on second.

The Reds sent in a pinch hitter who fouled away a stream of ninety-mile-an-hour pitches. Patiently he worked the count to 3–2. The room quieted, even Millie setting down her tray.

"Here's the windup," the announcer said.

The batter swung and connected, sending the ball up the middle, inches from the glove of the diving short stop. An outfielder raced to it as the runner rounded third. It was a magnificent throw from center, arriving at the plate with the clash of bodies. Runner and catcher lay in a heap, the umpire poised over them. Then the ball trickled away, and the bar erupted with deafening screams and baleful howls. The pirates shook their heads in disgust.

The bar began to empty. I dropped a twenty note on the table with the coupons handed me earlier. We hadn't made it to the door before one of the pirates rushed in.

"Millie! Better get out here pronto!"

A crowd gathered around the shiny Chevy Malibu that we parked next to. The headlights and taillights were shattered. Glass shards sprinkled the gravel. An earthquake fault line covered the windshield. Millie stood by the car, a hand to her mouth. She cried. "The bastard! He hasn't been outta jail a month."

The pirate who had befriended us sauntered over.

"Lover's quarrel?" I asked.

"Naw. They been married and divorced already. Her ex—Jimmy—he's mad at himself, at life. Got laid off at the mill five years ago. All those steel jobs got moved to Korea." He shook his head. "Once you've been a union steelworker, dammit, how're you gonna wash cars for a living and look yourself in the mirror? How're you gonna support your family cleaning hubcaps?"

A few people around us nodded understandingly.

"A man loses his pride, he's not got much left. That's when Jimmy started beatin' on Millie. After the divorce he hung with a bad crowd, next thing you know he's caught in some burglaries. And would you believe," he gestured at the car, "that Chevy was his pride and joy before the divorce? Rebuilt every piece himself."

Back in our car, I said to Smith, "I guess that about settles it. The lack of money caused the break-up of Millie's marriage and untold unhappiness to others. Do you still deny money can buy peace of mind?"

10 THE LADY SINGS

Smith formed that enigmatic smile of his. "This fellow, Jimmy, had food and shelter enough. Did you not hear right? It was his *pride* that was wounded. His emotional attachment to that superceded his material deprivations. Aside from him, that place was filled with reasonably happy people—a roof over their heads, their bellies full, and surrounded by friends. What more is there?"

"Quite a lot," I replied. "We've got to assume that those rich people in the sky-boxes must be even more contented, since they had the option of going to a sports bar, but decided, instead, to go to the stadium. Their choice couldn't be irrational."

Smith chuckled. "People engage in self-deception all the time, but let's forget that." He stifled a yawn. "I'm sleepy."

We stopped at the motel for Rex and drove back to Route 40 and over the Ohio River. Smith slept soundly through all the traffic noise. When we stopped for dinner I called my former college roommate in Chicago. He was expecting my visit, but not an additional guest.

"Well?" Smith looked up from the table. He'd eaten little and seemed pasty-faced.

"We're fine. He's got room for both of us," I said. "He's a corporate lawyer now, mucky-mucks in high society. We'll play it by ear and decide what we want to do when we get there."

Smith frowned. "Wouldn't it be prudent to plan further ahead?"

*　　　*　　　*

We drove through the night, stopping once for a nap and to refuel. Finally, the Chicago skyline loomed ahead in the stalled traffic. The city was overwhelming, not just in size, but in the cacophony of sounds and the relentless push of humanity against steel and concrete. We nudged forward an hour and a half before reaching our downtown exit. Twenty minutes later we pulled into the garage of Jed Wheeler's apartment on Michigan Avenue. We grabbed our bags and rode the elevator to a dizzying height.

"Rich!"

Jed opened the door before we rang. He ushered us into a spacious living room, decorated in white leather sofa and chairs, white rug, and white lighting. A picture window overlooked Lake Michigan twenty-five stories below. I introduced Smith as the "retired professor Smythe."

Smith peered out the window at the tiny freighters plying the waters. He smiled.

"Not bad for a south Georgia boy, is it?" Jed laughed. "Remember how dirt poor I was in college, Rich? Quite a change, huh? Sally and I will move to the suburbs when we have a family, but no point in facing that commute now." He bent down and opened his arms. "Come here, Rex, let me give you a hug."

Rex's tail was doing its imitation of a conductor's baton, keeping pace with a lively scherzo.

"You're sure he's welcome?" I asked.

"You kidding? We never had fewer than four or five dogs when I was growing up. Needed at least that many for hunting." Jed stood, giving Rex a final pat, "Tell me about your trip."

I shared the highlights, omitting mention of Smith's channeling.

"What would you like to do in Chicago?" Jed asked.

"I'd love to see something cultural," I said. "Something edifying. You know, mingle in the high society of the Windy City."

Jed laughed. "That's totally my wife's department. Sally will figure something." He picked up the phone and punched a number. "Sal? Rich and his friend just got in. They need suggestions on cultural events." Jed listened for a minute. "You got it!" Jed said, and hung up. "Saturday night, a Gala performance of the Lyric Opera."

"Splendid! Splendid!" Smith said.

"We've got season tickets, but Sally knows I'd rather stay home. She's pretty swamped also."

Smith poked me and whispered. "Ask him how much they cost. We're on a tight budget." Our budget *was* a concern: Smith was totally broke and I was getting by on last semester's salary.

Jed waved his hand. "Forget it. We might not even have used them. I'll get to stay home and watch the Braves on TV."

I looked at Smith's duffel bag and was certain it contained nothing he could wear to an opera. Jed read my mind. "I've got a tux that'll probably fit him," he pointed to Smith, "and if you've got a suit, you'll be fine."

✳   ✳   ✳

We spent the rest of the week resting, or at least Smith did. Never have I seen anyone sleep as long and yet so fitfully. The channeling was, as Julia said, exhausting. He would arise groggily, every few hours, to take Rex for a walk. "It's my job while we're here," he insisted. "You've got more important things to attend."

I was anxious to reach Julia, to share our adventures: our conversations, and our frightening accident. I dialed her number often, letting it ring. No pickup. Why are artists so averse to simple mechanical devices like answering machines? I spent the first free afternoon re-packing the station wagon. Our careen down the embankment left a tossed salad of books, clothes, and camping gear. The tapes I made of Smith's conversations were strewn about the back. These I collected, labeled, and packed in a covered box.

The next morning I brought up my dissertation files and sat at Jed's kitchen table. The pages seemed foreign to me. Did I write this? If I did, it must have been in a dense fog. After five hours staring at a computer screen, hands poised over the keyboard, I packed my papers and left the apartment. I lost myself in museums, discovering a Georgia O'Keefe print at the Art Institute gift shop which I had packed for shipping. The abstract was called, "Black Cross," done on one of O'Keefe's early visits to New Mexico. The dark cross was hewn of thick beams, and so dominated the foreground that only a small portion of it was visible. In the background, rolling bare hills basked in a sunset. The painting moved me deeply. I got out pen and paper.

"Dearest Julia," I began, "The lone cross suggests that humanity's presence can be felt even in the most barren deserts. I hope you…"

I tore off that sheet and began again. "Dear Julia, This reminds me of your beautiful paintings, the shapes magnified, the details simplified. It brings out essential beauty, and…"

I sat for a minute, then crumpled that sheet, too. Finally, I wrote, "Julia, Thinking of you. Rich." I shoved the note in the envelope and tucked it in with the package.

✳   ✳   ✳

It was Saturday night and Smith was in a surprisingly cheerful mood. Over an early dinner he regaled Jed, Sally, and me with his experiences at the Paris Opera.

"Took in the whole season, I did! Spring of ... well, doesn't matter when." He rapped his knuckles on the table. "There's nothing—I say nothing—more deeply affecting than serious opera. Poetry, music, acting—all coming together, a most delicious pleasure."

Jed and Sally nodded. I was unable to relax, keeping a vigil over Smith's tendency to forget what time period he was in. All that sleep made him talkative, and he prattled on.

"Oh, and the politics were so dangerously amusing," he said. "You see, the Queen favored the Italian opera and His Majesty the French. It became an 'Opera War'—a delightful fracas!"

Jed's eyebrows furrowed. "My history may be a little rusty, but there hasn't been a King and Queen of France since..."

"Oh, doesn't matter." Smith waved his hand airily as if to dismiss any trifling irregularities. "Personally, I've always found comedies to be the best. The acting's better," Smith intoned, sipping tea. "It's impolite to say, of course, but *castrati* are perfectly insipid as actors, scarcely tolerable. Though I imagine tonight's female roles will be sung by women."

There was puzzlement as Jed and Sally looked at each other. We groaned in unison. "Another of your sick jokes," I said, attempting to cover his gaffe.

"What? What did I say?"

"Come on, let's get ready."

Jed and I outfitted Smith in the borrowed tux, and we set off for our night of culture. The Civic Opera House entrance was crowded with cars and stretch limos. After circling the block to no avail, I resigned myself to valet parking. It cost fifteen dollars, plus a three dollar tip for ding and scratch "insurance."

Smith looked aghast at the prices. "This is not prudent. Not at all."

The performing arts hall was a magnificently gilded art-deco structure, built in the boom of the nineteen twenties and adorned with carved gold leaf angels on the crown molding. Giant oil paintings, bronze statues, and pink marble columns rose in the entryway. We climbed the broad staircase to the first balcony. Smith looked the part of a gangly teenager at a prom, arms and legs an inch too long for the borrowed tux, and limping slightly from constricted shoes; the collar constrained his neck.

The hall was packed, and for Sally's eighty-dollars-a-head tickets we were ushered to the first balcony, second row. I turned to the man on my left, studying the program: "Have you seen *Eugene Onegin* before?"

His wife leaned over. "Once. And you?"

"No, it came out a century after my time," Smith said, pulling on his collar. The woman tilted her head a quarter-inch to the right.

"Never saw it either," I said quickly, drawing her attention to the program notes. "Did you enjoy it?"

"It's fabulous!" the woman responded. "Tchaikovsky's music captures Pushkin's wonderful libretto. Hope you brought a hanky!"

The conductor was greeted by spontaneous applause and the lights lowered. His baton sliced the air and I didn't need program notes to tell me this was Tchaikovsky—ebullient, romantic, over-blown and foreshadowing. Eugene Onegin, the vain and pompous protagonist, appeared in the garden, urbanely self-confident and proud. He was confronted by Tatyana, the pure but homely country girl who loved him deeply and sincerely. He scorned her, and in a fit of boredom shamelessly flirted with his best friend's fiancée. In typical Russian fashion, this affront could only be settled by his friend throwing down a gauntlet. The boom of dueling gunfire ended the second act, and Onegin cradled his dying friend in his arms. The woman next to us looked over.

"Was I right?"

I nodded. "I'll need a hanky."

"Remind me to tell you something when it's over," the chatty woman said, moving to the aisle.

We shuffled through the crowd to a reception area. The humming of voices accompanied my mental processing of the first act. I'd found Onegin in myself, spurning the love of a good woman. Is that what I'd done to Julia? How many times had I been unable to love, to reciprocate the most basic of human emotions?

Waiting in line at the bar, Smith inclined his head toward two young women in front of us.

"Isn't it wonderful?" beamed the shorter one. "I've *got* to get the CD."

The taller one shrugged. "It's not nearly as good as Pavarotti at the Met. Once you've heard a world class production, it's hard to listen to this."

Smith turned to me, a grin spreading on his face. "Nothing can please that woman!" he whispered. "She's superior to everything she possesses! She's like that jaded Venetian, Senator Pococurante, that Voltaire describes so amusingly in *Candide*. You're familiar with *Candide*?" I shook my head. "No?" Smith frowned. "I should think someone of Voltaire's genius would be required reading."

Nearby, two elegantly dressed couples gave each other a loud greeting. They were talking so animatedly that we couldn't help overhearing. One of the women asked, "What about Thanksgiving? *Do* join us in Aspen, it will be so much fun!"

The man who appeared to be her husband said, "We're having the Marburys as well. You remember Roger and Celia?"

The other woman responded quickly, "It's a lovely offer, but I'm afraid we can't even think about it. Francis doesn't know when he's getting back from Andover, and Andrew's been invited to join his friend William on safari in South Africa. Frank has a trip to Europe around then, so we thought we might all meet in London. It's so complicated."

"Oh, I understand completely," the first woman recovered with a wave of her hand. "We barely made it tonight. Marcia had her dressage lesson this morning at six, and I rushed from that to get Philip to a game at St. Stephen's. On top of everything we had to let Elsa go last week."

Smith listened intently, his face glowing. He winked at me, as if I should glean some important meaning from this banter.

Reaching the front of the line, I ordered a beer.

"We don't serve beer," the bartender said. "Wine, champagne, cocktails, that's it." He looked beyond me to the next customer.

"Okay—um, wine then," I said, blanching when I saw the price.

I heard Smith's voice behind me.

"A wee dram, please."

"What?" the bartender asked.

"Scotch. Plain, no water."

I whirled, spilling wine on my sleeve. "You will not!"

Smith grimaced. "Er. How silly. I forgot. Water then."

The bartender handed over a Perrier. I dropped a ten onto the counter for both of us, groaning inwardly. Threading our way through the crowd, we heard snatches of conversation:

"...a six-thirty tee-off. Any later and the course will be jammed."

"The market's moving, but where? Hong Kong was down five percent."

"We'll dock in the British Virgins for a day, then sail to Bermuda."

"Jerry got reamed in the divorce. In terms of alimony, he's cooked."

"Jameson's livid about the merger. His parachute is nothing like Fletcher's."

Smith had loose hold of my arm. He squeezed it like he'd just won a bet, at my expense. He leaned over, about to say something, but the bells chimed, the lights dimmed, and we started back to our seats.

The final act was as ornately tragic as the first. Onegin reappears, morose and melancholic, having wandered for four years mourning the death of his friend. On his return to St. Petersburg he attends a ball hosted by his aging cousin, Prince Gremin, only to discover that Tatyana, now a poised and refined woman, is there as Gremin's wife and Princess! In a deep baritone, the Prince pledges his devotion to Tatyana, now that she has made him so happy by her purity, charity, and good nature. Crestfallen, Onegin covets the love he once spurned. He pursues Tatyana with his usual vanity, thinking surely to win her back. She still loves him, but remains true to her husband. In the climax she rushes off-stage, leaving Onegin broken and destroyed as the curtain falls.

The audience stood, applauding through two curtain calls. I sat transfixed.

Smith read my thoughts. "'Tis well known," he bellowed over the clapping, "that the misfortunes of the greater part of men have arisen from simply not knowing when they were well! When it was proper for them to sit still and be contented." Smith shook his head sadly. "Do you know what Milton said?…"The mind is its own place, and in itself, can make a heav'n of hell, a hell of heav'n."

Our neighbors turned to leave.

"Excuse me. You were going to tell us something?" I asked.

The woman turned. "Tchaikovsky was so moved by Onegin's fate—and so terrified by superstition—that he married a woman he didn't love simply to avoid spurning her!"

"Oh God," I said, "life imitates art! But it worked out? Love triumphed?"

She laughed. "Heaven's no! He was miserable!"

＊   ＊   ＊

We pushed through the crowd into the outside air. Thermal waves rose from the concrete sidewalk; it was humid and hot. The avenue was congested with chattering groups as we ambled toward the valet parking pickup.

We were waiting in line for our car when I heard the first shot—a loud crack in my right ear, sounding like a two-by-four slapped on wet cement. Smith and I recoiled, out of phase with the bullet that shattered the window of a parked car next to us. Safety glass crunched onto the sidewalk.

"Watch out!" someone screamed.

A second explosion ricocheted off the street lamp next to us. People scattered, forming a retreating wave. I propelled Smith behind the trunk of a tree. Fifteen feet to the rear a security guard struggled for a gun held by a small, dark-haired man. The guard's cap lay on the ground. The attacker was lighter than the guard but fought intensely and with better training. A mesmerized crowd closed a circle twenty feet away but pulled back each time the gun swung in its direction. Smith and I retreated slowly.

The assailant kicked to the groin, doubling over the guard. He raised the butt of his gun and smashed it to the head of the guard, who collapsed. The assailant whirled and the crowd recoiled. He vanished down an alley, black hair bobbing as he ran. In a minute the street was packed with police, and the injured guard was lifted into an ambulance.

"That was way too close," I said to Smith, driving home. "It's hazardous out there. Road rage one day, robbery the next."

It was only later, when the magnitude of our near escapes sank in, that my mind turned toward a darker path to truth. For that night, anyway, I slept soundly.

11 WEALTH AND HAPPINESS

We left Chicago the next morning, once again heading west. Given the summer heat, I chose to follow a northerly route, passing over the prairies in Iowa and South Dakota, and crossing the Rockies in Montana and Idaho. After that, we'd head for the coast and follow it to San Francisco, where I'd drop Harold at his sister's house across the bay in Oakland. It wasn't the most direct route, but I didn't need to beat any deadlines. The Yosemite cabin would not be mine for another two weeks.

The Illinois sky was clear, a thin haze hanging on the horizon of the city fading behind us. At this time of day, commerce was heading into the metropolis, not out, and after an hour of dense suburban traffic, the road opened into farmland. I stretched my back, rotated my shoulder blades, and eased my grip on the steering wheel.

The moment seemed ripe to make sense of our experiences at the sports bar and at the opera. I pressed the record button on the tape recorder and glanced at Smith. He anticipated me, saying: "Surely you teach your students about diminishing returns?"

"Of course," I nodded. "If it's a warm afternoon, the first glass of ice-water I drink has a bigger impact on quenching my thirst than the second glass, and the second more than the third. By the fourth glass I'm getting very little additional benefit, or maybe even a negative benefit if I feel bloated. That's diminishing marginal utility."

"Well then, this applies to wealth as well," he said. "That's why the great source of both the misery and disorder of human life seems to arise from over-rating the difference between poverty and riches. It's quite scientific: our observations satisfied you, didn't they, that vast sums of money are not required to produce the most intense fellow-feeling? Tell me, what did these experiences cost?"

"The sports bar cost $20," I said. "The opera, including the value of tickets, parking, and drinks, came to about $200."

"My point is," Smith said, "it cost *ten times* more at the opera than it did at the sports bar. Was the return ten times higher? If not, then there are diminishing returns to wealth, and my thesis is that it diminishes ever-so-rapidly."

I shrugged. "Makes sense."

"Of course. Don't you think it possible that in the ordinary situations of life a well-disposed mind—take those Pirates' fans we met at the sports bar—could be as calm, as cheerful, and as contented as any of the high-heeled set from the opera?"

"There's no scientific basis for saying so. Surely you prefer wealth to poverty?"

"Wealth deserves to be preferred. But it doesn't deserve to be pursued with that passionate ardor which drives us to violate the rules of prudence or justice, or to corrupt the future tranquility of our minds. If wealth alone becomes the object, there is always someone with more, and 'having' is nothing if it isn't the 'most'! The pleasures of the rich, consisting of vanity and superiority, are seldom consistent with perfect tranquility."

I let these ideas settle; there was a logic to it, yet I had a litany of doubts.

"My second point," Smith said, "Is that an increase in wealth produces only a *temporary* surge in good feeling, because sooner or later we accommodate ourselves to it. Happiness restores itself to its prior—let us call it its 'natural'—level, just as a pendulum finds its balance." Smith shook his head. "Power and riches can keep off the summer shower, not the winter storm, and they leave you always as much—and sometimes more than before—exposed to anxiety, to fear, and to sorrow; to danger, and to death."

✻ ✻ ✻

The flat rectangles of Iowa farm fields whizzed by on our linear path. The sun was high overhead. We resumed the conversation.

"You can't compare the happiness of the rich and poor in any absolute sense," I said. "Besides, actions speak louder than words. When poor people acquire wealth they stop going to sports bars and they start buying sky boxes and opera tickets. They drop the bowling league, and take up golf. Their *revealed preference* is for things of the rich."

Smith nodded. "Yes, this is what I call the great 'deception' of the human mind, that the poor race after the luxuries of the rich. This disposition to admire, and almost to worship, the rich and the powerful..." he paused for emphasis "...is the greatest and most universal cause of the corruption of our moral sentiments!"

I stirred in my seat. Overhead a pair of buzzards flew lazy circles. We passed a billboard advertising a Pancake House.

"Okay, I'll bite," I said. "How does this corrupt anyone's morals?"

Smith replied as if mating in chess, "The candidates for fortune too frequently abandon the paths of virtue. Unhappily, the road which leads to the one, and that which leads to the other, lie sometimes in very opposite directions."

We pulled into the Pancake House, found a shady spot for Rex with his water, and went inside. Smith used the rest room while I bought a newspaper and found us a booth. A small caption in the Entertainment section simply read, "Opera Marred by Shooting." It was a small blurb, apparently added to later editions. Police reported no motive for the attack, nor was any intended victim identified. The security guard was released from the hospital with minor injuries. A black wig was found in a trashcan in the alleyway, but investigators were unwilling to disclose other leads.

I sipped my coffee. Something didn't make sense. The robber—I presumed it was a robbery attempt—had picked an odd setting to practice his profession. Wouldn't a deserted locale have been better, somewhere without security guards milling about? Then I remembered all the wealthy people at the opera. Perhaps the economics made sense: the higher risk he took went along with a potentially higher reward. It made intellectual sense but my gut told me there was something else I'd missed.

After lunch we headed back onto the highway. I said to Smith, "This ... this 'deception' of mind you spoke of earlier—that people corrupt themselves unwittingly—any such deception would defy the foundation of much of modern economics." I paused. "Most economists ascribe to a model of economic man who is 'rational.'"

Smith seemed unperturbed. I decided to gently provoke him. "Do you have the gall to presume you're wiser than the masses? Isn't that pure snobbery?"

Smith stretched. "Rocking your boat, am I? Moral philosophy, at least as I practice it, examines motives," he said. "That's the key to this riddle. You, however, focus on the external behavior and ignore motives. But to what purpose is all the toil and bustle of this world? What is the reason for avarice and ambition? It is the *vanity*, not the ease, or the pleasure, which interests men in acquiring things. The rich man glories in his riches because they naturally draw upon him the attention of the world."

"And why does any of this constitute a deception?" I asked.

"In what constitutes the real happiness of human life, the poor are in no respect inferior. The beggar, who suns himself by the side of the highway, possesses that security which kings are fighting for." Smith turned to make sure he had my attention. "If the chief part of human happiness arises from the consciousness of being beloved, as I believe it does, sudden changes of fortune seldom contribute much to happiness."

We approached a populated area with billboards hawking everything from luxury cars to pantyhose. Smith grimaced. "To found a great empire for the sole purpose of raising up a people of customers, is a project fit only for a nation of shopkeepers!"

"That may well be," I said, "but at least it'll help us find a place to sleep." It was four o'clock, time to give Rex a run, and I could tell the long ride was tiring Smith. I pulled off at the exit and our luck held: the motel took pets.

After dinner and a shower, Smith and I lounged in our pajamas, Rex at the foot of my bed. Out of habit I flicked through the cable television stations. The channels assaulted us, each louder and more jarring than the one before. Smith watched and his face grew dark. On the shopping channel a saleswoman was animatedly hawking manufactured-diamond bracelets. Smith scowled. "How many people ruin themselves by laying out money on these trinkets? Eh?"

I lowered the volume and Smith went on. "Think how these trifling conveniences soak up the most anxious attention, and are ready to burst into pieces and crush in their ruins their unfortunate possessor!"

I laughed. "A rather dramatic way of putting things."

"More to the point, where is the prudence in all this? Where is the self-command to delay gratification? Without saving for the future, this country can scarcely hope for future prosperity!"

Smith, this wizard of elocution, seemed always ready to anticipate the next step, add a nuance, shade a hair. "But there's a redeeming side to all this vain search for material happiness," he went on, yawning. "It's this deception which rouses and keeps in continual motion the industry of mankind."

"We strive harder? Professor Smith?"

No answer. Smith had fallen into a deep sleep.

I punched the remote, searching for a Chicago station. The evening news was almost over, judging from the light banter of the anchors. My shot of Drambuie made me mellow. I dozed, unwilling to make the effort to crawl under the sheets.

A slick newscaster with a polyester smile faced his co-host. "Brenda, what's the latest on the Opera shooting?"

I cracked an eye.

"Mark, the mayor's opponent, who was among the crowd when the shooting occurred, is turning this into a campaign issue. He released a statement today charging that, 'Not even the city's most public places are safe anymore.' The mayor's office denied the allegation, and said Chicago's streets are, quote, 'Safer than ever.'"

As she was speaking, the visual switched to a grainy black and white security tape shot outside the Opera House. A small man with a wig of thick black hair was striding with decided intent, a hand inside his windbreaker. His face again seemed disturbingly familiar. His eyes darted left and right, the thin nose defined and hard. The video replayed.

I turned the volume up and Smith tossed in bed, covering his ears.

"Brenda, why all the media attention to this story? Presumably a foiled robbery, with no one seriously hurt. Certainly not remarkable in this city."

"Mark, what started as a minor incident now has officials scrambling. No one at City Hall is willing to speak on the record, but WCYX has confirmed that the FBI was brought in on the case. There's one piece of evidence the police have not released, a flier or poster recovered from the scene."

The reporter smiled with obvious enjoyment. "Confidential sources tell us it contains references to the terrorist group, 'People Over Profit.' That group claimed responsibility for bombing the Russian consul earlier this year. They've also promised to disrupt the trade summit in San Francisco next month."

The male anchor raised his eyebrows. "Any leads on the suspect?"

"Mark, investigators are trying to locate where that black wig was bought. There's one other thing. Police interviewed several witnesses who claim to have seen the suspect fleeing the scene in a vehicle. An older model blue sedan."

II

TRANSFORMATION

"[K]een and earnest attention to the propriety of our own conduct … constitutes the real essence of virtue."

—ADAM SMITH,
THE THEORY OF MORAL SENTIMENTS (FIXXX P. 244)

12 THE SEARCH FOR PROFIT

Des Moines, Iowa

Dear Julia,

*As you can see in this panorama postcard, these flowing lands
make for easy driving. Easy for the mind to wander, and wonder.
There's so much I want to ask. Smith sleeps most of the time.
Thanks for forwarding my mail to Sioux Falls. We'll be there later
today. Thinking of you,*

Rich

We drove on, jogging north into South Dakota. I parked at
the Post Office in Sioux Falls to collect my mail sent General
Delivery. There were two letters, one the size of a small note
card. The envelope was penned with a calligrapher's swirl. I
opened it immediately.

Dear Rich,

It's been quiet without you and Harold. I wonder how your trip is going. My neighbor told me my phone's been ringing off the hook. I could kick myself for not having an answering machine (that's taken care of now). I've been hauling loads of paintings to the gallery. The opening is Friday. Wish me luck!

There is more to say, but hope I'll have a chance to say it when you get back. The Reverend sends regards.

Warmly,

Julia

The other mail was an official-looking business envelope, with a return address of the Adam Smith Chair of Economics, Cambridge, Massachusetts. I braced. True to form, there was no salutation:

Burns:

What the hell are you doing? It may seem trivial to you, but World-Chemm was expecting a report a week ago. Not to mention I have yet to see your final chapter. Have you heard of email? The telephone? CALL ME.

—Bob Lattimer

P.S. I suppose I should mention, WorldChemm received death threats from some idiotic Bolshevik group. Seems they're opposed to WorldChemm's Russian buy-out. Quite a pain in the ass, having security around me every minute of the day. This is what they pay me for, I guess.

*　　　*　　　*

Sioux Falls was a hundred miles behind us, the flat prairies stretching ahead to the curve of the earth. Smith and I spoke little. He was tired and lowered his seat back, snoozing for much of the time. Rex mimicked Smith's exhaustion, resting with his nuzzle pressed on the back seat. It was just as well that Smith occupied himself thus. I didn't feel like talking, nor did I want to share my fears.

I mulled over the strangely familiar picture of the attacker I'd seen on television last night: a grainy black and white video of a man clutching a gun in his windbreaker. Where had I seen him before? The reference to "People Over Profits" jogged my memory to the Faculty Club lunch with Wayne and Carol. If Lattimer was a target of POP, then what about me? It seemed too bizarrely coincidental that Lattimer received death threats while I was forced off the highway in Maryland and shot at again in Chicago. And what of my stolen dissertation drafts? How did these pieces fit together?

Why would anyone want me dead? I was hardly a celebrity like Lattimer, and my work on the WorldChemm formula would be reason enough to kidnap me, not murder me. If I wasn't the target, then what about Harold? Who would want to kill an unemployed truck mechanic with no close friends? Did he have past enemies? Debts from a loan shark? Highly unlikely. I reached the inescapable conclusion: WorldChem's formula held the clue. I needed to discover why someone wanted to kill me, rather than steal the formula once I'd finished it. First, I needed to stay alive.

In his current condition Harold was vulnerable, rendered incapacitated by the channeling. Next to me, Smith's head was thrown back, eyes tightly shut, a faint snore emanating with every deep breath. I glanced instinctively in the rear view mirror, assuring myself that no car threatened. I rolled my neck, pondering how POP might next strike. The permutations grew rapidly. I shook my head in frustration: maybe I was just being paranoid, after all.

✢   ✢   ✢

We stopped overnight at a motel several miles from the highway, and drove on the next morning for a few hours. Along the broad Missouri River we found a rest area where I spread out a late-morning brunch of peanut butter sandwiches, carrot sticks, and fresh fruit. Smith was livelier, eating heartily, and when lunch was nearly over, I started the tape recorder.

"Forgive me if this sounds a bit critical," I said, "but it seems you're partly to blame if people don't understand you. If wealth doesn't pave the road to happiness, why didn't you say that in *Wealth of Nations*? And why talk of self-interest as a guiding principle, which today people could only interpret as selfishness?"

"Richard, calm yourself." Smith munched on a peach for dessert. "Four hundred pages—that's the effort I spent explaining the motives for human behavior in *Theory of Moral Sentiments*. No one in my day was so befuddled as to imagine only wealth or self interest mattered to me. If people don't read me, is that my fault?" He pulled out the peach pit and tossed it gently aside. Rex ran off after it and soon was grubbing in earnest.

"Doesn't seem that *Moral Sentiments* made much of an impression," I said.

"On the contrary, it was an instant classic, translated into French, German, even Russian eventually. All the great philosophers—David Hume in particular—wrote with high praise." Smith's voice faded and he became lost in thought for a moment. Then he turned to me and said, "You know, I think you'd enjoy meeting my friend David. Everyone does. I really ought to get you two together."

"Very funny," I said. I was now quite fond of the curmudgeon. His learned outbursts didn't faze me anymore. Rex attentively watched the family eating at the next picnic table, no doubt hoping some part of a sandwich would fall to the ground.

Smith sighed, laying back on the grass with his head propped between his hands. He surveyed the heavens dreamily. "My book on *Moral Sentiments* is what made my reputation ... allowed me to retire from academics; I was barely forty! Yes, I gave up tenure at Glasgow University to accept an offer to tour Europe as the tutor to a rich young lad. Something of a rite of passage for the boy, and I'd never been there either."

From his tone, it sounded like this stood out as an eye-popping experience. He said, "Yes, that book, and my friendship with Hume, is what opened doors for me in Paris, what allowed me to spend evenings with Doctor Quesnay and other reformers like Jacques Turgot. I remember them well. Doctor Quesnay had been the physician to the King's mistress—Mme. de Pompadour—as well as founder of the Physiocrats. The Physiocrats were ingenious at modeling the economy, the first to do so, really."

Smith's eyes sparkled. "It was the mid-1760s, and that small clutch of us were promulgating revolutionary free market principles from the safety of our salons, despite official censorship in France. Then brave men like Turgot actually got a chance to put some of these ideals into practice as finance minister, for a brief time, anyway—breaking down the trade restraints of the feudal lords! Removing the monopoly of the guilds! Had the King allowed Turgot to continue ... well, who knows what might have happened? Is it too great a stretch to wonder whether reforms might have staved off the French revolution? Might have saved Louis XVI's neck—*literally?*"

I was useless at French history, and made a vow to read up when I had the time. When would that be? Smith was smiling, a downturn at one corner of his mouth. "I was happy to go home, though, after two years on the continent. I missed my mother. I spent the next ten years living off my pension, writing *The Wealth of Nations.*"

I'd read something about that, early in my search to disprove Smith's channeling. "That's why some people say *Moral Sentiments* was the scribbling of a naïve youth," I said. "They say you subsequently became wiser from your stay in Europe, that the emphasis on self interest in *Wealth of Nations* reflects that maturity."

"Nonsense," Smith retorted. "My sixth edition of *Moral Sentiments* was published fourteen years after *Wealth of Nations!*" He sat up. "Do you think I'm so sloppy I'd let my *magnum opus* go to print if it erred on human nature, or contradicted my applied text on commerce?"

Two members of the family near us looked over.

"You're alarming them," I said.

"All right, then," he whispered. "This issue didn't arise until eighty years after my death, when I couldn't defend myself."

I smiled. "Keynes once wrote that so-called 'practical' people were ruled by little else than the views of defunct economists. Are you saying that people are actually ruled by the *caricatures* of the views of defunct economists?"

"Quite." Smith eyed me, softness in his smile. "It's been a long stretch, but I think you're finally learning something—ha!"

*   *   *

By late that afternoon, the prairies gave way to the windswept buttes of the Badlands. The famous Black Hills loomed ahead as distant gray silhouettes. Tomorrow we'd do tourist duty, visiting stony presidents on Mount Rushmore, and the next day we'd visit Custer's last stand at Little Big Horn, Montana. With this in mind, I found a campsite outside Rapid City, well off the highway. I'd be harder to spot than at a motel by the freeway. Besides, I enjoyed camping, and found the routines refreshing.

The little oasis was parched, and I put out a big bowl of water for Rex, then set about making camp. Erecting the tent was a breeze, and Smith watched with amused detachment.

"Tell me again why we're here and not at a motel?" he asked.

"It builds character," I replied.

I'd not yet confided to him my theory that I was the target of two assassination attempts. Besides having no proof, I didn't want to put a strain on him worrying about me. Our discussion that morning, however, about Smith's time in France combating feudalism, and the bloodbath that emerged from the French Revolution, reminded me he was no stranger to controversy. Whether it upset him or not, I'd have to level with him about the attempts on my life, so he could decide whether to stay with me on the trip.

After Smith put his things in the tent, I said, "Maybe you'll understand what I'm about to say. Here, have a seat."

He sat, looking at me with round eyes. This wasn't going to be easy.

"I've figured something out," I said. "It's about those shoot-ings."

His eyelids narrowed. He said in a calm, unconcerned tone, "You mean, of course, who is trying to kill me?"

"Kill *you*?" I gasped.

"Oh yes, I noticed," he said. "Not hard to piece together, really. That fellow in the blue car had eyes one couldn't forget. Seemed to bore right through you." He grimaced. "I saw them again in that Opera happenstance."

"You're just a voice from the past—for God's sakes, they're after *me*!" I insisted. "They think I've got the formula."

"Ba!" Smith's eyes gleamed. "A trivial piece in a much larger puzzle. I'm the one they want silenced."

My look of incredulity made him say, his eyes half shut, "Who would benefit if I disappeared into oblivion? Who would rejoice at my annihilation?" He pounded the earth with a hand. "All the same groups as in my day! Big corporations, big government, big church, anyone with usurped power or wealth—they'd all have motive enough: any business, like that WorldChemm, wanting to manipulate prices or courting pro-tection from competition; any bureaucrat reveling in power; and a multitude of others, like that POP group."

Smith rolled his head. "These people will never go away. They're all mercantilists, in various guises—trying to win their own gain at someone else's expense—rent-seeking! And I'm the one standing in the way." He put a hand on my shoulder, like a father might. "Rich, it's ideas that change the world, that lead to revolutions—and mine have done it before. My return has stirred the pot." He paused. "Of course, my ideas are cari-catures to this generation, so even 'profit' has become a dirty word."

Smith's outburst stunned me. I slouched over to my camp chair and parked in it, a scowl on my features. Smith retreated, amusing himself by throwing a ball for Rex. Calling my formula "trivial" got to me, but even worse was the self-assured pronouncement that *he* was the target of the attacks. What an ego that man has! It seemed pure silliness. Yet ...

hmm. I scratched my head, wanting a good shot of Drambuie; I constrained myself. Smith's last comment on "profit" being a dirty word made me pause. It was true, I remembered, that POP stood for "People Over Profit."

Profits. I sat up as if waking from a dream. *Smith and profits!* My mind explored the possibilities. As lucid as Smith's theories were, they could bewilder the uninitiated. Could Smith's famous insight on profit be the cause of our troubles? Paradoxes amused Smith, and one central paradox was the notion that high business profits in the short-run could actually be *good* for consumers.

In markets with healthy competition, a rise in demand for a product, say oil, pushes up the price. The higher price signals that the buying public prefers more of this product, and it allows current producers to reap large, "extra-normal" profits for awhile. But without barriers to entry, new competitors are lured into these high-return areas, bringing in additional resources of land, labor, and capital. In time, the resulting increased supply of oil causes the price to drop back to its low, *natural* level. In the long run, consumers benefit from more oil at its lowest possible price.

Any such "natural" order, however, is easy to miss. To an outsider, the topsy-turvy marketplace is incoherent, even threatening. Prices skyrocket one day because of sudden bursts in demand; they plummet the next because of new discoveries of oil, or changes in technology for extraction. The apparent chaos invites government intervention to "fix" a system that appears broken—"fix" by having government set prices. Yet Smith had faith in the self-regulating market, which, like an "invisible hand," directs resources toward higher profit areas without the need for centralized control or planning. Attempts to interfere with natural prices, wages, and profits can generally only make things worse. This conclusion rests on two critical assumptions, first, that markets are competitive, and second, that no externalities, like pollution, cause harm to others.

Smith's "natural" order is terrible news for oil producers, like Mammoth Petroleum Company, because its profits are constrained by long run competition. The only way Mammoth can earn high profits again is to improve product quality (offer better oil additives) or to devise cheaper ways of processing and marketing oil. This is one of Smith's great insights: *the perennial search for profit leads to unending innovation and business transformation!* Every business re-makes itself to survive.

Yet innovation is costly, and it may be easier for Mammoth to revive its flagging profits by making an end-run—by trying to restrict competition! If successful, this reduces the flow of oil, elevates prices to consumers, and richly lines Mammoth's treasury. This is what John D. Rockefeller was accused of doing in the "robber baron" era, before his Standard Oil trust was broken apart by the courts in 1911. It's what the OPEC oil cartel continues to try to do today. The predictable *collusion* of producers is what made Smith so brutally cynical about the motives of businesspeople: this class has an abiding interest opposed to competition.

The result of this is that some countries have capitalism without any real competition: an alliance between those in power and their friends in business creates a system of "crony capitalism." Those who benefit become more powerful politically, making reform of this corruption even harder. The poor and downtrodden naturally come to associate capitalism with conspiracy, exploitation, obscene profits, and the violent political repression needed to maintain these. Little wonder that someone untrained in economics, seeing just a fragment of the puzzle, could fail to grasp the socially useful role of profits in a truly competitive marketplace. That radical group, People Over Profit, probably focused on profits in a corrupt system, and somehow mistakenly projected Smith as symbolic of all that was evil in it; this would justify killing him.

Yet how could POP know of Smith's channeling? And what danger did Smith represent to them? My mind bubbled. If POP were after us, Smith's story made some sense. On the other hand, WorldChemm's formula could be worth a pile of money in the right hands, and I couldn't dismiss the notion that this was really the cause. Probably both our lives were in danger.

Smith sat beside me. "Figured it out?"

I nodded.

"Not sore at me, are you?"

"Why didn't you tell me about this before?" I asked.

"Would you have believed me?" He sighed. "What am I to do—go away? Let Harold take his mind back? Even if I did, the fellow who's after us wouldn't know I was gone, and might harm Harold anyway. Perhaps it's better to finish the job I came to do."

*   *   *

Smith napped while I walked to the camp office. I shoved a handful of quarters into the pay phone. It was a Tuesday afternoon, the only time of the week Lattimer devoted to meeting with students at his Cambridge office, a suburb of Boston. The phone answered on the first ring with Edda's voice.

"It's Rich," I said.

"Rich!" There was a moment's hesitation and she lowered her voice. "Oh my gosh, I've been so worried. You can't believe what's been going on here." Edda filled me in on the death threats received from POP, the heavy security placed on everyone in the office, and their frantic search to find me. Then she put me through to Lattimer. A moment later I heard the gravelly voice of the ex-Marine.

"Goddamn it, Burns, I ought to string you up by your toenails! In Korea I learned how, too. Hang on."

I heard voices in the background and Lattimer telling someone to come back later. I suddenly felt important, but not happy about it. In a moment, Lattimer was back. "Where're you calling from?"

"A pay phone, in the Midwest."

"That's goddamn helpful. Look, the feds have tapped this line, so they'll know where you are. Might as well tell me."

I told him.

"Look, Burns—"

"I know who's after you," I interrupted. "It's that guy we met at lunch in D.C. Your ex-student, what's his name—Max Hess?"

"You're a day late," Lattimer said. "The FBI was here yesterday having me identify that video of Hess taken in Chicago. How'd you figure it out?"

I recounted our adventure with the shooting on the highway and how we'd been at the Opera. "I recognized Hess from the security video, wearing that black wig," I said. I didn't mention anything about my pirated dissertation drafts.

Lattimer didn't dwell on my comments, saying, "Helluva way to try to kill someone, under those lights and cameras, almost like he wanted the attention. We could see him stalking you, once we knew what we were looking for. The FBI launched a manhunt for you after I recognized your picture on that video. What the hell have you been doing?"

"Thinking about things," I said.

He coughed. "Look, Burns, the FBI knows a lot more than they've said publicly. POP means serious business. You need to get up here, pronto."

"To Boston?"

"Your life's in danger, dummy. WorldChemm agreed to put you up in a safe place. You can finish your last chapter in quiet. Their security guys 'n gals will get whatever you need from the library. Dammit, I've got too much riding on this, Burns."

Lattimer never changed. His concern for my life translated into concern for my precious privatization formula.

"Listen," I said, "I know who POP may really be after."

"They're after me and you, bud," Lattimer interjected. "I wasn't kidding when I said even Hess knew about WorldChemm's bid."

"No," I said urgently, "Remember I kept trying to tell you about the old man who came to my door in the pouring rain?

It's him. He's the one they're after." I was about to say, he's Adam Smith, when Burns interrupted.

"Look, Burns, get yourself up here and you can tell me all your theories later."

"Can't you listen for once?" I fell silent, waiting.

"Get a move on, boy!" Lattimer said. "Call me as soon as you know your flight. I'll have some of WorldChemm's goons meet the plane."

*   *   *

I'd found out everything I needed. Nothing surprised me, and nothing pleased me. I could head to Cambridge and into Lattimer's clutches, or take my chances on the road with Smith. It wasn't a difficult choice. I'd find my way to Yosemite one way or another, but it wouldn't be the way anyone expected.

Within twenty minutes the station wagon was loaded, with Rex in his harness in the back seat. Smith watched curiously but pitched in without complaint or question. I headed to the freeway, stopping briefly at a convenience store to fill my tank and to withdraw my limit at the cash machine. Then I pulled onto a county road, turning south. After a hundred miles we found another ranch road heading west. With Smith navigating, we crisscrossed empty lands, south and west, seeing few souls.

When night came I rolled the windows down, letting the wind strike my face and arms to keep me awake. There was lots of ground to cover, in terms of distance and in making sense of today's discoveries. Smith tried his best to stay awake also, keeping me company. His eyes were sunken but alert.

I asked, "How does a person become a callous killer, an evil monster like Max Hess?"

"Before we can feel much for others," Smith replied, "we must in some measure be at ease ourselves. If our own misery pinches us very severely, we have no ability to think of others."

Hess' gloomy eyes and fidgety behavior gave me the impression of interior wretchedness. I told Smith the story Lattimer told me, how Hess had experienced deprivation and poverty in Bolivia for a summer, and came back a changed man, on a mission against capitalism. That led to his falling out with Lattimer, and Hess' termination from graduate school.

"It's a tragedy," Smith said, "that your Professor Lattimer found no way to share Hess' heartache. For if you have no fellow-feeling for the misfortunes I've known, or none that bears any proportion to my grief, we become intolerable to one another. You are confounded by my violence and passion, and I am enraged at your cold insensibility and want of feeling. That rage at Lattimer's indifference is what drives Hess." Smith turned to me. He tapped my shoulder gently. "It's time you started thinking about feelings, and sharing sentiments."

With that enigmatic line, Smith closed his eyes, and I was left to ponder on my own. I didn't know much about feelings, but I would need all my logic to uncover how we got into this mess. If Smith were the target of Hess's attacks, how had Hess come to know of him? Besides myself and Julia, who knew of Harold's channeling? I had good questions, and few answers.

13 FEELINGS ARE REAL

When the sun rose the following morning my odometer had turned nine hundred miles. The Midwest lay far behind. I'd kept a vigil, and unless Max Hess had mastered the art of driving in blackness, we'd made this moonless journey in isolation. The Colorado Rocky Mountains were in the rear view mirror as we descended to Utah's southern plateau. A stunning terrain of sandstone monuments, deep canyons, and towering granite cliffs passed us, the morning sun reflecting off red, orange, and purple formations. We stopped for fuel and food in Moab, and pushed westward, but tourists were out in force by now, meandering, gazing at the sights.

I tapped the steering wheel. "Too busy for my liking."

Smith nodded.

My eyes were wired open with caffeine, but my body flagged. An hour later I saw a faded sign for a state park. The unpaved access road wound through a juniper forest, and a long descent brought us to a small campground, Kodachrome Basin. A sign told us it was teasingly named by a National Geographic photographer for its evocative colors and shapes that cried out for artistic expression.

"It's a winner-take-all society," I said to Smith, "those bigger national parks at Bryce and Zion get all the tourists when the rock chimneys and limestone arches here are just as beautiful, and nearly deserted. Quite inefficient, if you think about it. But perfect for us."

The motley groups of campers, enjoying the isolation of this dry spot, ignored us. I stretched and yawned deeply.

"Not a bad spot to hide," I said.

❋   ❋   ❋

We slept the next day and a half, exhausted by our Midwest exodus. By the following evening I was more-or-less back to normal. Smith, moping, barely touched his dinner. He'd lost weight, and cinched his belt. I tempted him with a candy bar and he took a bite, laying the rest aside.

"Can we talk?" he asked.

We settled in the tent, Smith on the air mattress I'd bought for him. I sat cross-legged with the tape recorder at my side. Rex guarded the front flap, panting briskly.

"I'm set," I told him.

"That long drive gave me a chance to meditate about things. You asked what made that Hess fellow tick, what could lead him to do something heinous, like murder. It made me recall that just before my time there was a fellow, Thomas Hobbes. Hobbes was a brilliant man, yet in one respect, he went down a path I spent my life refuting."

His voice trailed off then surged back. "Hobbes is the one who popularized what you call the 'me' mentality. It is a view that moral judgment can be based on my own self-love only. To me, that view is repugnant."

"I would guess that view is fairly widespread," I said. "I doubt many people have read Hobbes, though."

"Who reads today?" Smith nodded. "Well, according to Hobbes, life in nature is a condition of constant war. Man is pitted against each other man, and because of that, life is 'solitary, poor, nasty, brutish and short.' That is how Hobbes explains the rise of the state." Smith sighed. "You see, in his book, *Leviathan,* Hobbes assumes that man takes refuge in society not because of any natural affinity he bears his own kind, but simply because without it he is incapable of living in safety."

"It's a powerful concept," I said.

"It misses a central point: beating in the heart of every person is the *desire* to be beloved! To please another! That's the way we were made. Use your common sense. Look"—Smith blew out air with disgust—"what happens to an ape given food and security but deprived of other contact? It shrivels and dies! If that's true of chimps, magnify it ten times for humans who express themselves in language, art, and music. Knowing and understanding—experiencing a 'fellow-feeling' with another—is essential for life. Without that, what are we?"

I wouldn't let go of nagging doubt. "From the vantage of evolutionary psychology, survival is all that counts," I said. "Social behavior may simply be 'hard-wired' if it helps us form alliances to propagate successfully. Even altruism can be so construed."

"You can follow that line, if you wish," Smith said, "but wouldn't that mean there's no 'right' or 'wrong' except insofar as it relates to your own self-love and survival? One might as well say all your choices in life become mere transactions."

I mused. "How can we love, if love is just a transaction?"

"Exactly." Smith rolled on his stomach, then pushed himself to his knees. "The argument should consider whether feelings for others can be authentic. I say they can. Where's my *Moral Sentiments*?"

I handed it to him.

"This is important enough that I started my book with it. Listen to my opening paragraph." He recited:

How selfish soever man may be supposed, there are evidently some principles in his nature, which interest him in the fortune of others, and render their happiness necessary to him, though he derives nothing from it except the pleasure of seeing it.

He laid the book aside. "This is the crux of the matter: I say we desire the happiness of others, and it is upon this foundation that morality is built. I'm not saying people don't use others, don't connive, and aren't insincere. Certainly that happens. But even the greatest ruffian, the most hardened violator of the laws of society, like that Max Hess fellow, is not altogether without such feelings."

In the distance I heard the tentative bay of a coyote, an opening to a longer song. It was every bit as mystical and romantic as the call of loons at dusk. I knew that I lamented Julia, but what was that coyote howling for?

Smith kept up a monologue, and I missed some of it. He was saying, "Now, don't misunderstand. We can't feel the same affection for everyone; sympathy diminishes as the distance between us widens. Still, genuine sentiments are possible."

Smith looked pensive. "You, for example, can't seem to believe that the affection in your life is real. Is that not why you're so miserable?"

I rose. Once again Smith put me under a microscope.

"You're a fine one to talk," I snapped. "You never married."

There was anguish on his face and I regretted my words instantly.

"I'm sorry," I said, ending the inquiry by striding out of the tent.

I walked aimlessly to the edge of camp. The light of a few stoves flickered, but the Utah night stars were fully visible in the blackness. The canyon bowl acted like a giant collecting telescope, concentrating galaxies into brilliant clusters that seemed within reach. Soon I heard footsteps.

I didn't look around, but said, "I thought I loved, but when I examined it…" My voice trailed off.

Smith said, "You mean, when you picked it apart rather than living it?"

"Yes, I questioned my feelings, to see if they were real."

We stared at the constellations a few minutes, then walked slowly back to the tent. I lit the propane lantern, poured myself a small shot of Drambuie, and we sat back on the cushions. Rex curled at my side.

"What if we delude ourselves?" I asked. "Most people think their *dog* loves them, but subservience and tail banging is just instinctual behavior to survive in the pack." I patted Rex's head.

Smith laughed. "You're no different than a dog, eh? Hmm. Let's try something." He rummaged in the tent and picked up the local newspaper I'd bought earlier. He handed it to me. "Did you see this?"

A banner headline took up a third of the front page: "Durango Fire Kills Two; Boy and Girl Orphaned." I grimaced. "An electrical fire in a mobile home," I read aloud. "The handyman who rewired it was charged with manslaughter." A gruesome picture showed the children strapped onto stretchers while flames lapped in the background. The boy lost an arm and his sister's leg was badly injured. "It's tragic," I said.

"Some sentiments were aroused in you?" Smith asked.

"Of course. I feel repulsed by the violence suffered by these innocent children. Makes me want to do something to help."

"Yet why should you care about these unknown children? You've no pecuniary or survival interest in them," Smith said. "I say you have an authentic reaction to them because some part of your imagination resonates with what they're experiencing. We need not dissect the evolutionary origins of this to note that it exists."

It was hard to relinquish the role of a devil's advocate. I shook my head. "Perhaps I'm reacting to the picture *as if* they were my children. In that light, one could explain my concern as the selfish gene at work again."

"That's an incredible after-the-fact rationalization," Smith said. "You were in immediate sympathetic alignment and it happened too fast to be a rational, self-promoting response. *The Theory of Moral Sentiments* confronts this point directly." He thumbed through the book again and quoted:

> *Those who are fond of deducing all our sentiments from certain refinements of self-love, think themselves at no loss to account, according to their own principles, both for this pleasure and this pain. Man, say they, conscious of his own weakness, and of the need which he has for the assistance of others, rejoices whenever he observes that they adopt his own passions, because he is then assured of that assistance; and grieves whenever he observes the contrary, because he is then assured of their opposition.*

He paused. "Now listen well:

> *But both the pleasure and the pain are always felt so instantaneously, and often upon such frivolous occasions, that it seems evident that neither of them can be derived from any such self-interested consideration.*

"Surely, no one who reads you could misunderstand," I said. "You've rejected any theory that ascribes all motivation to self-love."

Smith nodded. "Exactly. Natural sympathy with others enlivens my joy and alleviates my grief. The affection we feel for others is in reality nothing more or less than this habitual sympathy."

An unfamiliar set of emotions engulfed me. For a moment I stopped intellectualizing. I said, "So ... so love is real?"

Smith was startled, then he laughed. "Oh goodness, I see where this is heading. Dear me, are you 'in love' with Julia?"

I nodded. "I feel like Harold channeling that 'voice' and unable to do anything about it. All I can think about lately is

Julia—her eyes, her smile, the scent of her skin, her laugh, the toss of her hair. It's driving me crazy."

Smith nodded, putting his hand on my shoulder as a father might. "Being 'in love' is a passion of the imagination that is perfectly natural, and even pardonable, but I'm afraid also a little ridiculous, at least for outsiders to observe."

"Forget it, then," I said, feeling foolish.

"It is not being 'in love' that constitutes to me any great virtue," Smith said. "Think of all the vices which commonly go with it! Think of the occasions in which it leads to distress of every kind, to ruin and infamy—its consequences sometimes even fatal to young people in this day and age." He rubbed his cheek thoughtfully.

"No, at the risk of intruding into your affairs," he went on, "I should say you must go beyond this feeling. You must take this passion of being 'in love' as the foundation upon which to develop other passions which accompany love and which do interest us—namely, humanity, generosity, kindness, friendship, and esteem." Smith looked at the sky through the rain fly of the tent. He said softly, "In such measure as you may find the courage to share it, my boy, that's what real love is."

*   *   *

I was lost to my thoughts as Smith got ready for bed. The story of the Durango fire again caught Smith's eye as he folded the newspaper. He read it a second time, a crease forming on his forehead. He tapped the paper, getting my attention.

"Barbaric!" he muttered. "The whole town has turned against the handyman accused in the fire. Reminds me," he said, "of the incident in Toulouse."

My look of incomprehension produced a knowing reaction: his mouth formed a mock grimace, as if exhorting me to study more. His eyes, however, burned. "An innocent man," Smith said, "a Protestant, was accused and then condemned in the death of his own son. That verdict was purely the result of mass hysteria and religious prejudice in that French Catholic town. It caused an uproar all over Europe. Voltaire rose to defend the man, alas—too late to save his life."

Smith put a hand to his scalp, scratching. "Maybe it's not too late this time," he said to himself, his eyes darting about. "If Voltaire were here, it would not be too late for that handyman."

Smith often muttered absent-mindedly, and I took no more notice this time than any other. Perhaps I should have taken more active interest, but I didn't, and that's what got me arrested a few days later.

14 LETTER TO JULIA

Smith slept late the next morning while I attended to duties of pot washing and trash hauling. Our grueling drive on the preceding days, from the Black Hills of South Dakota over the Rocky Mountains of Colorado, and into Utah, had made me anxious for Smith's health. That, and our long session last night, were reasons enough to rest another day. I had several matters to ponder, the first of which was to assess the risks of going on to Yosemite.

How serious a threat was POP? The two attacks on us nearly succeeded. Yet the attempts also seemed reckless and even amateurish, perhaps the work of a splinter group or even a rogue like Max Hess acting alone. On the other hand, POP bombed the Russian envoy, which indicated they could have access to the deeper pockets of those who wished America ill. If so, they could have sophisticated know-how. It made sense to assume the worst, that these terrorists had technology to find Smith and me in all the logical places. That meant the northern route through Montana and Idaho we started on, leaving a trail of credit card receipts, was now probably a watched route. That meant Harold's sister's house in Oakland could also be under surveillance. It meant my mail at home and the college could be intercepted. It meant calls to Julia could be monitored.

I ran my fingers through Rex's fur, pulling out briars. Was I paranoid? I bought every newspaper I could find over the past several days, but coverage of the Opera shooting had vanished. Not a line of print anywhere. Perhaps the story died a natural death with Max Hess's clean getaway.

I stowed dishes and sat at the picnic table with paper and pen. There was so much I wanted to tell Julia about what I'd experienced, how things that eluded me my entire life were coming into focus, and, most importantly, how I felt about her. But I found it impossible to put into words. After struggling for ten minutes, I wrote:

Dearest Julia,

It feels strange writing a complete sentence to you. There's so much to say yet I don't quite know how to say it. Smith, by the way, has been a help—way beyond my expectations. I want to thank you for your instinct in bringing him to me.

I'm sending this note care of the art gallery for a reason. I don't want to alarm you unnecessarily, but Smith and I, and perhaps even you, might be in some danger. I don't trust the phones or I'd have left a message on your new machine! Have you seen anyone hanging about when you went to collect my mail? Or over at Harold's? Please be careful.

Missing you,

Rich

I stamped the envelope and wandered over to a neighboring campsite, where the occupants were getting their gear loaded into the back of a pick-up. They were headed north, I discovered, and I asked if they would mind posting my letter when they got to Idaho later that day.

"There's a mailbox over by the camp store," the man volunteered. "No need to drive it all the way to Boise."

"My friend collects postmarks," I said. "She'd love getting one from there."

*　　*　　*

Later that afternoon Smith and I settled into folding chairs overlooking the clay-hued canyon. A carload of campers was moving in next to us, a trio of women in their early thirties. Smith seemed particularly interested in a red-haired one, and rose to extend an offer of help. It was bemusing, thinking of how endearingly inept and bumbling Smith was with anything practical. The red-head declined with a polite thank you, and in a few minutes the three women had efficiently set up camp. With a wave, they set off on mountain bikes down the canyon road. Rex trotted behind until I called him back.

When I'd regained Smith's attention, I said, "Here's what I've learned so far: Hobbes says there is no absolute right or wrong, that all action derives its moral authority from concern for our own self-love. In the modern view of evolutionary psychology, emotions are just tools for survival and procreation." I went on. "You, on the other hand, argue that concern for others is authentic, and that moral judgment can be deduced from studying our emotional reactions, using our sympathy. Is that about right?"

"That's basically it, yes," he said. "I envision a society in which the least amount of government control is needed. For that to happen, humans must have within themselves the ability to reflect on what is right and wrong, and the desire to discipline their self-love accordingly. Certainly this desire must be nurtured; the unfolding of a conscience happens only over a lifetime."

"How did people react to Hobbes?" I asked.

"Mixed," Smith said. "The church reviled him for removing God from the moral equation, for denying the existence of God's laws. Rationalists attacked him because they believed that *logic* could uncover the natural, categorical laws of morality, like the laws of calculus and geometry."

"Do you buy that?" I asked.

"About 'natural' laws of morality?—yes, of course. After all, where do you think Thomas Jefferson got the idea for your Declaration of Independence? He wrote—'We hold these truths to be self-evident that all men are created equal, that they are endowed by their Creator with certain unalianable rights"—but where did these 'rights' come from? They came from *natural law*—the principle that human beings are bound to a common body of moral laws no less powerful than the physical laws of gravity and electricity."

My ignorance of history showed again. Smith patted my shoulder. "Unlike the rationalists, I say *emotion* and *experience* are at the heart of discerning absolute moral judgments. Don't misunderstand, logic is an invaluable tool, but analytics alone can't determine right and wrong. David Hume demolished that notion during my lifetime."

"Is that why today we separate *positive* economics, that part having to do with facts and theories, from *normative* economics, that part having to do with values?"

"Precisely. That's all David's doing. Which reminds me," he said, "I really ought to get you two together."

Smith didn't often repeat himself, and I thought I'd heard that line before. "One channeled spirit is enough, thank you," I replied.

"No, really." Smith stroked his cheek thoughtfully. "There are quite a few of my friends you need to meet. Perhaps now's the time, before it's too late. I still can't believe no one reads Voltaire. Quite shameful."

He became melancholic, and had I paid closer attention, and taken his last words as prophetic, I might have saved myself a good deal of trouble. I might have tried to convince Smith to leave well enough alone, to leave justice to the proper authorities of this day and age. I might have even gotten us the heck out of there. As it was, I took Smith's remark as a meaningless aside.

Lines formed on Smith's forehead. "Promises! Promises! Oh, Jupiter." He turned away, apparently engrossed in memories. I'd never seen him like this.

With difficulty he left his private thoughts. He pointed to the book on my lap. "This is important," he said. "Look—look at the title of my book: *The Theory of Moral Sentiments*." His became professorial. "Examine each word for its meaning. First, what is a 'theory'? A theory generalizes about cause and effect. The remainder of the title tells you about what: generalizations about 'moral sentiments.' Moral sentiments are emotions or feelings about right and wrong."

"I'm getting the idea," I said.

"I called it 'the' theory of moral sentiments to make it universal, and to indicate that I drew heavily upon my teachers and colleagues of the Scottish Enlightenment."

I shook my head. "Seems so removed from the 'invisible hand' and the self-interest of the butcher and the baker."

"To an untrained ear, perhaps. But never forget that economics started as moral philosophy," Smith said. "Morality must be explored before discussing its *application* to the realm of commerce."

He dropped his head. "I can't go on." He rose and turned away. "I have my own thoughts to attend to now."

✻   ✻   ✻

The next day was beautifully clear: a breeze freshened the air. I decided to stay put in our hidden camp another day. In the morning I cataloged the tapes of Smith's talks. By mid-afternoon Smith was awake and chipper, and whatever had troubled him yesterday seemed long forgotten.

"Get out of here," he said. "I can clean up camp as well as you."

I looked at him doubtfully.

"Shoo!" He waved his hands like he was herding a flock of chickens. "You've been cooped up too long on my account. Go enjoy yourself."

Relieved, I dressed for a hike in the canyon, and packed a knapsack with a quart of water and some cheese and crackers. Promising Smith I'd be back by sunset, I set off briskly up a narrow trail, letting Rex lead the way.

The arid Utah countryside offered startling vistas of deep gorges and scruffy hillsides, punctuated by improbable chimney rocks jutting to the heavens. I imaged how Julia would paint these exotic landscapes. Everything was bigger than life and brighter when I shared it in my mind with Julia. I carried on a schizophrenic conversation with her for an hour until I realized that is why they locked people away. Toward sundown I spotted a coyote trotting up a trail on the side of a hill. I expected to hear its mystical call later that evening, and kept a handle on Rex's collar until it was well out of sight.

It was seven-thirty when I crested the hill overlooking camp. The normally placid encampment seemed eerily lit and over-active. Then I realized it was because a rescue vehicle was there, emergency lights circling. I began running before I consciously knew whose campsite they were at. It took twenty minutes to scamper down the face of the canyon, and several times I nearly tumbled.

A medic was putting equipment back in his truck as I got there. Smith was collapsed on a cot.

"What happened?" I asked, out of breath.

The medic held up my empty Drambuie flask. "Seems grandpa's been nipping all afternoon."

The red-haired woman from the campsite next to us came over. "He kept calling me his sweetheart, 'Miss Campbell,'" the woman volunteered. "Seemed to make him very sad when I told him I wasn't." She shook her head. "My name's Compton, not Campbell."

I turned back to the medic. "How is he?"

"He'll sleep it off. But I found these liver pills in the tent. He'll need some help for a week or so."

"I'm not his girlfriend," the woman insisted. "My name's Compton."

"I'm very sorry," I said to her, "he was obviously mistaken." I turned back to the medic. "Perhaps he needs a hospital."

"He refused. Said he didn't have insurance. Anyway, the nearest hospital is three hundred miles."

Caring for Smith would be difficult, I realized, remembering his earlier collapse at the Faculty Club. It wasn't something I could do alone. I made a swift decision, and headed at a trot to call Julia.

*   *   *

When the sleeping form awoke the next morning, Rex's ears were back, and he began the strange canine ritual of growling, circling low to the ground around the comatose figure on the cot. I put Rex on his leash and led him to the car. When I returned, Smith opened his bleary eyes.

"Again, you and this Smith fellow try to kill me," the voice said weakly, a little spittle coming from the side of his mouth. It was Harold! I helped him sit up and gave him a pill with water. After he swallowed I brought a smile to his face by saying I'd reached Julia last night at the gallery.

"She'll be here tomorrow," I said.

"Looks—looks like a smile on your face, too," he said.

15 ANOTHER GYPSY TALE

The following evening Harold staggered to his feet and insisted on going along to pick up Julia at the airport. If I wasn't so worried about leaving him alone again, I'd have refused. I helped him into the car, and we drove the hour over to Cedar City. There was no easy way for Julia to fly in from Virginia, and it took most of her day on a circuitous route through Atlanta and Salt Lake City.

She appeared from the air-conditioned plane looking only slightly ruffled, and still beautiful, despite an arduous trip. She gave Harold a warm hug, and I watched with a twinge of jealousy as she gave Rex a kiss on the snout to stop his bark. Then came the awkward moment when neither Julia nor I knew what to do, whether to hug, shake hands, or kiss. I resolved the issue by reaching for her flight bag and giving her a smile. "Thanks for coming," I said.

It was ten o'clock before we reached camp. My offer of help to Julia was dismissed with a laugh: "Even we English know a bit about roughin' it," she said. Within ten minutes, she'd sorted through her luggage, pulled out her tent, and erected it in the dark. She unrolled her ground pad and sleeping bag, and stowed her gear.

Harold went to bed and I waited by the picnic table for Julia to finish. Despite her earlier sparkling appearance, I could see she was starting to fade. Looking at her, so tired, I recognized the depth of her sentiment, and commitment, at least to Harold. I realized, once again, that I desperately wanted her to feel that way about me. Despite my best efforts, I'd grown more emotionally dependent on Julia than I'd been able to admit. Would I have the courage to tell her?

I got out my new bottle of Drambuie, which, by precaution, I now kept locked in the glove box of the car, and poured two glasses. "I've got just the thing you need to unwind," I said softly, holding a cup in her direction.

A half smile drifted off her tired face like a leaf dropping from a tree. Then she waved, disappearing into her tent. I drank one of the glasses, staring into the moonless sky. It seemed to stare back. After a while, though I rarely ever allow myself more than one, I sighed and drank the other glass as well.

*   *   *

Julia slept late the next morning. I fixed eggs and bacon which sat and got cold. When she appeared, she put her hand on my arm, saying, "Sorry about last night, I was too tired to be sociable." She gave me a smile, and reached for a plate. She was famished, eating enough re-heated eggs for two.

After an initial euphoria at seeing Julia the previous evening, Harold woke in that foul mood which had plagued him since his "return." Dark circles ringed his eyes, and his skin was pallid.

With Julia there, I felt stronger about insisting, "Harold, let's go see a doctor."

"Nah. Nothing a doc can do about this voice inside."

"You can't help anyone if you go and die on us," Julia said, winking. Eventually the three of us began to chortle, causing other campers to look in our direction. The levity must have been good for Harold, who finally took a bite of eggs.

"Tell us about your family," I asked him. "You've got just one sister?"

He nodded. "More, but only one I know. Timisoara is the town where I was born, in western Romania. Six kids, and I was the youngest. My father was a salesman, traveling on the road. We had to flee during the last year of the war." He swallowed a chunk of bread, quiet for a moment. "My mother and sister and I got separated from the family during an evacuation. There was so much shouting and pushing, Nazis everywhere in the train station. We wound up in a refugee camp, and I was ten years old when they brought us to Ellis Island. The immigration officer asked my mother's name, but she didn't speak English. She gave him the name of our city." He put his teeth together and hissed the pronunciation, "Ti-mish-wahra."

He went on. "The officer was busy and didn't know how to spell that, so he just wrote 'Timms.' My mother couldn't read, and after what she'd been through—losing my father, my other sisters and brothers, all probably dead—what difference did a piece of paper make?"

"Couldn't you do something?" Julia asked, drawing her fists up to her chin. "There were committees to help find family members after the war."

Harold laughed ruefully and shook his head. "Gypsies don't go to authorities for help, we're always accused of stealing or fighting. No, we keep to ourselves." He sighed. "I had my wife, now I have no one besides my sister in Oakland." He took a pinch of salt and tossed it over his shoulder. "Like this—we were all thrown to the wind."

After eating Harold seemed in better spirits. "I'm sore from lying around," he said. "Think I'll go over to the nature center. You love-birds enjoy a quiet moment without me. Back in a bit."

He ambled off, looking remarkably fit for a man who'd collapsed just a few days before.

His absence gave Julia and me an excuse to burrow into my tent, keeping the flap open to catch whatever afternoon breeze arose. It occurred to me that the two of us hadn't been this alone since our last dinner in Fredericksburg. Yet today we accepted Harold's moniker of "love-birds" with just a slight glow of red cheeks.

We lay on the air mats, an awkward gulf separating us. We were silent a few moments, then both began speaking as if the curtain had risen on a stage. The resulting mishmash made us laugh.

"You first," she insisted.

I no longer hesitated. Foremost, I wanted to apologize for doubting her, and I wanted to thank her for getting me together with Smith. There was so much to say about our trip West, the two murder attempts on us, Smith's wonderful ramblings, the WorldChemm formula, and now, our hiding from Lattimer, the feds, and POP. I could see a growing warmth in her eyes that was missing at our last dinner.

A half-hour later, Julia said, "You know, your professor, Lattimer ... he sounds an awful lot like your father."

"It's crossed my mind. I'm jumping through hoops for someone I want approval from, but who is totally incapable of sharing any emotion I might want. Yes, that's occurred to me." I breathed out heavily. "That's the reason I left Cambridge. Hearst College isn't on a par, but it represents a break, an independence I had to assert."

Julia's eyes examined mine. "There's something I don't understand. This formula you're working on for Lattimer: why give it away to WorldChemm? If it's worth what you say, why not sell it?"

"I don't know," I said, stumped for a moment. "It's just the way we do science—we share our findings at meetings and publish our discoveries. Knowledge is pooled, which is why there are huge externalities to academic activity. That's why society supports us." I went on, thinking about it as I spoke, "I guess nowadays, many academics start their own private companies, to internalize the benefits of their research. I guess I'm more traditional."

"Hmm. And Adam Smith—what have you learned from him?" she asked.

I glanced at her. "I'd always assumed that my mind could guide me," I said, "that being highly rational would help me make all the right decisions. Among the things he's taught me, Smith showed me that's only part of wisdom, that feelings are also real and also matter. I finally understand a quote from Hume that one of my teachers posted in high school: *'Reason is the slave of the passions.'* I finally get it."

"There's more," I said, telling her of the landscapes I'd painted in my mind while thinking of her. When I was done, she kissed me, and I felt more relaxed and happy than I could remember, just to hear her breathing next to mine.

When we awoke from a catnap I remembered Harold's sardonic reference to gypsies. It hit me that Smith as a child had been kidnapped by gypsies—the "Romany wanderers"—and now he was channeled through a gypsy from Timisoara! Pure coincidence? I turned to Julia, whose eyes fixed on me.

"Has it occurred to you..."

"Timisoara," she said. "That's the key, isn't it? Where the Romanian revolution started in 1989. I remember the television news of Ceausescu trying to repress those brave demonstrators. His brutality led the army to rebel and join the people. It was the beginning of freedom in Eastern Europe. That's symbolism Adam Smith could hardly pass up!"

We drifted back to sleep, a puzzle solved.

*   *   *

Julia and I woke to find an empty campsite.

"You don't think?" she asked.

"I do think."

Harold had been gone since one o'clock in the afternoon. It was now past six and there was no sign of him. He'd disappeared, and we imagined the worst. I glared at Rex, sleeping by the tent, as if I expected him to have made Harold his charge.

"Get up, lazy dog, and get to work!"

The first thing I checked was my new bottle of Drambuie. It was undisturbed, locked in the glove box. We ran through the campground, checking the nature center and every bathroom. No Harold anywhere. The docent at the nature center was solicitous, offering to watch Rex for the evening, which made life simpler. I left a note pinned to the tent and Julia and I piled into the wagon. The few miles into town flashed by as I kept the car gunned.

The sheriff's department was a brick annex attached to a much older courthouse. The only person inside at this hour was a round young man with thick black-rimmed glasses. He wasn't wearing a uniform, which probably made him the dispatcher. He looked up from a desk that held the radio, a computer screen, and a couple of other gadgets, and removed his hand from a family-sized bag of potato chips. He looked at Julia, then me.

"I'd like to report a missing person," I said.

He didn't reach for a form or act interested. "Missing since when?"

"Since this afternoon."

"You've gotta wait twenty-four hours," he said, glancing away from us toward a wall clock, then to the computer screen. He reached for a handful of chips.

"The sheriff—where can we find him?" Julia asked. Her tone had the terse hardness of a Brit keeping a stiff upper lip. It was lost on the fellow, whose eyes said he'd seen tougher, and more interesting, cases than ours.

"Down the street at Lotta Mama's." He watched us leave with all the animated interest of the machines surrounding him.

The sheriff's cruiser was indeed parked in front of the diner. The sheriff sat in a booth where he could look out on the street, and, although he'd watched us enter and head right for him, he didn't rise. His brown uniform fit his lean build, suggesting he was aware an elected official had an image to maintain. His white hair was clipped short, and the tanned lines on his face placed him at sixty. He wasn't anyone you'd take lightly.

In front of him, a platter held the remains of a meal. He pushed the plate aside, and waved us to sit down. We introduced ourselves, and in rapid sentences outlined the problem of Harold's drinking and his sudden disappearance. The sheriff's eyes were alert without showing emotion.

When we were done, he spoke quietly, working the thick white porcelain cup of coffee between his hands. "You're from Virginia?" he asked.

We nodded.

"Well, I can see why you folks are worried, but there's not a lot I can do. Law says, if a grown man wants to go out for a few beers, not much I can do to stop him."

"But it will kill him!"

He nodded. "Might. He wouldn't be the first. Look, I'd like to help, but unless he's been missing a day, my hands are tied."

Pleading seemed pointless. "Where's the nearest bar?"

"None real near. This here's a dry county." He took a sip of coffee and set the cup down. Then he took out his pad and pen, and pushed them toward me. "You can write this down. You go up to Rocky Flat, there's the Bird House, that's twenty miles. On the south side is the Lonesome Dove Cafe, about twenty-five miles. Going west, you'd reach the Silver Mine Bar, oh … figure thirty-five miles."

His eyes narrowed. "Course, a lot of guys like the Old Durango Saloon, that's about thirty miles on past the Silver Mine. Out West, thirty miles is nothing, and the girls are friendlier." His left eye flickered, which one could almost have taken to be a wink.

"Durango?" I said. "Where those two kids were orphaned in a fire?"

"That's the place."

I tore off the sheet of paper and handed the notebook back, thanking him. When we were almost to the door, he called out. "Thought you said he was on foot?"

I turned and nodded.

"Well, I reckon he could have hitched any which way he wanted then."

*   *   *

Afternoon turned to dusk as we emerged from the Silver Mine Bar. Julia leaned against the outside of the car and flung her arms on the roof. She groaned. We'd spent the last three hours crisscrossing the region, checking the closest bars first. The odometer had spun 130 miles and we'd found no trace of Harold. It was hot, my lips were cracked, and my body felt like a bag of wet sand.

Julia held out the three-by-five inch snapshot of Smith she'd taken the day we left Virginia. None of the bartenders or waitresses had recognized it. She put it back in her purse. "Is it worth going on to Durango?" she asked.

"Looking for a needle in a haystack?" I waved my arm across the road. "He could be anywhere. Could have caught a ride with any of these truckers and be in LA before morning. Could be halfway to Oakland. He could be back in camp fixing dinner."

I hated to give voice to my worst fear, but I did anyway. "Could be kidnapped by Max Hess, taken down one of these back roads, and buried without a trace."

We sat in stony silence. The sun headed toward the horizon, and evening sounds emanated from the desert.

"What did that sheriff mean," Julia asked, "'the girls are friendlier' in Durango?"

I pulled an atlas from the front seat and spread it on the hood. Durango. It was just across the state line.

"Nevada!" I exclaimed.

"Oh, God, gambling and prostitution!" Julia's eyes widened. "You told me that woman in camp kept saying she reminded Smith of his old girlfriend. In Nevada there'll be a woman to fit any delusion he wants."

In a moment, we were speeding west again. I hit my hand to my head. "I've been a dope. I think you're right that Smith has taken over Harold's mind again, but I don't think it's a women he's after."

I pointed to the newspaper that was left in the front seat of the car, and which I'd pushed aside in my rush to drive into town. "Smith left that, thinking I'd see it," I said. "It's the story of that fire in Durango. Two people were killed and the handyman charged in their deaths. That's what's been bothering Smith, and he must mean to do something about it." I remembered those odd mutterings Smith made about wanting me to meet his contemporaries "if it wasn't too late," and I worried what he would do. My apprehension scarcely prepared us.

We reached the sign welcoming us to the State of Nevada. In a few more minutes we pulled into the parking lot of the Old Durango Saloon, sending a billowy cloud in the air. The dust settled over the pickup trucks, and a smaller assortment of cars and sport utility vehicles. We could hear the wail of a country band. I looked at my watch: it was nine o'clock.

The saloon could have been taken from a western movie set. A garden of prickly pear cactus circled the building's entrance. Sidewalks of seasoned timber led from the parking lot to the front of a bleached two-story structure, from which a large wooden annex extended. We stood on the porch taking in the horns and antlers adorning the entrance. The music was loud and shadowy forms danced inside. I felt out of place, but pushed through the door with Julia at my heels.

A massive bar sprawled the length of the room. Waitresses hovered by a workstation, loading trays with drinks before disappearing into the crowd. At the other end of the room a band played a fast two-step. Solid-built men in blue jeans and short-sleeve shirts filled the room, their women in short skirts and tight blouses. To the left an archway led to gaming tables and slot machines in the main hall.

Julia squeezed my hand. "I'm going to the loo. Get me something to drink?"

"Sure."

I edged to the bar, jostling for a spot. The line thinned and I placed my order. A leggy blonde wearing a cowboy hat perched on a stool near me. Lips the color of a fire engine parted.

"Howdy," she said, feasting mascara eyes on me.

I nodded politely, feeling my face flush.

She crossed her legs, displaying a patch of thigh under her miniskirt. Her calf rested against my leg.

"By yourself tonight?"

"Not really. Got the wife." The words tumbled from my lips, surprising even myself, but they seemed to do the trick. The woman shifted away. I picked up our drinks and edged back from the bar. I found Julia near the entrance and recounted my adventure with the cowgirl. Could Smith stand the pressure of this sales pitch? What of the booze that flowed like water?

"I checked the big hall," Julia said. "Even popped my head into the men's room. No Smith, anywhere."

We found an empty table from where we could survey the room and sip our rum-and-cokes in temporary despair. We were numb, listening to the plaintive music, too tired to face the next step. We'd come all this way, sure to find him. What now? It was possible, but most unlikely, that Smith had simply returned to camp. Unless he was upstairs with one of these cowgirls—which would be completely out of character—our options had just about run out.

When the waitress arrived to take our dinner order, Julia took out the picture of Smith. The waitress glanced at it and shook her head. She stopped to pick up a glass at the next table and asked, "Tammy, you seen this guy?"

The woman "Tammy" had white hair piled into a bun six inches high. Behind wavy glasses, her eyes bulged like over-sized marbles. Stacks of quarters lined her table, and she was fingering them into paper rolls. She reached for the photo with one hand, studying it.

"Sure, I've seen him. He was here tonight." Her husky voice gave a clue that smoking, as well as slot machines, was a pastime. "Sitting right at the bar. Don't know where he got to." She looked around the room. No Smith.

We plied Tammy with questions, but she had no more to offer. "Easy to miss someone around here if you're playing, or drinking," she said.

"Doesn't look like the watering ever stops," I said, surveying the packed room.

Tammy nodded, "It's on account of those folks that got burned up in that fire last week. Randy and Sue Takoda." She leaned toward us. "His two brothers are sitting right over there."

I looked with interest toward a long table near the back, where eight or ten men hunched over bottles of beer. The two men in the middle had thin lips and uncombed blond hair. There were plenty of empties on the table, but the two broth-ers weren't smiling.

"The man who started the fire's locked up over at the jail," Tammy said. "That's why we've got a full house tonight. The circuit judge's coming tomorrow for an arraignment. Then they'll have a hearing for the kids." She added, matter-of-factly, "Ever see what drunken cowboys do to a lawbreaker?"

Just then the band finished its set and the crowd dispersed from the dance floor. A waitress with a tray of drinks walked beyond the bandstand and stood before a wood panel wall at the far end. As if by magic, the wall parted and she walked through into a darkened room. The door slid shut behind her.

"Look at that," I said. "A private room. Let's check it out."

A stony-faced man with a thick neck parked his torso in front of the door. He was wearing gray pants and a white shirt emblazoned with a drawing of Old Durango Saloon. "You can't go in there," he said.

"We're just looking for someone," I said. "It'll only take a second."

He didn't budge. "You can watch the open tables if you want to see some action."

Julia frowned. "Can't we just peek?"

He didn't reply, and his impassive eyes suggested we'd better move on.

Behind the closed door to the private room we heard the murmur of voices and laughter. The waitress reemerged with a tray of empties, and as she did so, the tones grew louder. Julia and I gaped at each other.

We heard Smith!

16 A FULL HOUSE

The bouncer's eyes followed us back to our table. Tammy watched also, and after we sat down, she leaned over.

"House rules don't allow spectators in those high-stake games, honey."

"We've got money. How do we get in?" Julia asked.

The woman cracked her lips, like she'd heard something funny. "It's a regular Thursday-night poker game. The mayor's pretty particular about who he plays with."

"How long does it go on?" I asked.

"Relax and have another drink." She leaned back. "Lynching won't start 'till one or two."

We couldn't stand the smoke and noise any longer and went outside to sit on the deck. Julia wrapped her arms around her knees. At last we'd found Smith, but why had he led us here? I knew Smith well enough to suspect there was a reason, and that it probably had something to do with those orphan kids and that handyman. But what? Julia's mind worked toward the same conclusion. "Smith is reasserting himself and it's important enough for us to be in on it!" she said.

"Well, let's get going."

In darkness we picked our way over piles of cardboard boxes, overflowing trash cans, and abandoned vehicles cluttering a service alley behind the Old Durango Saloon. We climbed over a chain link fence to gain access to the back and luckily encountered no barbed wire at the top. Lights shone from the open rear windows of the building, and we could hear voices in the breeze.

"Wonder what the penalty for trespassing is?" I whispered to Julia.

"It's a lot less than the weight on your conscience if anything happens to Harold!" Julia led the way with cat-like eyes. I trailed, holding her hand. We were weaving, and it occurred to me we were tipsy after our hour of sipping rum inside.

"Ahhh!" Julia tumbled to the ground and I on top of her. We had sprawled over a truck tire.

"My ankle's twisted," she whispered hoarsely.

Her face was next to mine, and through her thin cotton dress I felt softness and warmth. Her hair and skin were luminescent, and gave off a flowered fragrance. Her pulse beat rapidly and I didn't think, but gently bent to kiss her lips. After a second of surprise, she kissed back, and I wanted to savor this moment and forget where we were and why.

"You pick such romantic spots," she said when we stopped for air. We giggled in this tangled cuddle, feeling suddenly light and happy.

Julia's face looked skyward, past me, and her eyes narrowed. "There!" She pointed to the wrap-around balcony on the second floor. "We can climb the fire escape."

"Let me help you."

With an arm around my neck, Julia and I crept up the stairs. She winced with every hop. The parapet was shielded by an overhanging roof, providing some cover. Two open dormer windows overlooked the private gaming room below. We tiptoed to the edge of the closest window and peered inside.

A circular card table dominated the center of the room. The green felt was sprinkled with stacks of red and blue poker chips. Overhead, a chandelier of wrought iron and elk antlers emitted a weak glow of light. The periphery of the room lay in shadow. Five men and two women fingered cards at the table. Smith was there, sandwiched between a red-haired woman and a large round-headed man who might have been Humpty-Dumpty. Smith's forehead glistened with perspiration, and I was relieved to see bottled water, and nothing else, set in front of him. His left hand clutched a fistful of cards. His other hand lay in repose on the shoulder of the red-haired woman, in whose direction he gazed approvingly.

The bet was making its way around the table, and the round-headed man said, "The bet is to you, Voltaire."

The man in question sat opposite Smith. He had pink scrubbed cheeks and hair neatly combed off his wide forehead. A pointed nose projected from a thin face, giving him the studious look of a high school science teacher. The man collapsed his cards into a neat stack, and set them on the table. Fingering first a red and then a blue chip, he settled on the red and tossed it into the center of the table. We could hear the clink of the chip landing on others as we inched closer to the open window.

The wager went from Voltaire to a baby-faced man wearing a khaki shirt, opened to the third button. Unruly black hair flowed over his forty-year old shoulders. Dark eyes glanced this way and then that from a deeply sunburned face. Everything about him, including the copper bracelet on his wrist, and the turquoise and silver ring on his index finger, gave the impression of someone who cared little for hierarchy, except the hierarchy of time: his nails looked bitten to the flesh. His shirt pocket contained a number of pens and a small notepad, as if the owner was accustomed to jotting things down in a hurry. "Rousseau raises," said the man, referring to himself in the third person. He took his last two chips and tossed them into the pot.

"That puts me out," said the red-haired woman sitting next to Smith.

After a silence, the large-headed man prodded with his elbow and said, "Come on Smith, don't go wandering off in your mind. It's your bid."

"Oh, you may depend upon me," Smith said, promptly folding his hand. Each person in turn tossed cards face down until the bet got back to Voltaire. A dimple in his chin appeared when he smiled, as he did now, tossing another chip on the pile.

"Voltaire calls?" said Rousseau.

"I paid for it. Show your hand, Rousseau."

Rousseau tossed his cards on the center of the table. "Pair of jacks."

Voltaire smiled again. His neatly manicured fingers set his cards down gently, revealing two queens. "The ladies have it."

"Mare's ass!"

Rousseau stood like he was going to pick up the table and throw it over. "Am I the only one to see this conniving? That's the second time Voltaire knew my hand." He began to inspect the room carefully, peering under the table, then turning his head to the ceiling. Julia and I ducked out of sight just in time. From our hiding place we heard someone make a crack at Rousseau's expense and the room broke into laughter.

Julia's eyes were saucers. "These people," she whispered, "they're names from history. Rousseau the philosopher, Voltaire the famous writer."

"Adam Smith idolized Voltaire," I whispered back. "What's going on?"

"My God, do you think..." Julia's voice trailed off. She pinched me and grinned. "I can't *believe* it. I've only read about mass channelings."

The room began to spin as I confronted the surreal scene before me. It felt like I had fallen down that rabbit hole in *Alice in Wonderland*. My head hurt. What did they put in those drinks?

"Sit down, Rousseau," the portly gentleman on Smith's side was saying. "It's a friendly game tonight, in honor of Smith's visit. Look, I gave Smith some chips, I'll give you some, too."

Smith frowned. "David, you can scarcely afford this."

I whispered to Julia, "I'll bet the fellow next to Smith is David Hume, his best friend."

Hume cupped a handful of chips in his stubby hand and set them in front of Rousseau. Rousseau lowered his head, tension seeming to evaporate. "You do spoil me with kindness."

"He's a viper," Voltaire said, gesturing. "That snake will bite."

"Rousseau suffered from paranoia!" I whispered to Julia, remembering one of the ten questions I'd posed to Smith as a test of his truthfulness.

"Let's take a break," Hume said, rising to his feet. "How about a toast to our old friend?" He raised his glass. "How many years since our last reunion—well, doesn't matter. To Smith." There was a chorus of good wishes and the sound of glasses clinking.

When the noise subsided, Smith rose to his feet. "I'm most grateful you could join me, at least for a few hours. This poker game is a fitting opportunity, with all the town's distinguished citizens in attendance—the mayor, the school principal, the newspaper editor, even the village doctor." He nodded respectively toward Hume, Voltaire, Rousseau, and the doctor, an elderly gentleman wearing glasses.

"You'll be speaking through the minds and lives of these poker players, gentlemen, and have all the things they know at your disposal," Smith said. After all, when people nowadays open their mouths, aren't they just parroting ideas from our epoch—quoting you, Voltaire, or you, Rousseau? How would anyone know if it's channeling or not?"

"Hear! Hear!" said Voltaire.

Now my head was really hurting. I didn't want to argue with Julia about whether mass channeling existed; I just hoped I didn't have to convince anyone else of it.

"The debates going on in this town tonight are not new ones," Smith said. "It's possible we can shed some light."

"Why reinvent the wheel?" agreed Rousseau.

Smith went on, "Of course, nothing you do tonight could oppose the will of the person whose mind you're using. But we're here to see if we can make a difference to this town—to those orphaned children, and to that handyman."

The two women, completely baffled, were looking at Smith with question marks in their eyes. They had no clue what was happening. Hume took notice and said, "Don't mind Mr. Smith, ladies. I'm still the mayor here and this is a little game of charade we're acting out tonight, just a game of pretend. These boys and I go back a long way—a long way."

Hume stood behind the woman who'd been seated on his left. She wore a long dress and pearls, her black hair pulled into a high bun. From the way she flirted with Hume, she might have come with the rental of the room. "You boys go ahead and enjoy yourselves," the woman said, reaching up to hold Hume's hand. "That's what you're here for. Have some fun! We've seen a lot weirder and wilder than this, haven't we Belle?" She laughed, looking at the redhead, who nodded readily.

"That's my Contesse," Hume said, giving the first woman a peck on the neck. He went to the side table where a fresh batch of drinks was prepared, and picked out a whiskey. "It's going to be a hot day tomorrow," he said, taking a sip. "That circuit judge has some hefty decisions to make."

"Quite right, quite right," Smith said. "Well then, if you're done with poker for the moment, it's time we got down to business." He turned to his right. "Doctor Quesnay, shall we start with you? Can you tell us about the children's progress?"

The dignified gentleman with wavy white hair and bushy eyebrows rose to his feet. Small oval eyeglasses perched on a pug nose.

"Who's that?" Julia whispered.

"I think it's one of Smith's friends from France," I whispered back. "Smith told me Doctor Quesnay was the leader of a sect, the Physiocrats."

The Doctor stretched his back as if the weight of the world had been upon it. He expelled a breath of air. "Well, Emily and Paco are improving steadily from their burns. They'll be ready to leave the hospital next month. The question is, where will they go? The judge has two options: The children's grandmother lives forty miles from here, out by—out by, you know—Rousseau's commune." He coughed. "Well, if it's still there."

Rousseau looked over, scowling.

The Doctor continued, "The grandmother wants the children, but she's quite poor. The children would share her bedroom. It's possible some of us, you know, the town leaders, could help build a small addition." There was murmuring around the room. Doctor Quesnay cleared his throat. "And, there's an aunt on their mother's side who lives in Los Angeles. She also wants the children. She's well off, has a house in the suburbs, plenty of extra room."

Hume nodded. He had retrieved a cigar from his pocket and was holding it unlit in his mouth. "Your work is most appreciated."

Rousseau sprang to his feet, almost overturning his chair. He pulled back from the table and began pacing, the heels of his boots making a loud clack each time they hit the wood floor. He drew up. "I may be the only one to feel this way," he said, "but I'm unapologetic about insisting—no demanding—that these children be given the right to grow up in the country. Their grandmother's house, even if it is small, is right next to our good spread of land. It has trees, a small creek, everything those children need."

"Rousseau, be reasonable." Voltaire looked at him with the eyes of a surveyor. "Your commune is practically deserted.

These young minds will but half-develop in that wilderness. It's fifty miles to the nearest school."

"Emily and Paco need to learn from their own experiences in nature," Rousseau exclaimed. "Can't you see the natural goodness and beauty inside them? Left alone, that nobility will flourish. They need that experience before book learning and theories."

Julia turned to me, her eyes wide.

"And what of their minds?" Voltaire was asking. "Their reason?"

"Where will they learn a trade?" Hume asked. "How can they make a living?"

"They'll be a master of all trades and mastered by none," Rousseau replied. "They'll fish by the stream, plant corn, and paint their bodies with colors."

"Like Robinson Crusoe?" Smith asked. "All alone against the world—how romantic. But surely we *do* need others: cannot both parties gain from voluntary trade?"

"As soon as one man needs the assistance of others," Rousseau retorted, "property becomes owned. Equality disappears, and slavery isn't far behind!"

Smith's lips tightened. "Aren't you forgetting we need others not just to divide our labor, but to share our sentiments? Look around the room. Society is more than a practical construct, it is a beautiful thing."

Voltaire clapped his hands together three times. "Bravo, Mr. Smith. Tell us, Rousseau, where will these children learn of civilizing art and music, and the social graces?"

"Civilization corrupts!"

Voltaire turned away. "Bahh! You and your noble savages!"

"I never said that!" Rousseau said, his eyes blazing.

Smith whispered to Hume, "He is more capable of feeling strongly than analyzing accurately."

Hume nodded with a smile, returning to the card table. He stood again behind Contesse, caressing her long neck. "Surely,

Contesse, you'd never pass up nights of dancing with me in town to live in the country?" he said.

"Of course not. Unless my boyfriend found us together!"

"Then just tell him it was Mr. Smith with you. He'll believe all you did was talk." Hume and Contesse laughed, heads nuzzled and hands probing.

Smith turned to the woman on his right. "Am I beau to no one but my books?"

Except for flaming red hair and lips, the woman next to Smith was otherwise nondescript, wearing a lavender cotton frock. "No, you're sweet," the redhead said. She stroked his bald head. "You're funny, too! Calling me, 'Miss.' And my name is Belle, not Campbell."

Smith blushed. "Miss Campbell, I—I must tell you…"

"Don't tell her," said Hume, "show her!" At this he pulled Contesse to his chest and planted a loud kiss on her cheek. The whole table, with the exception of Smith, burst into laughter.

Contesse giggled. "My words are virtuous," she said, reaching around Hume's back with her right hand, "my actions aren't quite so!" Her fingers pinched Hume's buttock.

Smith swallowed. "Miss Campbell, my deepest apologies for this, this…"

The crowd was laughing hard by then, and so were Julia and I, slumped against the wall away from the window, trying to control ourselves. Julia cupped her hand over her mouth. Poor Smith, the guest of honor, bearing the brunt of these jokes. The strange evening, while being grounds for my rational mind to rebel, had given us a heartening view of Smith and his friends. Yet I waited for the sleights of hand in this magic show to be revealed. I wanted reassurance that none of what we saw and heard violated the laws of science.

When I could trust myself, I leaned toward Julia and whispered, "What happened to the regular poker players?"

"They're right there, probably playing a whole lot better than they otherwise would. Ahh." She'd momentarily forgotten her injury, and now extended her ankle and rotated her foot, wincing. "I can't explain it, Rich, it's like a dream. Maybe they'll take on these personalities for a few hours, and wake up tomorrow with a feeling of *déjà vu*. I don't know."

The laughing died away and we moved back to the window.

"Doctor Quesnay, you wished to add something?" Smith asked.

The elderly doctor removed his glasses and meticulously polished them with a cloth. He finished the task and carefully replaced them. "Yes, in regards to the children, I must agree with Rousseau. Sending them to their aunt in Los Angeles condemns them to a dull life of industry and commerce. Those are sterile occupations, adding not a whit to the nation's surplus. Agriculture, on the other hand—"

"Now just a minute!"

"Pfff!"

Hume and Smith interrupted simultaneously. Doctor Quesnay talked on, drowning them out. "The grandmother has fifty acres! Fifty acres of good, irrigated soil. Let me calculate what that land can produce." He went to the corner of the room and withdrew from his medical bag a large piece of paper, which he unfolded on the table. The sheet had three columns with crisscrossing lines.

"What in the world is that?" Julia asked.

My legs were cramping. I adjusted my position and looked closer. "A circular flow chart," I whispered. "It shows the stream of payments in society, like the circulation of blood in the body. Quesnay was a medical man, and devised that model, the first macroeconomic model."

Doctor Quesnay continued his calculations aloud while the others looked on. "Suppose an average seven-year run of good and bad harvests. Let us see—so much corn, and cattle, so much for hired labor, a payment to the landlord, so much for manufactures—let us see then." Doctor Quesnay shook his head. "You see?—the natural balance is disrupted by any intrusion. The rise of industry cannot but cause calamity to the productive sector, which is agriculture alone."

Hume shielded his voice, saying to Smith: "There's that religion of agriculture again! 'Mysticism masquerading as science' is what it's called!"

Belle broke in: "What's this got to do with the kids, Emily and Paco?"

"It's their future," replied the Doctor. "It lies in farming."

"Ah, my dear Doctor," Smith interjected, "you are about the most ingenious man alive, and your system perhaps the nearest approximation to the truth yet known. But surely these children, if they found careers in industry, would add to their own, and the nation's, wealth? Surely *labor* is the source of a nation's wealth, not nature!"

"Surely nothing!" Quesnay looked up. "Land is everything! My *tableau* shows it perfectly. Only in a perfect system, an ideal system of laissez faire, can the natural order be harmonized." His voice trailed off as he calculated.

Smith's comments at the Faculty Club came back to me. Smith said he was too practical to hold any dogmatic or rigid views, such as held by the sect of Physiocrats. So I wasn't surprised when Smith stage whispered to Voltaire, "The good doctor imagines a perfect system, yet I've never seen one! And many systems that *aren't* perfect work tolerably well."

Voltaire nodded. "I've said it myself. The best is the enemy of the good."

Quesnay stopped his calculation to look up. "What are you mumbling?"

Smith said, "My good Doctor, experience shows that the human body preserves, to all appearances at least, a perfect state of health under a variety of diet and exercise regimens." Smith patted his stomach. "Now then, wouldn't that apply to these children, and, by analogy, to the wider world of commerce?"

The noise of bar patrons increased, and we heard boisterous yelling. Voltaire took this moment to rise to his feet.

"Let's stop this squabbling!" he said. "There are more important matters to attend. What about the handyman, Amos Johnson? He sits in jail, and a lynch mob bides its time in the saloon. What protects him from the injustice of this town?"

17 JUSTICE

Belle pushed back from the card table, her eyes flashing. "Injustice? It's people's justice, and if the law won't act, we will."

"Now Belle, hang on to your hat," said Hume. "The circuit judge will be here tomorrow. Let the judicial process work."

Julia and I were still riveted to the window on the second story balcony of the Old Durango Saloon, listening in on this bizarre encounter. My knees and back were stiff from holding a rigid position without making a sound. Belle, the red-head next to Smith, held the floor and Smith was looking at her now with a removed gaze.

"Easy for you all to say," Belle continued. "I went to high school with Sue Takoda, and I've never cried so much. Amos Johnson rewired that house barely a month ago," she said. "He as good as killed Sue and Randy with his bare hands."

"You've no proof," Voltaire said, his voice rising.

"Common sense says he wired it wrong! Maybe there's too much thinking going on here." Belle crossed her arms and shot Smith a glance.

Contesse reached for Hume's hand and pulled him toward his seat. "Come on handsome. I thought we were here to play poker. How do you expect the house to make any money? You, too, Belle. Let's deal."

Voltaire moved in front of Belle. He spoke with a soft tone that masked none of his intensity. "Common sense is not so common," he said. "Would you convict without trial? Does a man have no natural rights?"

Belle shot back, "Will a guilty man go free to repeat his crime?"

"Better to risk saving a guilty man than condemn an innocent one."

Tiny muscles around Smith's eyes softened. "Who knows that better than you, my friend?" he said.

All eyes returned to Voltaire. He grimaced, looking down at Belle. "Ah, yes, I did my time in the Bastille. What a beautiful dungeon—and such a superior education it provided me. The cold and damp perfect for my health, overrun with delectable rats, if you could catch them. How lucky it was for those of us whose crimes were entirely fabricated, otherwise we might have missed those convivial years!" He slowly turned and sauntered back to stand by his chair.

Belle's eyes followed him back to his place. Contesse leaned forward. "That isn't the point. In this town, everyone knows the handyman Amos Johnson is guilty. Isn't what's right, the greatest good for the greatest number of us? We say the man's guilty," Contesse insisted.

"No, no, and no!" Voltaire exclaimed. "That's tyranny by the majority—a man condemned without proof—purely on prejudice or superstition. Let us look at the facts."

Hume stood. "What *are* facts? I ask you, what are the facts of this case? Such things can be known only with a degree of probability. Hence, cause and effect can never be proven, only assumed."

Smith tapped his water glass to get attention. "Can we ascertain this man Johnson's state of mind? His thinking?"

Just then there was a knock at the door. The bouncer standing guard outside cracked the partition. He beckoned to Hume, who left his seat and stepped into the bar. The group at the table eyed each other warily and there was an edgy silence for two or three minutes. When Hume returned, the wrinkles on his forehead pushed higher.

"You may get your wish, Smith," he said, gnawing on his unlit cigar. "Seems there's talk in that crowd of dispensing their own justice tonight. The sheriff's away in Reno, testifying on a case. His deputy at the jail isn't sure he can control them alone. I told him to bring the prisoner over here for safe keeping."

"In here?" cried Rousseau.

Hume eyed him. "Where's the last place anyone's going to look? Nobody's fool enough to barge in on my private game."

Thirty minutes passed while they smuggled Amos Johnson out the back door of the jail and silently brought him through the rear of the Old Durango Saloon. Julia and I tiptoed back from the window, stretching our legs and keeping well out of sight. I didn't know the penalty for trespassing, much less for spying on a high-stakes poker game. I wasn't anxious to find out, yet I couldn't bear to leave this spot. I was sure that Smith had brought together his friends to conjure up some way of saving this man's life.

A stooped old man shuffled into the room, and Julia and I resumed our painful crouch at the window. Every other step the gentleman took ended with a slight limp. As he got under the light we could see neatly pressed pants, a clean white shirt, and brown boots. A thin white mustache was the only hair he had left.

Hume beckoned him to a seat. "You're here for your safety, Mr. Johnson."

"It is possible we can help you," Voltaire added.

The man nodded and sat on the edge of the proffered seat. There was an awkward silence, and it was clear that the poker game was now of less interest to the gamblers than the bent figure before them.

"You were handyman at the Shady Grove Mobile Home Park?" Hume asked politely.

"Yessir, been there three years." There was another long silence, and I imagine the solitude of jail the last week got the man started, because he went on to offer, "Before that, I was forty-two years at the nickel mine over in Jasper. Retired about five years ago when they made me. But I like to keep busy. Been working my whole life."

"Isn't it true that you rewired Randy Takoda's trailer last month?" Contesse asked,

Mr. Johnson's mustache quivered. "It's true, but also it ain't true."

Hume raised an eyebrow. "Ah, you're a philosopher?"

Mr. Johnson looked confused. "No, what I mean, you can't call that rewiring! Not what I did. That boy, Randy Takoda, asked me if I'd give him a hand. He'd been blowing fuses, didn't even have a circuit breaker. But when I showed up, all he had was a big roll of aluminum wire. Said his brother found it behind the depot at the airbase."

Rousseau put out his hands to stop the man. "He shouldn't be telling us any of this! This isn't a trial, and what he says can be used against him later. We'll all be called as witnesses." He glanced quickly around the room. "You can never tell who's listening."

"There's that suspicious mind again," Hume whispered to Smith.

Mr. Johnson said, "Nah, I ain't telling you any different from what I already told the sheriff fifteen times. I'll tell it again to you." His voice trembled. "I told Randy I didn't want anything to do with aluminum. Man, that stuff's been banned for years. Said I wouldn't do it, unless he came up with copper."

There was a stirring at the table.

Hume asked. "What changed your mind?"

"Well, I started to leave. Then that little girl, Emily, took my hand and asked if I wanted to see her dolls. She had a bunch of them laid out. Each one looked dirtier and more ragged than the next. Must have been thrown away by other folk, I expect. Then I looked around the place. It was clean but the furniture was all torn, holes in the couch, rips in the curtains, you know. Both the parents worked; I know they did. But you can't get by on minimum wage, not with two kids. Probably didn't have health insurance."

"No, they didn't." Doctor Quesnay said. "But why not leave well enough alone? Do no harm."

"The old wiring was too dangerous," Amos Johnson said. "I couldn't leave them like that. I told Randy I'd do it if they'd replace it with copper as soon as they could get the money. He called me last week to say he almost had enough. Then that fire! It broke my heart seeing the picture of them kids in the paper. I wish I'd gone ahead and bought the dadburn copper myself, taking it out of my Social Security."

Hume cleared his throat. "Given the horrific results of the fire, your actions sound indefensible."

Belle nodded. "Just what I said."

Mr. Johnson hung his head.

Smith stood. "We all know the aftermath of this incident was tragic." He absently rolled a blue poker chip through the thumb and forefinger of his left hand. "But we cannot pass moral judgment solely upon the utility or disutility of an action's outcome. We sympathize with the motives of this man as being both proper and praiseworthy. He intended no harm, but rather good."

"He burned the house down!" Belle said. "Doesn't that mean anything?"

"An unintended consequence, for which he suffers deep regret." Smith rejoined. "It is only knowing his intentions *and* the outcome that we can form a judgment as to the merit of his conduct."

Voltaire's knuckles rapped the side of the table. "Well said. Well said."

Smith wobbled and dropped to his seat. He wiped the perspiration from his forehead. "For us to punish Mr. Johnson, we must find not only an injurious act, but also the motives for it. I cannot sympathize with the resentment of the public in this case."

"You'll ignore the fact that two people died, that those kids lost their folks?" said Belle.

Smith shook his head. "No. But an innocent man brought to the scaffold by false imputation endures the most terrible agony, worse than those who suffer for the crimes they actually committed."

Belle expelled a breath of air and slid her chair away from Smith's.

The band in the bar finished another set, and in that greater silence Hume said, "Let's move on, shall we? We're all a bit edgy." He picked up the deck of cards. "Contesse, maybe you're right, a few deals will relax us. Seven card stud, shall we?"

Without waiting for an answer, Hume dealt two cards down to each player. Following around the table once more, he flipped the next card face up. "High card opens," he said, taking a sip of his whiskey and winking at Contesse. She smiled back, placing her hand on his arm.

Rousseau examined his hole cards. His mouth turned down and his eyes formed small fireballs. He hesitated, gripping his cards, then tossed a chip into the center. Smith folded his cards, but the other players threw in a chip and checked in turn. Hume dealt the next card up, first to Contesse, then Doctor Quesnay, then Voltaire. He was reaching toward Rousseau when the latter lunged forward and slapped Hume's hand to the felt and kept it pinned.

With his free hand Rousseau flipped over his hole cards. "I can't play these! Hume's spied them already. I caught him red handed." Rousseau stood there trembling. "I know you're all against me!"

Hume lowered his eyes. "Surely not, my friend. We praise you, most of us do." He pried his hand free from the table.

Rousseau's eyes glistened. "You mock me! You're deceitful, and frivolous. You're all corrupted."

"Your pride is as hard as the hump of a camel!" Voltaire said.

Rousseau caught the remark and spun. "You sir, have reason without wisdom."

"Jean Jacques, that is unkind," Hume said gently.

Rousseau whirled back to Hume. "And you sir, honor without virtue."

Voltaire winked at Hume. "Did I not warn you of the viper?"

Rousseau's eyes swept upwards, appearing again to search for hidden accomplices. Julia and I had grown lax and were resting our elbows against the window jam. We lurched back but too late. My eyes locked with Rousseau's!

From Rousseau's mouth erupted a primal scream.

In an instant, the wood paneled door slid open, and the thick outline of the bouncer appeared in the passageway. Behind him, a wave of bar patrons, led by the two Takoda brothers, peered in.

18 CHILDREN OF THE ENLIGHTENMENT

Smith and I sat at a picnic table the following morning as Julia dished pancakes onto our plates from the hot griddle. The sun climbed in the sky. We'd been up all night, most of that time in an interrogation room at the sheriff's office. Being in danger saps one's energy, and once the peril passed, we were getting our second wind. Smith ate heartily, his face pink, his demeanor more peaceful than I'd ever seen it.

Julia and Smith kept up a non-stop commentary.

"Did you see that look on Rousseau's face?" said Julia. "When he saw Rich and me peering down at him, one would have thought he'd seen Satan himself!"

Smith was chagrined. "His discomfort was extreme, but I suppose he had it coming. Ingratitude, not Madness, is that fellow's middle name."

"Prudent men don't gamble in poker games," I chided Smith.

"I wouldn't call what he did gambling," Julia said, answering for him. "We never saw him do much more than ante."

Smith took a healthy bite of pancake, swallowed, and stared at me a moment. "I guess I owe you an apology." Smith waved his fork at Julia and me.

"For good reason," I replied.

Our brush with the law was humiliating. Julia and I were arrested, photographed, and fingerprinted, and let go hours later when the trespassing charges were dropped on the mayor's advice. Our experience was redeemed only by the fact that the diversion we created on the balcony allowed Smith and Voltaire to get Mr. Johnson, the handyman, out the side door to safety.

"I was pretty sure you'd find your way to Durango, but I had no idea it would turn into a federal incident," Smith said.

"The mayor could've been killed when that crowd rioted," I said. "Darn lucky he's a man in high standing."

Smith nodded, stroking his chin. "If you stand for anything, you will be attacked." His mouth widened into a sheepish grin. "I confess, I'd been trying to get you to meet my contemporaries, and that was an important occasion for it. Wisdom and virtue spring only from action."

Julia sat down with her own plate of pancakes. "Well, you wise and virtuous men would be quite wise if you washed all these dishes!"

The docent from the nature center showed up at that moment, leading Rex on his leash. He appeared no worse for his overnight visit with the nice lady. He couldn't stop wagging his behind, scampering around Smith and Julia and me like a contestant in a rodeo event. The docent, Mrs. Callahan, lived in a trailer behind the museum, and said she'd thoroughly enjoyed Rex's company last night. She was a spry widow whose main hobby, she told us, was treating campers like kin. "I've got 'family' now in forty-six states and eleven foreign countries," she said happily. We thanked Mrs. Callahan and vowed to send her a box of dark chocolate, her favorite, when we reached California.

Exhaustion finally caught up with us and we headed to bed, sleeping until late afternoon. With the sun low in the sky we set off for a stroll in the canyon. Julia was still limping from her twisted ankle, so she leaned on my arm and I felt like a knight with his damsel. Smith trailed behind with Rex performing his usual ritual of dancing in a circle, sniffing at Smith's heels, and trying to get attention.

After twenty minutes of ambling we came to a steep ridge overlooking a plain. To the unobservant eye the dry earth appeared inhospitable, yet there were signs of life everywhere: slithered trails in the dust, pocked holes in the cliffs, and shoots of plants climbing through cracks in rocks. We found shade behind a boulder, sat, and shared a canteen of water.

"It seemed like old home week between you and Hume last night," Julia said.

Smith nodded. "There's always catching up to do. It's no exaggeration to say, Hume and I lived at the most exciting time in human history—at least since the dawn of agriculture ten thousand years ago."

"Not more exciting than the present," I said. I raised my hand skyward. "Today we fly to the moon and Mars. Satellites and computers provide instant communication anywhere. Heart transplants and clones don't even get headlines anymore."

"Ah, youth! Such myopia!" Smith said, suppressing a giggle. "Inventions spring from the *imagination*, Rich. What you now call our eighteenth century 'Enlightenment' freed people from their mental shackles. Once imagination is freed, innovation is inevitable."

A look of abstract beauty formed on his countenance. "We—Hume and I—lived during that penumbra period when the world's thinking underwent a profound transformation," he said. "Many aspects of society were still shrouded in the veil of the Middle Ages, yet others grew inexorably toward the light of the Scientific Revolution. People of the Middle Ages clung to a faith in an afterlife, and why not? Society was strangled by rigid controls—imposed by the church, by feudal landlords, and by the government. And since rewards came only in heaven, who would bother to fight these inequitable details here on earth?"

Smith liked to fiddle with things as he spoke, and he picked up several small rocks and rubbed them together. "The Enlightenment revealed the concept that advancement was both possible and desirable," he continued. "These insights led to political revolutions in America and in France, and to economic revolutions in the Industrial Revolution. That's why you needed to meet my contemporaries, to see the context for my work. *Justice* and *freedom* are not simply words to us, but the ideas of progress. Many people had to die for these ideals to live."

He gestured expansively to the valley below. "A stiff price was paid for America's own nationhood," he said. "I tried my best to prevent that long, expensive, and ruinous war. The slaughter of so many innocents! Three infernal years I argued with Parliament against the madness of modern war. That was a key point of my *Wealth of Nations*, after all, a treatise on economic independence. Do you think it mere coincidence it was published in the spring of 1776? Coincidence that your Declaration of Independence came out four months later? Did you think of that? Hmm?"

Smith's voice deepened with anger. "The rulers of Great Britain merely amused the people with the idea that they possessed a great empire on the west side of the Atlantic. Pfff! This empire existed in their imagination only. It was, not an empire, but the project of an empire; not a gold mine, but the project of a gold mine; a project which entailed immense and unending expense. The effects of monopolizing the colony trade, to the great body of British people, brought mere loss instead of profit. It was surely time for our rulers to awaken from their dreams."

Smith raised his arms in frustration. "Rather than a war to keep America oppressed, I favored a constitutional union. Fancy that! In fifty years, we could have moved our capital from London to Philadelphia." He turned, downcast. "My arguments fell on deaf ears, and that first civil war sheared America from her mother country."

Julia was relaxed and happy; looking at her preoccupied me pleasantly for the next few moments. The sun and breeze felt wonderful. My attention reluctantly returned to Smith, who was saying, "America's founding fathers from Virginia loved my ideas on free trade. Of course, they did! So they could sell their slave-grown tobacco directly to Europe and bypass the monopolizing British middleman. A worthy objective, but at what price their hypocrisy? Freedom to sell their own wares as they chose, but on pain of death they could not allow a black man the same privilege! You see how people can take just a piece of my philosophy and twist it to suit their ends? I only wish those plantation owners had paid as much attention to my attacks on slavery: it took a second bloody civil war to eradicate those vile markets for involuntary labor."

Smith tossed a pebble over the edge of the ridge, listening. He heard nothing. "You see how important it is for you to put a face on all of us? History's not quite the same when you do, is it?" he said. "Hume's contributions to the Enlightenment are too numerous to elaborate, from philosophy to history to economics. Voltaire, as you know, deeply moved me; he and Rousseau inspired the French Revolution—the latter for the egalitarian spirit and self-empowerment stirred. Doctor Quesnay, the physician with the flow chart, was a most influential economist, yet hear me, I distanced myself from the Physiocrats on purely practical grounds: Imagine Quesnay saying manufacturing didn't contribute to society! Almost as absurd as Rousseau railing against the progress of civilization."

Smith went on. "It should be clear that Enlightenment figures didn't always agree, and we often vehemently disagreed. We shared the promise of searching for truth, wherever it might lead. The Scientific Revolution showed that we could understand, predict, and to some extent control the natural physical world. Hume and I applied these scientific methods to the *human* world, to uncover the laws of social organization— of morality and markets—akin to the laws of gravity."

Smith shook his head with a look of wonder. "It was a most revolutionary and optimistic time, I should say. These new inventions you rave about today are simply outgrowths of our innovative thinking. Mere effects of our causes!"

Pieces of this intellectual puzzle were falling into place, and although last night at the Old Durango Saloon was a surreal dream—a Fellini film that could not possibly have happened—I found myself accepting it all without protest. Strange how once I accepted Smith as genuine, the rest of it, implausible and unlikely as it was, did not phase me anymore.

Julia, listening quietly, finally spoke. "I hate to burst your bubbles, gents, but shouldn't we be dwelling less on the past and more on the future?"

Smith and I directed our eyes to anywhere but her. Julia faced us squarely. "I admit, I was the one who encouraged Harold to channel Smith. But I had no idea he would completely take over his mind." She smiled wanly at Smith. "No offense intended, but you're like the man who came for dinner and stayed the summer. Isn't it time to finish up?"

Smith and I exchanged glances. Julia went on, looking now at me. "It's time we got Harold to his sister's in Oakland. As in, tonight!"

Smith examined the ground intently while I feigned preoccupation with a cloud formation to the west. I finally brought my eyes to hers. "There's a lot of material left to channel," I said. "He comes up with something new every day. It's important stuff."

Julia's reply was sharp. "Well, he can say it just as well in Oakland. Being around his sister may bring Harold back to health, in mind and body."

I looked at Smith. He said nothing, but his brow was furrowed. With an imperceptible back-and-forth motion of his head he signaled a "no" to Julia's idea.

"All right," I said to Julia, "we'll start after dinner."

Julia softened. She snuggled against me, rocking her head against my chest. "Thank you."

Smith scowled, as if I'd deserted him.

I rose and started back along the canyon rim. Smith lumbered to his feet with difficulty, and Julia followed, holding his arm. Except for Julia's outburst, which was soon forgotten, we were in good humor and relatively at peace as we reached the camp store. The local newspaper snapped us back to reality. Pictures of Julia and me were blazoned on the front page! We were caught in the photographer's flash at our booking at the jail. Our names and home town in Fredericksburg were also printed.

"Damn!" I said. "Won't the Provost love that! Won't the Samuelson Committee love it!"

Smith gestured at the newspaper. "Still, you make a lovely couple."

"And what about POP?" My mind churned. "Saves them a bundle of legwork finding us."

I was convinced our two brushes with death were no coincidence. Max Hess was still out there, and could take down Smith, and me, and anyone near us. We'd been lucky so far. But our scrape with the law was now front page news, and it was the sort of "local celebrity" item the Fredericksburg newspaper loved to promote. The whole world could know where we were by tomorrow. Could we take that chance? Could we take the chance Julia might get hurt if she stayed with us? It was a half-hour later when a plan formed in my mind.

After supper we packed the car with our gear. I sat in the men's room and composed a letter. "My sweet Julia—We can't go to Oakland for all the obvious reasons. Going with us puts you in grave danger. Forgive me for not leaving it for you to decide. You are sometimes too brave, and if you insisted on coming I could not have trusted myself to say no. I've arranged for Mrs. Callahan to see you safely on the plane home. Believe me when I say I love you, and Harold loves you, and I think Smith does, too. What a strange *ménage à trois*! Until we can be in touch."

I pocketed the letter and slipped it into Julia's purse when she went to the rest room. With the smiling docent waving goodbye, Smith and I hopped into the station wagon and sped towards the setting sun. Rex looked through the back window of the car. In the rearview mirror I saw Julia reappear from the washroom and look uncertainly at our disappearing cloud of dust. I nearly applied the brakes.

What I was doing was horrible and paternalistic, yet I knew if I'd told her our plans she'd have insisted on coming; I wouldn't have had the will to stop her. So I kept going and kept watching until she was a spec in the distance.

"She'll be furious," Smith said. "But you did the right thing."

"Will she know my motives?" I asked. "Or judge only my actions?"

VIRTUE

"[S]uperior prudence…
is the best head joined to the best heart."

—ADAM SMITH,
THE THEORY OF MORAL SENTIMENTS (1759)

19 THE SPECTATOR WITHIN

We reached California's coast after a long night's drive. We wanted anonymity, and with the tourist season in full swing, the misty wooded parks below Carmel were a wonderful respite from our Utah adventure. It would be an unlikely place for a terrorist to look for us. I needed time to think, to plan. With the September board meeting of WorldChemm approaching rapidly, I still had nothing to give them. Yet I felt strangely at peace. September would come soon enough.

Our camp at Big Sur was set amid old-growth coastal redwoods that towered over us, the tallest living things on the planet. The canopy made it barely possible for the sun to penetrate, and provided protection from the evening's drizzle. We slept solidly our first day there, catching up on lost dreams of the past two nights. The following morning we continued to laze, letting the fog burn off. Lounging in silence, we admired the giant forms reaching to the sky. When the sun reached high noon our stomachs began to stir. We inquired at the park office, and drove to a cozy restaurant hanging from a cliff overlooking the ocean.

The northern California coastline stayed consistently cool year round, making it possible to leave Rex unattended by the car, content with a bowl of water and some kibble. We went inside, and the gigantic picture windows overlooking Big Sur immediately brought Julia to mind, and how much I missed her in this romantic spot. Once we'd ordered lunch and our drinks arrived, I broached Smith, "Feel like talking?"

"Fire away."

I took out the tape recorder and set it on the table. It seemed like a month since we'd last used it, but in reality it was just a few days. During that time, Smith nipped my Drambuie and imagined that a red-haired camper was his old girlfriend. He collapsed and provoked Harold's return, then disappeared for a half-day and was finally discovered in a gambling saloon, playing no small part in a town riot. With all that, was it any wonder I couldn't remember what we'd talked about?

On low volume I replayed the last few minutes of tape, with Smith propounding that extensive government control in society isn't needed because humans naturally tend to counter-balance their selfish motives with other motives. People have a conscience, he said.

"That's it," Smith nodded.

"All right. The next thing would be, how do we get a conscience? Are we born with it? Or, as a modern person wants to know, is it for sale at the mall?"

"Don't be crude," he said, but I saw him smile. "Although we aren't born with a conscience, we *are* born with the drive to develop one, and given the tools to do so. To the extent that a conscience develops during your lifetime, you are said to progress as a virtuous person—as opposed to a pig, a rat, or a rock. A conscience unfolds: it is pursued, cultivated, and nurtured."

I pondered this a moment, then said, "Why should I care about developing a conscience? Why not rely on instinct and reason?"

Smith took a sip of soft drink and set the bottle down. "Well, your conscience is formed using both of these. One instinct we've discussed is that of self-preservation or self-love. I tried to show in my books that this instinct isn't evil. Within bounds, it is even virtuous, as I wrote about in *Wealth of Nations*.

"But my second proposition," Smith said, "is that humans also have an innate instinct to seek approval. We do this by being in *sympathy* with others. By sympathy I mean no particular emotion, either good or bad, but rather an understanding of the passions of another. It is the 'fellow-feeling' shared with others. Now, one could say that some of this derives from selfish motives."

Across the room a baby was being lifted into a high chair and fussed over by a mother. "Yes," I said, motioning to the infant, "that child is looking at her Mama as the nearest thing to God. It wants the coos of affection that approval brings. External approval and survival seem synonymous."

"The issue is deeper," Smith replied. "Your desire for your own *internal* approval could ultimately lead you to oppose your parents and peers. Your conscience could lead even to your death, like that of Socrates. The survival instinct cannot explain all human behavior, not even, perhaps, its most significant acts."

The beach below us was deserted except for a solitary surfer who approached the edge of the water, cradling a board under his left arm. His black wet suit hugged his waist. A long gray ponytail hung down his back. He seemed oblivious to everything but the incoming rollers. The man dropped the board to the sand.

We watched as he slowly pushed his arms into the sleeves of the wet suit and zipped it over his back. He moved to where the incoming foam swirled at his feet and then stopped. Fifty yards to sea the surf broke in a narrow band about a hundred yards wide. On either side of this band, giant island boulders rose out of the sea, jagged rocks menacing at the edges.

"Look at that fellow," Smith said. "See how he hesitates at the water's edge. There is conflict inside himself."

"It's a calculus of pleasure and pain," I suggested. "It's rough out there."

"Yes. He's having an internal dialogue about whether or not to enter the surf. It's a decision about right and wrong action. Notice that he isn't basing his decision on *our* approval, since he can't see us. The audience he imagines is the audience inside his mind. The conversation he has is with himself."

"Yes, I suppose that's right," I said.

"Well, that conversation with ourselves is how a conscience develops," Smith said.

The man on the beach made a decision. He reached for the surfboard, fastened his ankle leash to it, and trotted into the waves. In a moment he was submerged under a froth of whitecaps as he made his way to the breakers offshore.

I turned to Smith. "How could we develop fellow-feeling with that surfer?"

"We put ourselves in his place," he said. "Since I can't do that literally, I must get there through reflection. I ask the question, 'How would I feel being in his shoes?' It's the active working of *imagination* that makes sympathy possible. Imagination is our Creator's gift for becoming a truly human person."

Smith examined the waves below. He spoke slowly. "What I'll say next is subtle but critical: The sympathy of others is their approval that I am feeling what is appropriate to feel."

"Meaning?" I said.

"Suppose you are in a minor car accident which is fully covered by insurance. If you react as if your whole life were about to collapse because of this fender bender, it will be hard to find anyone to sympathize with you. Your reaction doesn't fit the circumstances."

"If your wife *died* in that car accident," I said, "your reaction is entirely proper."

Smith nodded. "You are alert to whether your emotional responses are, in fact, appropriate. You may alter your reaction, over time, as you come to see what is acceptable—what is within the bounds of propriety. A child who cries ferociously because of a slight scratch learns, is socialized, to minimize these tears and save them for a bigger wound."

"Becoming repressed little monsters?"

Smith laughed, "A Buddhist comes to see pleasure and pain as simply choices. Is the Buddhist repressing pain or not feeling it?"

"Point made," I said after a moment's reflection.

"Very well. Since I choose to moderate my feelings, I am conscious of my feelings and actions. I observe them, to see if they are, in fact, appropriate. I try to see myself as others see me. I become an *impartial spectator*, as well as an actor, in this drama."

Smith paused, then said, "This impartial spectator's view is critical for creating a conscience. When I look at my possible actions from the view of another, I learn that while I may be 'number one' to myself, I am not 'number one' to others who don't share my egoistic partiality to myself. Moreover—and this part is absolutely critical—we desire not only to gain the external praise of others, we desire to gain the internal respect and praise of *ourselves*. Yes, there is that final, but essential element—the rock onto which so many stumble—listen to me, we ultimately want to be *worthy* of our praise. We desire to be *praiseworthy*."

Just then the baby across the room began to howl.

"That baby hasn't learned any of that yet," I said.

We laughed.

The meal over, the waitress removed our plates. We lingered over coffee and tea, surveying the coastline from our hilltop perch. The sky was hazy with streaks of darker clouds racing through it.

Smith curled his lips and squinted, seeming to focus on some distant object. "No doubt, on many occasions, conscience loses out to the weakness in man." He turned to me. "Yet, the authority of our internal judge—our conscience, the great inmate of our breast—is very great. It is only by consulting it that we can ever see what relates to ourselves in its proper dimensions."

He leaned forward and patted my arm, "Let me give you an illustration. You are well aware, I'm sure, of optical illusions: objects appear large or small, not according to their real dimensions, but according to their proximity to us."

He pointed to the picture window overlooking Big Sur. "Take a look at that vista—an immense landscape of ocean, woods, and mountains. Yet, to our eyes, that vast panorama encompasses little more than these few panes of glass. Those colossal mountains appear, according to our eyes, much smaller than the very chamber in which we sit. That man on the surfboard is but the size of my fingernail. Our eyes deceive us!"

Smith was enjoying himself. "We remedy this defect of our eyes by adding *perspective*. We can form an accurate comparison between those mountains and this little room in no other way than by transporting ourselves, in our imagination, to a different place from whence we could survey both these objects at nearly equal distances. We can thereby form some judgment of their real proportions. Habit and experience teach us to do this so instantly and so easily that we are scarcely conscious of it."

Smith rose and began to pace. "In the same manner as our eyes, the selfish and original passions in our nature deceive us also. Whatever is closest to us feels most significant. This distortion is remedied through the perspective of *propriety* and of *justice*. These correct the otherwise natural inequality of our sentiments."

Smith rotated on the balls of his feet to face me. He had a deeply serious look about him. "Consider this: suppose a province in the great empire of China, with all its myriad of inhabitants, was suddenly swallowed up by an earthquake!"

I must have flinched, for Smith placed a hand on my shoulder. He went on. "How would a man, let us even specify, a man of *humanity* in Europe, who had no connection with that part of the world, be affected upon receiving news of such a dreadful calamity? Eh?"

Knowing him as I did, I refrained from answering an obviously rhetorical question. Smith went on smugly, "This man of humanity would, I imagine, first of all, express very strongly his sorrow for the misfortune of those unhappy people, and he would make many melancholy reflections upon the precariousness of human life, and the vanity of one's labors, which could thus be annihilated in a chance moment. He would too, perhaps, if he was a man of speculation, enter into many reasonings concerning the effects which this disaster might produce upon the commerce of Europe, and the trade and business of the world in general."

Smith smiled in a cunning way, narrowing his eyes. "And when all this fine philosophy was over, when all these humane sentiments had been once fairly expressed, he would pursue his business or his pleasure, take his repose or his diversion, with the same ease and tranquility, as if no such accident had happened."

I stared at him.

"Oh yes! The most frivolous disaster which could befall his own self would occasion a more real disturbance to his mind than the annihilation of millions in China. Oh yes, if he was to lose his little finger tomorrow, he would not sleep tonight, but—provided he never saw them—he will snore with the most profound security over the ruin of a hundred million of his brethren. Destruction of that immense multitude is plainly an object less interesting to him than a paltry misfortune of his own. This, my dear friend, is the painful truth: our *passive* feelings are almost always immediate, sordid, and selfish!"

"Then you've just eviscerated any notion of a human conscience," I replied.

"Not at all!" Smith said. "Bring this discussion into the realm of *action*. Suppose this man of humanity, acting in secret, could miraculously save the lives of these hundred million brethren? Suppose he could do so at the cost to himself of—a cost let us say, of—his little finger." Smith challenged me: "Would he do it? Eh? Would *you* do it?"

"Give up my little finger? To save a hundred million Chinese?" My reaction was visceral. "Of course I would."

Smith smiled broadly. "Well, then, a moment ago you were sordid and selfish. Now, you're willing to suffer physical pain and permanent disfigurement. What has made the difference?"

"We're talking about saving a hundred million people!"

"There you have it! You have just added *perspective*. In your imagination you visited some distant land, from whence you could feel not only your own minor pain, but also the travesty of your Chinese brethren. From the perspective of this impartial spectator your choice was decidedly easy: What choice would be praiseworthy in your own mind? What choice would cooperate, in some sense, with the laws of your Creator?"

Smith raised his index finger. "The key to a conscience is to exercise your moral imagination. Thus, while our *passive* feelings are almost always so sordid and so selfish, our *active* principles are by contrast often generous and noble."

Smith's mind seemed capable of peeling a single layer of an onion. I said, "That's brilliant, Smith. Ingenious. I'm damned impressed."

He rubbed his chin contemplatively. "We've barely scratched the surface."

❊   ❊   ❊

We rejoined Rex and drove from the restaurant lot, meandered south on Route 1 for less than a mile. The sharp right turn down to Pfeiffer Beach was easy to miss. The narrow road was unmarked and overlooked by most sightseers, but our waitress had alerted us to watch for it. Locals always tore down the sign to keep tourists away. We bumped down the one-lane road, which followed a dry canyon running between two hills. Occasionally a gravel driveway cut in, leading to a cabin or house hidden in the thick forest.

For a moment the road straightened, and I glimpsed a blue car trailing a few hundred feet behind us. My heart raced. Despite the enormous size of America's landmass, and despite the apparent tranquility of this spot, I knew that Max Hess still had a gun pointed our way. After a half-mile the car disappeared up a wooded driveway. Its profile revealed it too big to be a small sedan. I gave a sigh of relief.

After a few miles the pavement ended and the road turned to gravel and mud. We entered Pffeifer State Park and put five dollars into a self-pay envelope. The lot was empty save a Jeep with a rack on top, presumably belonging to the surfer we'd observed from the restaurant. A short walk led through a forest canopy to where the hillsides gave way to a pristine beach, about fifty yards wide at low tide. Just offshore the breakers crashed into giant, house-sized boulders. Natural arches in the rock caught the waves and lifted spectacular sprays of water in the air. The mist sprinkled down, turning into shimmering rainbows. The surfer engaged in his solitary craft, catching rolls and cutting through the channel in his black wetsuit. He could have been a seal.

Rex trotted to the surf's edge, barking and chasing as it momentarily receded to the vast Pacific. When it relentlessly surged forward again he raced back out of harm's way. It was exhilarating to be part of the push and pull of this cold ocean, on the edge of being overrun, yet also safe. We ambled up the deserted beach, following the ridge of purple kelp from a past high tide. Halfway up the beach we perched on a giant tree stump that had washed ashore in a storm.

I sat silently, wondering why Smith's seemingly clear articulations from lunch were mentioned nowhere in my economics textbooks. Why the "science of choice" taught only *half* the story—the "sordid and selfish" part of human behavior, and rarely or never the "noble and generous" part—nagged at me. The marketplace of Adam Smith existed not in some imaginary land of autonomous, amoral individuals, but within an interdependent social fabric in which virtue was extolled and a moral conscience constrained individual actions. To ignore these aspects could lead economists to incorrect and perhaps even dangerous conclusions. What were the implications of this for practical matters, I wondered, for the conduct of business?

As if he could read my mind, Smith said, "We must discover, my friend, what it is which prompts the generous upon all occasions, and the selfish upon many, to sacrifice their own interests to the greater interests of others. Think about that."

Lost in thought, Smith bent to pick up a handful of pebbles from the sand and began weighing them in his fingers. The wind picked up and the sky darkened. The ocean now boiled with whitecaps and the surfer struggled to stay up. I jumped off the log and wandered further up the beach. A sharp stick lay at hand and I used it to break the air sac on a giant purple kelp. There was a popping sound as the skin was pierced. I threw the stick away and sank into the sand.

Smith came up. "I've taken your wind away?"

"Surely no dictator, no terrorist—the Stalins, the Maos, the Max Hess's of the world—would for a moment act with what you call a conscience," I said.

"Precisely." Smith gazed up at a flotilla of prehistoric-looking pelicans, floating overhead along the shoreline.

"There's no shortage of examples," I said. "Look everywhere and you can find terrible evil."

"Yes." Smith turned back to me. He measured each word. "The man of the most perfect virtue, the man whom we naturally love and revere the most, is he who joins, to the most perfect command of his own selfish feelings, an exquisite sensibility to the sympathetic feelings of others. Take this character of feeling away and you will have a monster, such as those you mentioned. What would be the state of that society, ruled by such unconscionable chiefs?"

I didn't need to answer. Smith folded his hands behind his back. He let out a sigh. "Ahh! Hardships, dangers, injuries, and misfortunes—these are the only masters from whom we learn the virtues of self-control. But these are all masters to whom nobody willingly puts himself to school."

With this, he turned and walked to the water's edge. I had the feeling he was tiring. I left him alone. Suddenly he pointed, and I followed his finger to the surf.

"He's gone under!" Smith said.

A giant wave washed up on the beach. A surfboard rode the crest of foam and came to rest at the water's edge. The surfer was nowhere to be seen. Smith trotted down the beach. I followed at a run and quickly passed him, getting to the surfboard first. I pulled it onto the beach; the ankle leash was broken.

I was about to go into the water when Smith pulled on my arm, and said urgently, "Why don't we let him drown and steal his board? No one else is around. It would be easy."

I stood in stunned silence, unable to believe what I'd just heard.

20 A PARADOX

I whirled on Smith. "That's barbaric! I can't imagine doing that!"

"Exactly," he said, yelling at me over the wind. "You can't *imagine* doing it. Your imagination saved you from a terrible thing. Look, there he is!"

A body in a black wet suit was on its knees in the froth, thirty yards from us. We trotted down the beach to him, Rex in the lead. The surfer stood groggily, coughing. He wobbled in to shore. Smith crowed, proud of the trick he pulled on me. "Your reaction was to an external standard which has become internalized in you. This is the reaction of the impartial spectator."

"But if the spectator is just socialization," I yelled back, "we'd all be robots. If the society were racist, I'd be that, too. Moral relativism would rule the day."

We were almost to the surfer. "We haven't time to fix your misconceptions on that now," Smith said. "Let's give this fellow a hand."

The man was tall, heavily built, weighing easily two hundred pounds. I guessed he was in his early forties. With a wet and sagging arm around each of us he limped to the parking lot, and I returned for his board. The sun disappeared and the wind blew through my shirt, now sodden from the surfer. A chill went through me. The surfer was still spitting salt water when I got back to the parking lot.

"I can't believe I went out in that surf," he coughed. "I nearly bought it! My partners would have *killed* me." He managed a laugh.

We learned his name was Peter Chen, and he was also camping at Big Sur. He drove down last night from Palo Alto to try out El Nino's enhanced waves. Now he was in no position to drive anywhere. He slumped against his Jeep, hands on his knees.

After a few minutes Peter stood and shakily retrieved a backpack from his truck. "I need a painkiller for my shoulder and knee."

"Let's get you back to camp," I said. "We can put your board on top of your Jeep and come back later for our car."

Peter nodded wearily, and the three of us jammed into the front seat of Peter's Cherokee with Rex in the back. We plied up the narrow road from the beach and into the Big Sur camp. The old trail snaked around for several miles through the thick redwood forest. Peter said, "That's my spot, over by that creek."

"Pretty empty here."

"I come for silence," he said.

"Not so much that you won't join us for dinner? We have plenty," Smith said.

"I'd like that."

✻   ✻   ✻

We returned in a happy mood to our campsite a half-mile away. At sunset a fire burned in the grate and potatoes roasted in tinfoil. Peter sat on the picnic bench, one hand massaging his right shoulder, the other holding a beer. Smith stood by the fire, Rex keeping close watch. "How do you like your steak, Peter?"

"Actually, I don't eat meat. I'll be fine with the potato."

Peter's soft-spoken manner was in contrast to his large, athletic frame, and the deeply tanned and strong look of his closely shaved face. His hands were muscular, the nails carefully manicured. A long whitish-gray ponytail went half-way down his back.

"Must be nice taking off in the middle of the week to go surfing," I said.

"One of the perks of being boss," he laughed. "Actually, we're all on flex-time."

"Your business?" Smith asked.

"Computer chips. Specialty boards." Again he spoke softly, humbly. "Sixty million in sales, about forty associates. Just had our tenth anniversary."

Smith and I nodded appreciatively. "But you don't look…" I started to say.

"Like a boss?" He laughed. "Thank you. That's a compliment. You must be from back East?"

"How'd you guess?"

"The mindset—it's different. Got to be different to succeed here. You've probably heard about all those start-ups going belly up? Well, we haven't. In this market, creativity is vital, but so is efficiency. Not just in product design, but production, marketing, distribution. Loyalty and motivation are the key. Takes a different kind of workplace to bring that about, and a different sort of person to run it."

"Not that different," I said. "Still run for profit, I guess."

"No, it's paradoxical," Peter said. "We don't run it for the bottom line. That's not the way we succeed."

Dinner was over and we sat in silence. Smoke drifted upward through breaks in the canopy; stars glittered. We were full in the belly and pensive in the mind.

"Tell us about yourself," Smith said.

Again Peter's voice was low and unassuming. "The key experience of my life happened when I was nineteen, serving in Vietnam. I was a radar operator in flight control. My best friend Roy was flying in one day, and I stood out on the tarmac to welcome him back. Next thing I knew, enemy rockets were exploding all around. Then his 'copter was hit and Roy was cut in half. He lived just long enough for me to get to him, and watch him die."

He stoked the fire with a stick. "When you hold someone dying, there's no more bull. It's not a game anymore. There's no trying to be something you're not. No more trying to sound intelligent or witty. None of that matters. There's only *being*. That was the gift Roy left me."

The fire settled and Peter threw on a small log. "Being real means being connected, whole. It means being the same person at work as at home and at play. Life is integrated. Heck, when I came back I got plenty of experience working for others, some big companies, some small. In some companies the tension is so thick it's like mud. No one can be themselves. You smell fear in every corner."

Peter spoke so softly I slid closer to him on the bench.

"Bosses who motivate with fear make decisions they aren't proud of," Peter said, "and they justify it by saying, 'it's just a smart business decision.' But if it's so smart, why is everyone wracked with pain? Why is turnover so high? When they go home to their families they hide it all inside. They lead dual lives, one at work, another at home. They want to see themselves as good people, but they're trapped in a sick organization, an organization that doesn't let them be human beings making human decisions."

"Being in business means making hard choices," I said.

"People accept hard choices for the right reasons," he said emphatically. "So you ask, what are these right reasons? What is it that motivates people to work willingly with all their energy, and with sacrifice on occasion?"

"We've all heard about the fantastic stock options in Silicon Valley," I said.

"No question, people work hard when their contributions are recognized and rewarded. Stock options are important. But you'll miss something momentous if you stop there." Peter hunched forward and chose his words carefully. "The secret is this: people work harder when they appreciate *themselves* for what they have done. When the goal of the enterprise is worthy of their highest aspirations."

Smith nodded and leaned toward me. "When the impartial spectator inside themselves approves," he said.

Peter looked curiously at Smith and continued. "People work harder when you touch someplace deep inside, by having them buy into a dream bigger than themselves. That unleashes a creative spirit, and the mind and heart are integrated. So the company becomes, in a sense, the vehicle for the aspirations of the workers as integrated human beings."

"I thought the company was a vehicle for making profit," I said, remembering Milton Friedman's and Adam Smith's injunctions against "do-goodism."

"It has potential for much more than that," Peter said. "When people accept a bigger dream, there's a remarkable transformation. The workplace becomes alive, dynamic, charged with energy. Profit is the *by-product* of achieving that higher aspiration."

"Not just money, but something better?"

Peter laughed. "Have you ever seen a company mission statement couched in terms of making money? You won't find one, and the reason is simple: it doesn't engage people as efficiently as a higher aspiration will. You've got to touch people by aspiring to be the *first*, the *best*, the *biggest*, the *newest*, or trying *hardest*, caring *most*, by tying your success to that of a lofty and worthy social goal. Even Donald Trump, after his come-back, said money was never the object of his success, only its measure."

I nodded. "Of course, most companies proclaim something other than money as their goal. They say they want to 'serve customers.' But that's a gimmick, isn't it, for public relations?"

Peter shook his head. "Better not be. Workers and customers have pretty sharp detectors for insincerity and pretense. If the company is run solely for the bottom line, workers become cynical and disillusioned. To succeed, the higher aspiration has to come honestly from the heart. The mission statement doesn't mean a damn thing without commitment and action."

"It's hard to imagine Wall Street reacting favorably to this," I said.

Peter nodded. "We had funding problems, like all start-ups. But the irony is that people long for meaning in their work. When you provide a vehicle for that, they'll do anything for you and each other to keep it working. But why listen to me? Why not come see for yourselves?"

Smith nodded thoughtfully and I assented.

"It's arranged, then," Peter said. "Day after tomorrow at noon."

*   *   *

With supper over, Peter dropped me at my car. On the way back to camp I pulled into the parking lot of the camp office. I needed quiet time to think, and plan. As entertaining as the dinner had been, it was pure agony to be in these beautiful redwoods without sharing it with Julia. I missed her alluring eyes. She could make me laugh. Even her clean scent lingered in memory.

There was a pay phone outside the park office. It was late, and with the time difference, it would be seven in the evening in Virginia. The last time I'd called, to ask her to come to Utah, I'd been lucky to catch her at the gallery. This time I dialed there, and heard unending rings.

I feared calling Julia at home, in case her phone was tapped by POP, the FBI, or who knows who else. I pondered for a bit. There was a young couple two houses down from Julia who bought one of her paintings a year ago. I carried it over for them to hang. What was their name? Thomas? Tompkins? I tried to remember whether street numbers rose or fell going west on her street. I plied the pay phone with quarters and was lucky to find a sympathetic operator. She gave me the number of Robert and Sarah Thompson, two doors down from Julia.

Sarah Thompson answered the phone with the buoyant cheeriness of a garden club president.

"You may not remember me," I began, sounding foolish to my own ear. I took a deep breath and plowed ahead with a quick and false rendition of my dilemma: how I very much needed to reach Julia, but thought her phone out-of-order. A poor liar, I felt as obvious as an embarrassed teenager. But there was no point involving others in our danger; the less they knew, the better. I finished with a plea for her to get Julia to the phone.

"No point in that," she said quickly, following with a rough laugh. "She won't talk to you. My husband's traveling in Asia, so I invited Julia over for dinner last night. Boy oh boy, you are not a welcome name around here. Can't say I blame her. After she'd given you a second chance."

I lowered my head. "It's different this time. I did it for someone else."

"Uh-huh," she said, letting me know she believed not a word.

"Won't you even try to get her?"

"Look," she said, "I'll leave it up to her, but she's not home now. She'll be over this time tomorrow if you want to try again. I'm not guaranteeing anything, Mr. World Traveler."

*　　　*　　　*

It was eight the next morning before we rolled out of bed. A heavy mist lay over the tent, the picnic table, and the canopy of leaves. Even Rex didn't seem interested in stirring. We sipped strong coffee and finished the last of the trail mix. When the sun dried the dew from the tent we stowed the gear and set off. Once again we were on Route 1, winding northward around steep cliffs that fell precipitously into the Pacific Ocean. Several times we came around a hairpin turn to find the road blocked by work crews shoring up the bank from a slide. Below us waves crashed into the rocks at high tide. Just south of Carmel we pulled into Point Lobos, a craggy outcropping in the ocean, famous for its colony of several hundred sea lions that bark from an offshore island. The sign by the road noted that it was one of the largest marine sanctuaries in the world. We paid an entrance fee and drove to a parking lot overlooking the ocean. I left Smith sunning himself on a blanket with Rex, and set off exploring a trail that hugged the coastline.

Along the rocky shore a troop of spotted harbor seals lay in the sun, looking like enormous fat hand-rolled cigars, one drooping over the other. Occasionally a new arrival flopped in from the sea, belly hopping onto the pile. They were placid and content, unconcerned with the tourists kept a safe distance away behind a wooden fence.

A protected cove was carpeted with a beach of gray rocks, worn smoothly to the size of marbles. The tide started out, exposing more and more pools of squirming sea creatures. Purple, green, and orange anemones were everywhere, gradually closing their bracts up around their bodies as the water receded. I picked about the barnacles and limpets, stepping carefully, enjoying the sunshine and the invigorating sea air. Terns feasted on helpless prey while sea gulls fluttered overhead with pompous importance. In the shallow water hermit crabs peaked out of their stolen shells and crawled alongside sea snails and an occasional starfish.

I turned my back to the ocean and leaned over to inspect another frothy tidal pool. I heard an unexpected "whoosh," and before I could lift my head a wave crashed in with sudsy flurry. Salt water drenched me to the knees. I scurried onto higher rocks, amazed at the violence of the ocean, and grateful I hadn't ventured farther out. The energy coiled in those waters was remarkable.

My thoughts flashed to Peter's ideas of the previous night. Could there really be a similar unharnessed energy inside each of us? Could a business become more businesslike by allowing workers to grow in their humanness? It was far from the eye-shade business calculations that seemed to rule the world. Yet paradox seemed to be at the heart of scientific revolutions. Under my feet I felt solid and unmoving rock. But sub-atomic physics asserts that matter is 99 percent empty space, and what little mass there is, is in constant motion. By breaking apart that atom we unleash a torrent of almost unlimited energy. Wasn't that Peter's point? Getting to the core of the human soul and unleashing that power? It sounded fantastic. Even if it got started, was it controllable? Once workers were empowered, could they be contained?

I returned to the parking lot, finding Smith munching on an apple smothered with peanut butter. He particularly seemed to enjoy the peanut butter, once I told him the price and he discovered how filling it was.

After a week of camping, we needed pampering. I checked us into a motel near Cannery Row in Monterey and the first thing I did was take a long hot shower. Afterwards, Smith stayed contentedly with Rex, and I wandered down to the Aquarium to see the majestic sights. Dolphins in the large tank seemed to anticipate each other's movements, and the fish swimming in sync seemed equally adept at picking up hidden clues. I recalled how Smith said we were innately wired for "fellow-feeling" with others. Wasn't this something dolphins experienced?

Another exhibit catalogued the fall of sea otters, hunted to near extinction during the last two centuries because of the high demand for their pelts. This story followed the well-known pattern of the "tragedy of the commons": since sea otters are a common property resource—owned by no one—no private actor gains any monetary value in preserving them, and yet many gain handsomely from hunting them. As sea otters dwindle, there are unintended consequences, because sea otters eat sea urchins. Without a predator, sea urchins multiply and eventually eat their way through the underwater plant life. As the submerged kelp forests disappear, so do the multitude of vital fish stocks harbored within, and, in turn, so do the populations of birds that feast off fish. The short-run gain to hunters creates a much larger loss to fishermen and others in the long run. This downward ecological catastrophe was halted by an international treaty to ban the killing of sea otters in 1911. The sea otter populations were recovering slowly.

I tried to put all of this in the context of Economics 101. While Smith argued that markets were generally self-sustaining and self-correcting, the market's free-for-all scramble for profit proved unsustainable in this case because there were no clearly defined property rights. And trying to assign property rights in a complex eco-system like the oceans entails monstrously high transactions costs. Hence, the market in this case could not naturally sustain itself without some outside rules. There was a lesson here: seeing otters merely as profitable commodities, in isolation from their integrated environment, was a dangerous practice. Likewise, when economists advocate free markets in far off developing economies, it is often in ignorance of the complex legal and social environments operating there. Could this likewise lead to unintended consequences, to unsustainable outcomes? When tinkering, make sure you have all the pieces! Capitalism is an intricate, integrated system of markets, institutional structures, and social values. Its complexity could hardly be captured by mathematical models that deal with impersonal markets in isolation. Yet that is exactly what Lattimer, and I as his student, were presenting to WorldChemm on their privatization project in Russia. These ponderous thoughts weighted me down, and made me less than happy with myself.

I consoled myself with the hope that I might be able to reach Julia tonight. As ten o'clock Pacific time approached, I ensconced myself in a phone booth three blocks from our motel, quarters at the ready. When the line rang on the Thompson's end I held my breath ... and Julia answered! I didn't get many words in edgewise in that first call, with her telling me off in her soft but pointed British accent. I didn't really need to speak. I just wanted to hear her voice.

21 A NEW PARADIGM?

The next morning found us circling Monterey Bay into Santa Cruz, then cutting northward through the mountains. We wound through a magnificent stand of redwoods, eventually crossing the San Andreas Fault. Skirting San Jose, we headed up the peninsula toward San Francisco, following a parallel path to the cloud-covered Santa Cruz Mountains. Flanking us were rolling foothills, dotted with scrub oak trees and the occasional shiny glass-and-steel office park. The arid, gold-hued landscape carried a bleak beauty in its sparseness. Near the horizon a brown haze of smog and humidity lay over the San Francisco Bay as far north and east as we could see.

By eleven o'clock we arrived on the outskirts of Palo Alto.

"This is the stuff of dreams," I said, exiting the highway onto Page Mill Road.

I was excited, almost ecstatic at being in the heart of Silicon Valley. Ahead of us, along a long stretch of road, was Hewlett-Packard's headquarters. Massive low-slung buildings and factories were designed to create the feeling of a college campus. Across the road, up a side street, was Hoover Tower, landmark for Stanford University. Tens of high-tech research buildings sprouted around the campus like mushrooms. Farther along we saw the legion of support industries that make up Silicon Valley, the finance capitalists, consultants, lawyers, and business journalists. We toured, finding the manufacturing giants of the information age: Intel, Sun Microsystems, Cisco Systems, Motorola, and Lockheed Martin. Here is where hundreds of technology start-ups began, such as Apple, Adobe, and Netscape, but not Microsoft, which made Seattle its home.

"This is the heart of the new America," I said. "Least until the market crash."

Smith looked around with interest.

"Fastest export growth of any sector," I continued. "Phenomenal productivity—new chips introduced every few months!"

Peter Chen's specialty chip factory occupied a one-story warehouse building in the neighboring town of Mountain View. It was set off from the road with an assortment of trees and plants. A small sign said, "Ecosystem habitat regeneration." We parked and went in, tying Rex to a shade tree and leaving a bowl of water.

Peter greeted us at the door. He wore a neat pair of jeans, a white shirt with blue tie, and penny loafers. He had the same gentle smile and warm eyes, but today there were creases on his forehead that weren't there two days before. He ushered us past an open reception area. A woman in her mid-thirties stood by the counter, her eyes red. An older woman was beside her, an arm on her shoulder.

"Something the matter?" I asked, as we went into Peter's office. It was a small, eight by twelve foot room with a clear window facing the factory floor. There were two guest chairs which we sat in, and Peter settled behind an unassuming wood veneer desk.

"We've got a little crisis," Peter said, running his hands through his hair. "Well, why lie, it's a *big* crisis."

Smith and I looked at each other. "Perhaps we'd best come back," Smith said.

"No, you might as well hear it. Don't want you to get the wrong impression that running a business is only fun and games." Peter stood and shook his head. "Jim Macdonald of Macdonald Semiconductor, our largest customer, called a half-hour ago. He raked our account manager Barbara over the coals." He nodded in the direction of the woman at the desk who'd been crying. "It isn't the first time either. Every time he calls, my staff ends up in tears. Not just Barbara, but her assistant, our technicians, everyone. He wants to throw his weight around, like a damn emperor, just to feel people squirm and let them know who's boss."

"What did he want?" Smith asked.

"He demanded that his chips be given priority. He wants them this afternoon, instead of tomorrow as specified by our contract."

"An unusual request?" I asked.

"Not at all, we're constantly juggling to accommodate if we can. But today we've got twenty orders ahead of him. Some of these are from small start-ups that operate with tiny margins. They need their products just as badly as Macdonald does."

"You can live without the start-ups," I said. "But Macdonald's the big fish, I guess."

"He's thirty percent of our volume," Peter sighed. "He regards me as an equal but he's tyrannical with my staff. I've asked him to lighten up, many times. He doesn't listen."

"Anyone higher up in his company you can talk to?"

Peter shook his head. "He's the founder and CEO. He thinks money rules and he can get away with this bullying. Barbara can't take it anymore. Says she's going to quit."

"The consumer *is* king," I said. "That's the first law of competition. You can't cut off your nose on this one. I guess you'll have to hire a new account manager."

Peter walked to the filing cabinet and rested against it. He expelled a breath of air and thumped his palm against the metal. Smith and I glanced at each other, wondering whether this would be the time to make a graceful exit.

He straightened and returned to his desk. In a weak voice, he said, "No, I've got to face him." He sat and picked up the phone. In a moment he had Jim Macdonald on the line.

"Jim? It's Peter. About your request: I can't push up delivery today. No, I won't ... because we'd break our commitment to others. We'll have your product first thing tomorrow, as promised."

Peter took a deep breath. "One more thing, Jim."

In a few sentences Peter laid out the problem with Barbara and finished with, "I'm instructing my staff not to accept any new orders from you."

Peter gave a bleak smile as Smith and I sat in astonished silence.

We could hear yelling emanating from the earpiece. Peter grimaced and punched a button on his receiver. A voice bellowed from the speakerphone, "Cancel my business? I gave you twenty million in orders last year! You can't fire me, I'm the goddamn customer!"

"Jim, we've thought it through and you've had plenty of warning. I'm sorry it has to be like this. That's our final word."

Peter hung up. He was pale. He got to his feet and swung to face the factory floor. He rested his forehead against the plate glass window, his breath fogging the pane. He said softly, "The customer comes first? Not really. The employees come first."

"I love a paradox." Smith smiled. "Do go on."

Peter exhaled and turned to face us. "A mentor of mine, Paul Hawken, once told me, there's no way to instill a positive customer service ethic before you embody a positive employee ethic. Responsiveness in, responsiveness out."

"What does that mean for the bottom line?" I said.

"Our company lives by its productivity," Peter said. "We have virtually no absenteeism, low turnover, no pilfering, and our people thrive in the constant chaos of this industry because we face problems together. The old way of doing business, of hiring and firing people like cogs of interchangeable steel, leads to terrible morale. Fear serves as the motivator. People become too scared to risk, too frozen to innovate or cooperate. The culture becomes stifled with sycophants, bureaucrats, and spongers."

"Still, it took courage to fire your largest customer," I said.

"Barbara is like a sister to us. She'll be around long after Macdonald's workers jump ship."

Peter turned again to point out the window onto the factory floor. "I know I sound mystical, but consider how our company would be different if we let Jim Macdonald go on terrorizing us. And not just him, but think of all the hundreds of other small and large encounters of each week, each one giving us the chance to signal what our values are? If we chose profits ahead of everything, even ahead of our core values, then we'd make different decisions: We'd install safety and pollution equipment only to the minimum letter of the law; we'd tie workers to rigid schedules regardless of their personal emergencies. You know what would happen? Our workers would figure out pretty quick they're just pieces of meat, disposable items on the bottom line. The level of tension around here would mount. Workers would call in sick, from ulcers and mental stress, or just plain meanness. Our production crew would start making mistakes, and when we needed something *special* from our crew they would have nothing special to give us. What had we given them that was special? We would start downhill, little by little. So that's why there's a paradox. We follow our higher aspirations for what kind of 'family' we want at work, and customer service and profit are natural by-products of doing that well."

As suddenly as he had gotten up, Peter sat in the chair and covered his face with his hands. He stayed that way for half a minute before drawing his palms slowly across his features, squeezing his cheeks, eyes, and nose. He looked like he'd seen a ghost.

"I may have just made the biggest mistake of my career," he said. "It's all very fine to talk about empowering workers, but that means little if this company goes belly-up. That's hardly caring for workers in the long run."

Peter stood again. "Make no mistake, we can't be doing what we do unless we keep making a good profit." He motioned around the room. "You see how we're frugal. No fancy offices. No company cars. No management cafeteria or health club. We fly coach, except for Paula, who's five months pregnant. We keep health insurance down by reducing negativity and stress on the job. We struggle like all companies, and we have our share of problems. I just hope to God we make it through this one."

Peter headed for the door. "I need to tell people what's happening. We'll have to make some big adjustments without Macdonald's business."

He went out into the reception room and we saw him talking to Barbara. She hugged him. Peter motioned us outside and we entered the plant. "It's going to be tough, but I know we'll survive." Peter said. He sounded happier and more confident than he did twenty minutes ago.

"Doing the right thing has a deep affect on all the people involved," Peter said as we walked down a white corridor. "Good energy is unleashed and life expands. It's not just Barbara who's now willing to walk on coals for us, it's everyone else who hears about this. I mean, people learn fast that we don't bull."

"Your approach sounds pretty idealistic," I said.

"Yeah. We've had to let people go who needed fear as a motivator," Peter said. "They're so wounded they can't think for themselves, they wanted someone to tell them what to do every moment, and someone to watch them to see it gets done. No question our model won't work for everyone. But it's made us profitable, until now."

We entered a large production area with vats of cleaning acids. Peter cautioned us to not get too near.

"We're in competition with the world's leading companies," Peter said. "That forces us to be different. We do it by creating relationships, genuine ones."

Smith looked at him with a dreamy gaze. "A 'fellow-feeling' with others, is it?"

"Yes, but it has to be real. You can spot a phony in a heartbeat. I don't lecture this, I just do it. The beauty is, once you have relationships, everyone looks out for others."

Smith interjected softly, as if reciting something he had put to memory, "All is not lost, when one puts the people in a condition to see it has intelligence. On the contrary, all is lost when you treat it like a herd of cattle, for sooner or later it will gore you with its horns."

Peter turned to Smith, gazing at him. "That's beautiful."

Smith nodded. "The great Voltaire."

"Poetry aside, business can't be run by being nice," I added.

"No one said anything about being nice," Peter replied. "*Nice* is the falsity that gets people killed on the job from sloppy procedures. You've got to be forthright, straight out, in the moment."

We reached the design area where computer chips were being etched. Four or five workers looked up and nodded as Peter entered. Peter went over and picked up a silicon wafer. The intricate pathways were a beautiful contrast of emerald green and gold.

Peter smiled, "If we can make it work here, what's stopping others in less competitive arenas? I can't help but think we're a harbinger of things to come."

"You don't think conditions here are unique?" Smith asked.

"Not anymore," Peter said. "Look, I studied engineering at Stanford. We learned how Henry Ford revolutionized industry through mass production. He had a simple idea: switch from producing cars *in series*, one-by-one, to producing them *in line*, along a conveyor belt. Long production runs allowed Ford to hire unskilled workers to do the same simple, repetitive motions."

"Aren't those economies of scale still valid?" I said. "How can you compete with Taiwan, for example?"

Peter smiled. "We don't try. They make volume chips, commodities with low value added. We make specialty chips, with high value added. Speed and quality are more important for our business." Peter set the wafer down. "Ford's innovation has run its course, and it's easy to see why. Remember what Ford said, 'You can have any color Model-T you want, as long as it's black'?"

We laughed.

"Would consumers stand for that these days?" Peter asked. "Today everything is custom orders, short production runs, quick setups and turnarounds. That means even in factory jobs you need workers who can handle constant change, think for themselves, take responsibility, be pro-active in finding solutions. If you can motivate employees, you can cut out layers of high paid managers and supervisors telling workers what to do every step. Think what you'll save in time, money, and productivity. And if this is true in manufacturing, double what I've just said for service jobs."

I mulled these ideas as we walked back to the entrance. "Your breakthrough is simply realizing that worker productivity depends critically on how a worker *feels* about the job?" I asked.

Smith prodded me. "Good heavens, I pointed that out in *Wealth of Nations*. Seems hardly worth debating that a worker should work better in good spirits than disheartened."

Peter nodded assent. "Absolutely. But getting a worker to feel excited, loyal, and dedicated may mean turning a traditional company's management style on its head. You don't learn this in an MBA program and you can't put it in a memo; you have to live it."

Smith nodded. "Prudence, benevolence, and justice are the character of virtue. The truly developed person exudes these qualities, the latter two of which connect him to others in a genuine way."

"We show benevolence and justice to our friends, our families," I said. "It's not something economists typically put in economic models for running a business."

"Do you want to live your life in an isolated box?" Peter replied. "Is that the path to wisdom?"

＊　　　＊　　　＊

On Peter's recommendation we stopped for lunch at a bagel shop on University Avenue in Palo Alto. The spot was a haven for students hunched over books and newspapers while munching sandwiches and sipping lattes. From their clothing and demeanor, these students appeared to come from all parts of the globe, attracted like magnets to the education and industry in Silicon Valley. Peter told us there were more Ph.D.'s per capita here than in any other spot on the planet. We looked over the crowd and wondered who would be the next Hewlett or Packard, Gates or Jobs.

With coffee cups in hand we strolled downtown. A short walk from University Avenue took us to the small white garage where Bill Hewlett and David Packard began their fledgling electronics business just as the Great Depression ended. Winding our way back, we stumbled on a low-slung adobe building. A sign told us it was the public library. Smith and I looked at each other and silently nodded.

"You check the papers, I'll try the Internet," I said.

A half-hour of searching produced a mountain of information.

"Here's something," Smith said, holding up a newspaper article. "There's a trade summit in San Francisco next month, the same week as WorldChemm's meeting. That's no coincidence, I'm sure. POP has threatened to break them both up."

"Not just POP." I pointed to my stack of printouts from the web. "Environmental groups, labor unions, Marxists, the Republican far right and the Democratic far left: It's a coalition of odd bedfellows uniting against world trade."

Smith pondered this, then said, "I should like to be there."

I was more optimistic than I should have been. "Of course," I said, "but how can I protect you against that mob? Isn't it bad enough having Max Hess and POP shooting at us? Do you think that fanatic Hess will ever give up?" I asked. "And POP or no POP, I've got to finish my dissertation."

"Where to then?" Smith asked.

I smiled ruefully. "Harold's sister lives a stone's throw away in Oakland. But that would be putting you in the spider's web, wouldn't it? We can't risk it."

22 ONCE AGAIN THE INVISIBLE HAND

We crossed San Francisco Bay at its southern end, avoiding massive congestion near the city. Unlike the picturesque span of the Golden Gate Bridge, which opened onto a rugged and pristine Pacific, the southern bay was stagnant, dirty and industrial. The few rivers feeding it were moribund by late summer. San Jose sprawl took up the southern third of the bay, industrial parks and freeways eating into the wetlands. A persistent haze rested on the skyline, producing a cataract-effect on my eyes. It was hot and humid.

Passing Oakland produced a wistful moment, knowing that Harold's sister was just west of the freeway. Instead of exiting, we swung east toward the Sierras. The cabin I'd reserved for the month of August was still waiting. It was not a place I had contemplated going with a companion. It was to have been a solitary refuge, a haven to confront the demons in my dissertation. I planned strenuous hikes and climbs during sunny after-noons. Yet with Max Hess and POP after us, Smith stayed along for the ride, and I—well, I wasn't at all displeased.

It had been a long several weeks since we'd begun our trip in Virginia, and I reflected on the landscapes passed, the dangers survived, and the intellectual and emotional challenges surmounted. I'd left the East Coast confused, angry, and blocked. I could feel that subsiding, being replaced with surprising acceptance and calm. Life gave no guarantees, but this voice of Smith's had shown me I could choose how to live. Listening to the beckoning call of conscience, seeing through the interior eye of authentic sentiments, finding peace of mind from being, rather than having—these were all choices. I recalled Smith's line, "The beggar, who suns himself by the side of the highway, possesses that security which kings are fighting for." I knew he was right. But I struggled to reconcile these views with my ingrown attitudes, nurtured through years of attention to popular culture, advertising, and economic schooling.

As we passed the foothills near Walnut Creek and entered the flat, agricultural expanse of San Joaquin Valley, I put my simmering questions to Smith. "How did what Peter say square with your concept of an invisible hand?" I asked. "What did you think about profit not being the goal, but profit becoming the by-product of producing meaning for workers? Is Peter an odd-ball?"

"I'll leave that to the marketplace to decide," Smith said. "If he can increase productivity by appealing to his workers' higher aspirations, and—this is critical, of course—if his gains in productivity exceed his costs of doing so, then his profits will rise. Other companies must follow suit or lose out."

Smith paused. "It's an interesting experiment, and only time will tell if he's right. What he said strikes a chord in this sense: His conduct appears guided—disciplined, if you will—by a moral conscience."

The road narrowed, becoming congested with trucks loaded with agricultural produce. Heavily subsidized irrigation water brought rapid development to the central valley. Here, water was "liquid gold," taking the place of oil or diamonds in determining riches. We passed field after square field, each outfitted with large mechanical arms spewing water onto crops. A noisy processing station emitted a fog of noxious fumes, causing Smith to shield his face with a handkerchief. Rex whined and flopped down, exhaling loudly.

When we were past it, Smith said, "Think about my example of the butcher, the brewer, and the baker. Each seeks his own 'self-interest.' Suppose that it were possible for the butcher to sell an inferior cut of meat *without being discovered*. Will he do it, assuming he could get away with it?"

"Possibly," I said.

"Yes, but no scam is perfect, and customers might discover the fraud and shop elsewhere, putting him out of business. This is why competition is such a powerful disciplining force."

He paused, enjoying the storytelling. "But this isn't the end of it. Even if he could cheat you and get away with it, he still might choose not to. To do so might make him lose something he cherishes most of all, namely, his own self-image."

"And you've argued that self-image is worth more than money."

"It's essential for peace of mind, which is what happiness is all about."

"What if he cares more about money than peace of mind?" I asked.

"Then he would be a fool, and mind you, there are plenty of fools out there."

"And the invisible hand?" I persisted.

"The invisible hand of the market operates not only because of competitive pressures, but also because of the self command each of us brings to our behavior. *Trust* arises when you deal with people you know to have an internal self-image to uphold. A market works more efficiently because of this. Without trust, the economic machinery labors and grinds, starved of oil, and the monitoring and enforcement costs simply become prohibitive."

We stopped for dinner at a truck stop near Stockton, the sun lingering on the horizon. After the meal, I fished for my wallet. "I find it hard to believe many businesspeople wouldn't cheat their customers if they could get away with it," I said.

Smith examined the bills I deposited on the counter. "You're a mass of contradictions," he said. "Look, you just gave away a tip."

"So? The waitress worked hard for it."

"What if she did?" Smith replied. "We'll never be this way again. Why not stiff her and maximize your savings? Hmm? Your *conscience* says leaving a tip is the right thing to do. You must please yourself by listening to this conscience. Why is this part of your own humanity so evident, yet you deny it for the butcher and the baker?"

"There are Scrooges out there," I said. "I know a few."

"Of course. I merely assert that people have an inner spectator who helps guide their behavior, within a market and elsewhere."

We reached a stopping place for the night. Lying on our motel beds, we let the air conditioning soothe our bodies.

"You still awake?" I asked.

There was a murmured reply.

I reminisced. "After my first year of grad school we sat for oral exams, three of us at a time. The old fogy giving it was a tyrant, completely bull-headed. I remember him asking us, again and again in his thick German accent, 'Vat is capital? Vat is capital?' We gave him every definition we could think of, from Marx to Samuelson, and nothing appeased him. We all flunked and had to retake the exam the next year. By then the bully had retired and we passed with flying colors."

Smith sat up. "And your point?"

"I've thought a lot about capital since then," I said, enjoying my pedagogical role. "Economists used to focus on physical capital—that forklift over there, the pump on that irrigation equipment, buildings and roads, things you could touch. But in the sixties, economists discovered they were missing much of what explains economic growth, and they were forced to expand this narrow view by adding the concept of 'human' capital—the stocks of intangible assets brought by workers to production, things like education, training, and health. Today virtually all businesspeople accept the importance of investing in these types of capital."

Smith looked irritated. "This doesn't get to the heart of my point—the values with which people interact with one another."

"I'm getting to that. In the 1980s, human capital was broadened further to include social capital. It became recognized that economic activity takes place within social norms and institutions, and trust can substantially reduce transactions costs. Some economists have even said social capital includes virtue."

Smith cast me a withering look. "If you knew this, why did I have to fight you every inch of the way? It was like wrestling a python!"

"It's only starting to make sense," I said.

"Anyway, you could have learned all you needed about virtue and social norms from my *Moral Sentiments*," Smith sniffed.

"How much more is there?" I asked.

He didn't answer. Instead, he gave a deep sigh, and rolled over.

23 APPEALS TO HIGHER AUTHORITY

We reached the two-room cabin south of Yosemite the following morning. The "cabin" was a glorified camp shelter, a small log building used by hunters in past times as cover during bad weather. Nestled on the slope of a hill, it was well-isolated from its nearest neighbor. Water was hand-pumped, and cooking was carried out with dexterity over a two-burner propane stove. No hint of electricity or phone marred the pristine quiet. Its simplicity and inaccessibility made the retreat affordable, if sparse.

The next weeks took on a pattern of regularity. Smith arose first, fixing coffee for me and tea for himself. He retreated to the porch and rocked, watching the sun rise through the granite peaks. I took over the small broad-board table, spreading out my papers and books. I used my laptop computer sparingly, saving the battery.

At three o'clock in the afternoon we'd stop for a drive into the surrounding hillsides, where I'd take a hike with Rex while Smith snoozed on a grassy knoll. After dinner we'd light the lantern and it was more dissertation work for me while Smith read. Around ten o'clock we'd conclude the day with a stroll up the hillside overlooking the valley. I'd sip Drambuie and Smith would puff an unlit cigarette. On these walks, he regaled me with subtle insights or delightful turns of phrase that could only be pure and genuine Adam Smith. Thinking back, I regretted all the time I'd wasted, putting Smith through that stupid "test" of ten questions, all because I refused to accept him. That proposition was second nature to me now, yet I sensed our time together was drawing to a close. Smith himself became more wistful and melancholic with each passing day.

Twice a week we stopped in town to pick up groceries and ice, recharge my laptop battery, and do a load of laundry. While our socks were spinning, I'd call Julia from a pay phone. That would cheer up Smith as much as it did me. Ever-mindful of POP, we worked out a system. I would dial the home of Julia's neighbor at a predetermined time, and Julia would just "happen" to be at the Thompson's borrowing some sugar or dropping off a pie. We'd spoken three times since Monterey, and Julia almost forgave me for deserting her in Utah. I was feeling busy and happy, and the combination seemed to work magic on my dissertation.

A good theoretical model didn't require volumes of text, just the one essential kernel of truth that everyone else had overlooked—overlooked because sometimes it was too obvious to bother mentioning. What was unnoticed or ignored could have a huge impact, particularly in a fluid, developing market. Chaos theory, for example, showed how even the delicate flap of a butterfly's wings could unleash forces a thousand miles away. It was for such a nugget of insight that I searched.

The mark of a master craftsman, be it a carpenter who measures twice but cuts only once, or a painter, like Julia, who newly presents the fundamental nature of a bumblebee through subtle distillation, is the ability to identify what is important. Not an easy task, to be so clear and so knowledgeable as to find confidence in reducing down to essential, reso-nate elements. I could see my floundering in early drafts as I struggled to sharpen the essence of my dissertation down to the razor's edge.

There's only so much inspiration one can glean from star-ing at a pad of notepaper, so my occasional day-long hikes turned into unconscious extensions of work. By the end of the second week I had gasped to the top of the usual tourist desti-nations—Half-Dome, Yosemite Falls, and Vernal Falls. Each posed a different set of problems in getting to the top, and it was in overcoming these obstacles that I hoped to shake loose the essence of my dissertation. These were exhausting and exhilarating climbs, cresting summits to breathtaking panora-mas of mile-high glacial carvings. The exertion mirrored a river of thoughts, a cascade of water rushing against a dam.

Surprisingly, it was on an afternoon of modest hiking and barely breaking a sweat that the levee burst. We had driven over the Tioga Pass Road to Tuolumne Meadows. Snow peaks fed the Tuolumne River which meandered through the valley. The surrounding mountains were ringed at their base by cres-cents of pine forests. The mountainsides showed slivers of white where north-facing ravines still cradled snow banks.

Smith and Rex took off to explore the river while I hiked the meadow. Wildflowers carpeted the fields with a dazzling array of colors and shapes. A mile passed as my boots swooshed through the soft undergrowth of red, orange, and purple blossoms. My breathing merged in-sync with my steps. A calm descended, heightening my senses yet simultaneously taking me beyond them. My mind was free.

Imagination—seeing with perspective, changing focus—that was the key! Anew I surveyed the mat of wild flowers, the flowing river along its worn path, the snowy peaks, and the natural way in which they harmonized to produce the spectac-ular outcome in this meadow. Random events, such as a dry winter or a flash flood, might alter the specifics of the land-scape, but there was a synchronicity with which the living things and the elements combined anew to create a natural balance: the river carving a new bank, older trees dying, and new ones sprouting where conditions improved.

I saw the problem of stock valuation under uncertainty as an extension of the swiftly passing stream and the implications for a valley where wildflower investors sought the water of international capital. In a revelation, the insight for which I searched appeared. It was hardly luck or accident, for I worked hard to prepare the intellectual ground for this moment. It took imagination to break it loose.

"Yee-haa!" I skipped and yelled. "Yee-haa!"

I quickly took out the pencil and paper I always carried and began to write the equations that expressed those insights.

*   *   *

I stopped in town, humming and singing, anxious to share my epiphany with Julia. I was back in the car within a minute.

"No answer," I said to Smith.

"Same as yesterday," Smith replied.

Why would Julia fail to keep our rendezvous? My euphoria began to ferment into worry. By the time we got back to the cabin, worry had grown into alarm. For Smith's sake, I didn't show it. What could I do? Whatever it was, it would have to wait until morning.

I spent an hour on my computer inputting the equations I'd developed, then turned off the machine and set it aside. Smith and I had navigated so much philosophical territory over the last weeks that to distil its practical meaning took precedence that night. I recalled the first time we'd spoken in Julia's living room, how Smith said the wick and wax of a candle needed oxygen to burn, just as the economy needed the interplay of human beings to make it a society, the "fellow-feeling" that creates a foundation for moral conduct. At that time I couldn't fathom how that could be of any possible relevance to me, to economics, or to business. Now it provided the lifeline to a better, richer way of living.

Economics was a commanding discipline, capable of illuminating potent lessons for the world about scarcity, and our choices for dealing with it. The "economic way of thinking" broke through the sometimes illogical, and often muddled, preconceptions of students and politicians alike on a range of subjects. I had little doubt that our world was richer, and our choices clearer, because of the compelling insights offered by my chosen field. Yet Smith challenged me to wonder if the discipline was fulfilling all it could be. While modern economic theories exhibited logical elegance, did they address the interconnectedness of one to another, in social and moral ways? Could there be true understanding without that? Moreover, mainstream economics seemed to require nothing of the individual by way of personal change and transformation, nor did it acknowledge, encourage, or inspire anyone to care a whit for anyone else's well-being.

By contrast, Smith's classical view provided the insights for achieving greater material comforts, yet he had little faith that these would bring happiness. For the vast majority of mankind, happiness would unfold from inner growth and transformation, from relating better to others, using the moral imagination provided each of us. This was the road to peace of mind and happiness. *Being*, not *having*, was the answer. The transforming power of this message was extraordinary, yet it was hardly an easy path to follow. It would require a new way of thinking, acting, and living.

I put it to Smith that night on our evening stroll. Rex led the way, his nose following the ground as he maneuvered up the overgrown deer track a quarter-mile from the cabin. The moon cast shadows ahead of us.

"I've been struggling to understand all that you mean by a human conscience," I said to Smith.

He answered in a flash, as if it were the uppermost thing in the mind. "A conscience is man's internal capacity to judge his own conduct, and to align it with a sense of duty to a moral standard."

"But we never finished our conversation from Big Sur," I said. "How does a conscience differ from popular opinion, which could be racist or ignorant, or could simply reflect mob hysteria—like what happened in Durango?"

"Your moral standard is partly the product of socialization," Smith said. "But your imagination allows you to go beyond narrow, local concerns."

We came to the bluff where we usually rested to survey the valley. The gorge was quiet in the chilly air. Sitting on a log, Smith turned to face me.

"Here's an unhappy illustration from my own time," he said. "Before the revolt of our North American colonies, Britain had a monopoly of the Maryland and Virginia tobacco trade. Tobacco was global big business, every bit as prosperous as your pharmaceutical industries today. Glasgow, where I was teaching, was a booming port through which that colonial tobacco flowed, and my neighbors made fortunes from plying it. If I parroted the prevailing opinion of my friends in commerce, I would have rejoiced at that wealth."

Smith sighed deeply. "But it was the fruit of African slave labor. And slavery is one of the vilest systems, selling man, woman, and child like so many herds of cattle to the highest bidder! Although never enslaved myself, I could imagine its grim and profoundly unjust effects. Despite the enormous wealth it produced for some, I denounced the system on moral and economic grounds. So, while public opinion may be ignorant, biased, and distorted, the impartial spectator is set free from such limitations."

Smith elaborated. "Even so, in the heat of the moment and overcome with passion, one's spectator could lack the desired detachment and cool judgment. That's why experience gives rise to general rules of morality, so one does not have to rely on the impartial spectator on each and every occasion."

"Rules are based on tradition," I countered, "and human tradition could perpetuate horrible wrongs."

"True, the all-wise Author of Nature has made man the immediate judge of mankind," Smith said, "but remember this—there is a higher tribunal than tradition, the tribunal of one to come." He stood, and wandered to the edge of the forest, hands clasped behind his back, looking every bit the learned professor.

"Meaning?" I asked.

"You've met the great Voltaire, so you'll appreciate his quip, 'If God did not exist, it would be necessary to invent him.'" Smith smiled. "So our happiness in this life is thus, upon many occasions, dependent upon the humble hope and expectation of a life to come, where exact justice will be done to every man. This hope and expectation is deeply rooted in human nature.

"But even here on earth," Smith continued, "by acting according to the dictates of our moral faculties, we necessarily pursue the most effectual means for promoting the happiness of mankind, and may therefore, in some sense, co-operate with the Deity to advance the plan of Providence."

"I haven't heard you mention your faith before," I said.

"You won't find me wearing religion on my sleeve," he rejoined with a quick smile. "I expect that others call me a Deist—like your heroes Washington, Jefferson, and Franklin—a believer that God created the universe and its laws, and we must use our minds to discover them. We use reason to discern the remote consequences of our actions, to foresee the advantage, or detriment, which is likely to result. Reason helps us use self-control to abstain from present pleasures or endure present pain, in order to obtain a greater pleasure or avoid a greater pain in the future. In the union of these two qualities— reason and self control—consists the virtue of prudence."

I started to interrupt but he shushed me.

"Hear me now. Prudence, when it is directed to the care of one's own fortune or reputation is never considered an endearing or ennobling virtue. Such narrow prudence can perhaps make you rich, but it is not in being rich that truth and justice would rejoice." Smith picked up some pebbles from the ground and shook them absentmindedly, by now a familiar exercise whenever he searched for the right words.

A hundred feet away in the forest we heard the crackling noise of a deer, or perhaps a wolf, shuffling along its hillside trail. Rex's ears shot up and he let out a low growl. We kept still and in a moment the night was again ours but for a whisper in the treetops. A brilliant moon dazzled overhead in this place of solitude and pure enchantment.

Smith continued with his thesis: "No, I say, there is a *superior prudence*, one which involves wise and judicious conduct directed to greater and nobler purposes than to the needs of ourselves. Superior prudence is the former narrow prudence combined with greater and more splendid virtues: with valor, with extensive benevolence, with a sacred regard for rules of justice, and with a proper degree of self-command."

"You're describing yourself, aren't you?"

He didn't hear me. "It requires the utmost perfection of intellectual and moral virtues. I say to you, *superior prudence is the best head joined to the best heart!*"

I swallowed hard. This Smith fellow was not just an intellectual icon meriting a few caricatures and clichés, he was the founder of a moral framework for living: Not just the "father" of modern economics, he was its nurturing "mother" as well— a source of clever, pragmatic intelligence, and beyond that, wisdom. How different my classes could be next fall, I mused, using the entire corpus of Smith's views, not just an amputated limb—the invisible hand.

My meditations were interrupted by another rustling, this time from the bushes directly behind Smith. Rex gave a low growl. With the slight movement of a branch, a shadowy form emerged from the woods. For a second, I imagined a bear. Then into the moonlight stepped Max Hess, pointing a gun!

I opened my mouth but no sound emerged. Oblivious to this commotion, Smith kept up his monologue. "To strive for perfect wisdom and perfect virtue—"

Hess struck Smith in the back, sending him crumpling to the ground.

"Wisdom—ha!" Hess said, now pointing the weapon at me.

Rex bounded from six feet back, leaping toward Hess's out-stretched hand. The report of the gun threw Rex reeling into the brush. He whimpered and Hess fired another shot his way.

"Bastard," I screamed, rushing toward Smith's fallen form. He was alive, breathing shallowly.

"Move!" Hess barked.

I pulled Smith along gently, using his armpits for hand-holds, his heels dragging on the ground. Hess followed, keeping the gun pointed at my belly. In his other hand Hess carried my laptop computer, which he must have taken from the cabin before following us here.

We struggled up the steep hillside to a cave on the far side of the rise. Strewn signs of a camp indicated Hess used it as a shelter. In the moonlight I could see a white van pulled up under the camouflage of over-hanging branches on a nearby logging road. He'd switched vehicles, of course. Damn it! I'd become so lax, thinking there was no way Hess could find us once we'd fled Nevada.

"How did you find us?"

"Shut up." Hess hit me in the hollow of my back, catapult-ing me into the cave. He followed, dragging Smith by the scruff of his jacket. It was cold, damp, and dark where I landed in mud, and I could feel drips of water on my aching back. Beside me I heard Smith's labored breathing. Enough moonlight fil-tered through for me to make out Hess's form positioned over us, the weapon still at his side. Replaying the scuffle outside the Opera House in Chicago, I knew he could be fast and vicious in a fight. There was little chance of disarming him in my current position. I pushed myself onto my elbows, and was starting to sit up when a boot in my chest laid me out flat.

Having established dominance, Hess squatted across from us, leaning against the cave wall. His eyes gleamed, and he seemed poised to leap. After a moment, he grabbed my laptop computer. He pressed the power button, waiting for it to boot. Since the theft of my dissertation papers, I'd kept my files pass-word protected; that was of no use now with Hess pointing a gun at me. Without difficulty he navigated through my folders, and found the one I'd completed that day with the new equations. He grunted with satisfaction, then exited the program.

He proceeded to reformat my hard drive!

I stared in astonishment. He wasn't going to steal the formula. He was going to erase every trace of it. Hess saw my look. "Yes, your formula will soon be gone, and you, too."

"Others will discover it, just as I did," I said. "You can't stop everyone."

"I don't need to."

The computer finished whirling and Hess tossed it aside.

He spoke in a whisper, his words a ramble growing in intensity and volume. A litany of evils had been done, he alleged, by an unjust society. Western "civilization" prayed to the alter of capitalism, its religious icon the Almighty Dollar. People were puppets, jerked back and forth by the invisible hand of Benjamin Franklin on the one-hundred dollar bill. Given or withheld to stifle speech and thought, dollars made everyone conform to an over-blown commercial world that makes profane what is sacred. As Hess ranted I glanced at Smith: blood oozed from a wound in his back.

"I said 'no' to the whole Spiel and your friend, the 'Great Doctor Lattimer,' attacked me for it," Hess said. "When I told the truth about Che Guevarra and the plight of the people in Bolivia, did the Great Professor listen? Did he learn? Did he try to help those who cannot help themselves? No—instead he sabotaged my scholarship. Before I knew it, I was on the street."

"You're good at playing the victim," I said, finding myself in the uncomfortable position of defending Lattimer. "There were other graduate programs; other things you could have done with your life."

"Silence!"

It was clear Hess intended to kill us, but in his madness he seemed intent on first crusading his causes. We spent the remainder of the night listening to Hess's diatribe against globalization, the evils of multinationals, and the treachery of the World Trade Organization. A swarm of bats chirped on the ceiling, and steady drops of water from underground springs completed the chorus of background noise. Hess was finally silent.

"If you're going to murder us, at least tell me how you found out about Smith," I asked.

"Finding you was a lucky coincidence," he said. "You fell from the sky. I was seeking the cell members for POP and was using the lists of other friendly organizations. And although universities have done their best to purge Marxists, there are still some gold mines ... your colleague in International Relations, Doctor Wayne Brown?"

I swore under my breath.

"Yes," he continued, "I went to Hearst College to get him into POP. Can you guess who nearly knocked me down on my way to his office? You!—walking so intently you did not watch where you were going. I recognized you instantly because I had seen you with Lattimer at the Ebbett Grill in Washington. What a wonderful chance, so I followed you to the library. You forgot to erase the computer screen, and I saw the book title by Smith that you were seeking."

It occurred to me that he was the "former student" asking about me at the library.

"My youthful looks are very handy," he said. "After a week, your friend Doctor Brown was calling to tell me about the lunch at the Faculty Club with you and this not-so-amusing fellow Doctor 'Smythe.' As I was saying, you both fell from the sky."

"The bastard," I said.

"Oh, do not be so severe. We never told him our plans for you and Mister Smith. And what about you? You left your dissertation papers in the recycling so that I could find them? That was idiotic."

He was right on that score. I was a brick-head to have imagined myself in an ivory tower in placid Fredericksburg, insulated from the "real" world of power politics and multinational muscle. Our only chance at survival was to keep Hess talking, anything to tire him out and give us a moment to take him.

"How did you find us here?" I said.

Unlike the first time I asked it, this time Hess didn't hit me. He sat back, watching with bright eyes that revealed nothing. Finally he said, "I found your picture with your girlfriend on the front page of the newspaper in Nevada. But that track was old by the time I got there. Still, I knew you would be at the WorldChemm meeting in San Francisco—you wrote that on another sheet I pulled from your recycling bin."

I cringed again.

"And while I did not know the importance of this, I also saved your brochure about cabins in Yosemite you threw away. I went to the West Coast just exactly as you must have done. Our people back in the East were very alert and they watched and they waited. Then ... we had luck." He paused to smile. "When your girlfriend started to make little trips to the house of her neighbor each other night, how so, we asked? Strange, no? She does so much baking and she always lacks flour?"

I cursed. I'd been a fool, risking Harold's and Julia's lives when I could have taken them to the safe house in Boston that Lattimer offered. I refused because of my own selfish need to exert my independence from him.

Julia—was she all right?

Hess seemed to intuit my concern. "Your girlfriend. She is very beautiful."

Anger obliterates judgment. I didn't care if Hess shot me as long as I could make him hurt first. I tensed, ready to spring. Hess stood quickly, extending the gun. "Very soon anyway, you are dead."

My anger dissipated and Hess said, "After one of your telephone meetings with your girlfriend, one of our clever members went into the house of the neighbor and stole just one thing—the portable telephone. Out in the yard he dialed *69 to make the call come back. What a surprise! Somebody at a pay phone in Yosemite Park answered."

Hess enjoyed this. "Then, for the first time I remembered the brochure about the cabins that you threw away. I should have followed that lead sooner; I could have found you in half the time. So I came to Yosemite and waited in town, watching the phone until you showed up, exactly on time like a train."

I lowered my head. Hess said, "Let me give you some advice, which will not do you any good whatsoever, but in this business to be consistent means you die. You have to do something unexpected, you must have a rigid rule not to repeat yourself. That way, you cannot become analyzed or predicted. That is why the CIA, the FBI, and Interpol have never caught me. And this is not because the bastards have not tried."

*   *   *

It was near morning.

"Why should you even believe Harold's the real Adam Smith?" I gestured at the prone figure. "He's a delusional old man. Kill me, if you must, but let him go."

Hess looked at me wearily. I thought about lunging for his gun, but he was watching intently. Finally he said, "You are forgetting my training in economics, which makes me able to puncture your deception. If he is not the real Smith, you would not waste your time with him, you would not offer to die in order to let him live. Your own actions reveal what he's worth."

I needed to do something, anything, to keep Smith alive. "But he's misunderstood," I said. "Smith doesn't glorify profits at the expense of the downtrodden. Read him yourself! I've got his books in the cabin."

"I have read Smith," Hess sighed. "It is clear he does not endorse high profits that are undeserved."

My mouth was open. "But if you knew that…"

I looked again at Hess's boyish face, and it suddenly looked twenty years older. My question must have caught him off guard for he shifted in place, looking down. In that instant I saw behind his back to the entrance of the cave: A form crouched there!

"What might have happened," Hess finally asked, "if I could have read Adam Smith so much sooner? Smith is a man who understands the world, and the real people living in it. In him—all of People Over Profit's concerns are addressed."

"You *like* Adam Smith?" I said, completely confused.

Hess's mouth had a grim twist to it. "Yes, Smith does not propound a capitalism for the sake of corporations, but rather a commerce for the sake of people. I know all this now, but only by accident. When I went to graduate school to find answers, I was made to memorize dry formulas for efficiency that do nothing to help the poor. The discipline today seems ruled by technocrats—mathematicians without a conscience."

"And your response," I said angrily, "is simply to hate, to tear down, to kill? Why not work to build something better?"

Smith, who had been lying unconscious, began to stir. I watched with peripheral vision as the crouched figure in the tunnel began moving forward slowly, covered by background noises in the cave. The figure stopped a yard from Hess's back. It was Julia!

I said to Hess, "If you *like* Smith, then why in God's name kill him?"

"Because it's too late for me," Hess replied. "I'm not starting over at my age."

A glimmer of hope came to me. "It's never too late. Groups like POP are started by well-motivated people, it's just a question of educating them."

Hess gave a laugh, an aberrant laugh. "My simpleminded, naive American! POP has now become a front, a sham, a hoax. You and this Scotsman will be worth a lot more dead to others." Hess raised the handgun to Smith's head.

I tried to keep my voice calm, but it cracked anyway. "A front for whom? What others?"

"A tool of the Russian mafia," Hess said. "Privatization of Russia's aluminum assets will make a small group of them stink-rich, but only if overseas bidders are excluded. POP was infiltrated to mobilize the public against foreign multinationals, and scare leaders into thinking political upheaval is imminent if bidding is opened from the West. I was perfect to run

POP because of my Maoist connections. That helped convince the CIA and others of POP's threat."

"But you're Che Guevarra's man!"

"I was. Even a tiger grows new stripes."

"But why? You do care about the poor!" I said.

"I don't care, anymore," he sighed. "I am sick of poverty. In a few months I will be rich enough to disappear to Bali for the rest of my life. As long as I do my part to keep the Russian aluminum industry free to be exploited. I'm not so different from you, am I? Only difference is, you lick Lattimer's boots."

Smith was awake and spoke slowly, in obvious pain. "Free does not mean 'competitive.'"

"That is it," Hess said. "With an aluminum monopoly there will be no limit to the riches for the kleptocrats running that country. It's the same old story, isn't it?"

He cocked the hammer on the gun. "With friendly faces in government," he said, "and international mergers giving companies back the market power they lost when trade was first liberalized, nobody wants Smith raising his voice against them."

Hess tightened his grip on the gun. I tried to think of something, anything to say or do. But it was too late.

Hess squeezed the trigger.

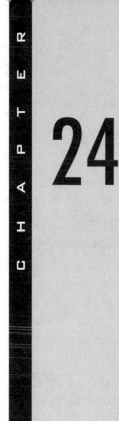

24 SAYING GOODBYE

The crash of gunshot ricocheted in the cavern. Smith lurched for Hess just as the gun fired, getting one hand on the barrel. I leapt onto Hess and swung at his throat. Hess was stronger and more agile, and in a second he threw us both off. He brought the gun up and was about fire again, pointing at Smith, when behind him Julia swung forward with a rock into the side of his head. The gun clattered into the darkness of the cave, and Hess crumpled to the floor.

Dazed, I felt Julia hugging me, then she bent over Harold.

"He's shot in the stomach," she said. Blood oozed from the wound.

We carried him down the hill to the station wagon, and gently lifted him lengthwise into the back seat. Julia crouched next to him, stuffing a handkerchief to stem the bleeding. For a moment I debated running back to the cave to tie up Hess. But those minutes could mean death for Smith. I swung instead into the driver's seat and we took off in a whirl of dust and gravel.

Despite Julia's compress, Smith's blood was leaking from his wound onto the back seat. He was conscious but dying, and the violent jostling of the station wagon made it worse.

He swallowed. "Save the tapes," he said in a hoarse whisper.

We careened down the pass at a deathly frightening speed. Several hundred pounds of camping gear lay in a spaghetti heap in the far back.

"The tapes," he said, closing his eyes.

"Forget the damn tapes!" I yelled.

In the rear view mirror I saw a smoky white van in the alpenglow of dawn a mile behind us. My old station wagon was floored, but could do little in these mountains.

"There's more," Smith whispered.

Then his head dropped, and it was the last thing he said.

"Damn!" My eyes watered. I pounded the steering wheel. "Goddamn!"

The white van gained fast; in a minute it was upon us. Hess swerved over and began to draw alongside. Luckily, a pickup truck appeared around the curve ahead, flashing lights and blaring its horn. Hess retreated and I breathed a sigh of momentary relief.

Hess's vehicle advanced again over the yellow line. No oncoming traffic stopped it from drawing near. When it was a half car-length back, I jerked the steering wheel left to cut him off. He braked in time to avoid being thrown against a cliff. Stunning scenery whirled by as I see-sawed the station wagon across the road, keeping Hess from passing. I alternately stomped the gas pedal and braked, and after a minute of this could smell smoky pads. I was no race car driver, but it was working to keep Hess back.

Without warning the road straightened and widened. The granite peaks lay behind us as we descended at break-neck pace to the valley floor. Hess had plenty of shoulder now on which to maneuver and pull alongside. He raised the pistol, pointing it at me. This was our highway duel in Maryland all over again. I slammed the brakes but they'd burned out. There was a blistering explosion, glass breaking, and metal tearing. Then all went black.

*   *   *

I woke in a fog. It was bright, too bright, and someone was caressing my face with a warm cloth. My body felt suspended in a cloud. My right eye inched open to Julia's smile. She planted a kiss on my cheek. It was clear I'd died and gone to heaven, for nothing had ever felt so wonderful as this.

"He's awake," someone said, "the morphine's wearing off."

I struggled to sit up and found myself in a cramped hospital room painted a shade of military green. A doctor and a nurse, both in uniform, stood at the foot of the bed.

I looked to my right to find Smith in the bed next to me, an I.V. solution dripping into his arm. He said, "About time you quit goofing off around here." It was no longer the voice or accent of Smith, but that of Harold.

"How long…"

"Three days," Julia said, gently straightening my sheets. "You suffered a concussion and a broken leg in the crash. Harold's doing fine; he's lost a lot of blood but the bullet just missed his kidney."

Julia could read my anxiety.

"Max Hess is dead," she said. "A truck pulled into his path, not expecting to find a van hurtling along on the wrong side of the road. Hess died instantly. The truck driver's okay, but I think you'll be wanting to buy a new station wagon," Julia said with a light-hearted grimace. "By the way, you're both at this military base under aliases. The Feds don't want POP getting another chance at you."

"But ... how did you find us?"

"Shhh—try to rest," Julia said softly.

"You saved my life." My head began to sway again.

She held the side of my face. "I planned to come out when my exhibit closed. Then my neighbor Sarah's house was burgled, and I knew POP would find you sooner than that. Sarah was terrified of staying home, so she moved to a motel; that's why no one answered the telephone. There was no way I could reach you, so I just came."

She flew to Fresno, rented a car, and arrived at the cabin a little after eleven o'clock that night. Finding my station wagon there, but the cabin ransacked, she feared the worst and began searching the surrounding woods, to no avail. She was ready to try in town when she heard whimpering from the side of the hill.

The fog from my mind lifted and I suddenly remembered. "Rex?"

She nodded. "I'm so sorry, Rich. I found him nearly dead on the trail; I held him until he was gone. He followed you as far as he could, which means he saved your life every bit as much as I did. Once I found him it wasn't hard to follow the tracks you made up the side of the hill."

✳   ✳   ✳

Later that afternoon, after lapsing into a sleep, I awoke to find myself alone again with my hospital companion. I slowly swung out of bed and steadied myself on the handrails. Putting weight on my good right leg, I gingerly hopped over by the other bed, careful to avoid the I.V. pole and other paraphernalia by it. I sat in a chair, and propped my left leg with its cast on a cushion. I looked up at the figure in the other bed on whom I'd grown to depend so much.

"You told me something, our last night at the cabin," I said, "You told me, 'There's a higher tribunal than tradition, it's the tribunal of one to come.' I've been thinking about that."

"I never said that!"

The voice was Harold's. He looked at me wide-eyed. "If you're talking to that Smith fellow, he's gone. Haven't had any dream or voices in my head since I woke up here three days ago. 'Cept for my stomach, which hurts like blazes, I feel great."

They say stress does strange things to a person. I lowered my head and tears began to fall and they kept falling. After a moment Harold reached over and put his hand on my shoulder.

25 WORLDCHEMM

WorldChemm's headquarters were located a block north of the Convention Center in San Francisco, and just a quarter-mile from the old laboratory where the company started as a materials supplier in the second world war. The old site was a company museum now, used for special events like today's Board meeting. It was no easy matter getting there, with the international trade summit in full swing at the Convention Center. In attendance were several thousand official delegates, including forty heads of state, leaders of the International Monetary Fund, the World Bank, the World Trade Organization, and numerous presidents of international businesses.

In addition to these, twenty thousand protestors occupied the city, sleeping in parks and milling about the streets. Signs and sing-a-longs separated the peaceful protestors from the extremists in raucous bands who confronted police with insults spewed over bullhorns. Protest banners unfurled over white traffic barricades in the slow drizzle. Police in black riot gear patrolled every corner, but were outnumbered by solemn protestors trying to form a human chain to block arriving delegates.

On the other side of town a coalition of non-governmental organizations, the NGO's, staged a counter-summit to detail the hidden costs of globalization—the loss of indigenous cultures, the deforestation of rainforests, the polarization of society into the super rich and super poor. Although voluntary free trade creates more winners than losers, this fact does little to assuage the injuries of those on the short end, and these groups were out to bring that home.

Feeling like I was breaking a union line, I entered a black limousine provided courtesy of WorldChemm. Lattimer was waiting in the back seat, along with several other board members.

"Hey, Burns, you made it!" Lattimer said. "Not that I was in the least worried."

Actually his face looked as if he hadn't slept for a week.

"You could've called before yesterday," he whispered, a twinge of reproach in his voice. "Helluva lot of people been looking for you."

I smiled but offered no apology.

As the others looked out the smoky windows at the throngs of protestors holding banners, Lattimer whispered again. "This better be good, Burns. My ass's all over the place covering for you."

The limousine's sticker identified it as an "official" vehicle, easing us through police checkpoints. But the very sight of a black stretch limo proved irresistible to a crowd of marchers, who in an instant opened their knapsacks and pelted us with tomatoes and raw eggs. Two patrolmen on horseback quickly dispersed them.

"Fools," Lattimer muttered. "Blaming the IMF for poverty is like blaming the Red Cross for war!"

*   *   *

WorldChemm's executive boardroom held forty chairs, with only a few empty ones as the meeting time drew near. In the audience were several Samuelson Committee members including Susan Mitchell. I gripped my presentation in my left hand. With my right hand I tapped a cane nervously against my leg cast.

Senior Vice President Milton Jones stood at the lectern to open the meeting.

"I'm sure you're all aware of Dr. Robert Lattimer's distinguished career promoting free markets worldwide. I would ask him to come forward and introduce this morning's speaker."

Lattimer strode to the microphone amidst loud applause. It was clear these bigwigs had come to see him as much as to hear me. The appeal of celebrity that surrounded the holder of the Adam Smith Chair of Economics intimidated even corporate executives accustomed to operating in the media limelight.

"Ladies and gentlemen," he said, looking down from his six foot two inch frame, "Unfettered markets can transform the world, can liberate billions of people from their shackles. The sooner this happens, the better. Many countries are listening, and indeed, this is a momentous time. The iron curtain is down—a new millennium begins!"

There was another round of applause. Lattimer gestured to me on the platform. "My protégé's model provides a means of analyzing asset market risks during this time of transition. I'm sure you're more than just a little interested in a specific application to the Russian aluminum industry. Without further ado, Richard Burns."

"Ladies and gentlemen..." my voice creaked. As intimidated as I felt, I was also at peace. For what seemed the first time in years what came out of my mouth was not only an intellectual statement, it also made sense in my heart.

"Professor Lattimer's contributions to our discipline are outstanding, and we owe him a great debt. He fought an enormous battle against the waste, the inefficiency, and the oppression of governments controlling every aspect of life. Advocates for freedom can indeed rejoice in a new world. There is little doubt that stabilizing macroeconomies, liberalizing businesses from the onerous corruption of bureaucrats, and privatizing industries run by governments—the famous 'S–L–P' approach—is in the broad vein defensible."

There were expectant smiles in the audience.

"And yet..." their smiles faded, "...and yet, this approach may miss something critical. It provides the necessary conditions, but perhaps not the sufficient conditions, for sustainable development. To leap from one extreme—that of economic despotism, as we have seen it in the Soviet bloc—to the other extreme of anarchy and 'cowboy' capitalism—without first tilling the soil with justice—can only questionably lead to long-run success. Markets are the means to an end, not the end in themselves."

There was a concerned muttering in the audience. I saw Susan Mitchell scribbling on a legal pad. My heart pounded, and a trickle of perspiration dripped inside my shirt.

"I prefer give-and-take," I said. "If you have questions—please ask." I stepped back from the microphone to search for a handkerchief.

A man in the second row raised his hand. He had a double chin and a deep, kindly voice. "Might you address the practical implications of what you're saying?"

"Of course, of course." I stepped back to the microphone. "You may be surprised to learn that a hundred years ago America's economy was more integrated with the world economy than it is today. We had freer trade in merchandise, fewer restrictions on labor immigration, and capital sought its own reward without restriction. And what happened? In the first half of the twentieth century the planet embroiled itself in two world wars and a great economic depression. It took fifty years of political struggles to reopen the world economy to where it is today."

There were nods in the audience from those few faces that I judged were in their fifties and sixties. Most of the younger crowd looked at me curiously.

I pressed on. "Isolationism can reappear—and has—just look outside the window!"

Although muted by the heavy drapes on the windows, we could hear the chanting of protestors on the street, the raucous sound of bullhorns, and the wail of sirens.

"If the next generation perceives that this corporation—and global capitalism in general," I continued, "is part of the economic problem, not part of the economic solution, they will seek redress. That is why, before it's too late, we must ourselves focus on the fundamentals of what sustains global capitalism within a civilized society." Remembering Smith's dictum on superior prudence, I added, "Any answer we offer to the next generation must satisfy their hearts as well as their minds."

The V.P. of WorldChemm interjected. "What does this have to do with that formula you've developed?"

I looked at him. "Mr. Jones, before capitalism came to England, that country had already fought numerous battles for justice. These resulted in the Magna Carta and the British Bill of Rights. Where are the institutions in today's unbridled developing markets—the places you would grow your business today—that safeguard justice and promote virtue? Think about these differences: in America we have reasonably honest courts and laws. Our most successful entrepreneurs—the Carnegies, the Rockefellers, the Dukes—endow schools, libraries, and foundations which give back to future generations. Well beyond these, we have thousands of civic groups, non-profits like the Boy- and Girl-Scouts, churches, charities, and community associations, all working to elevate the attention of society to something greater and beyond ourselves—all promoting the goal of virtue."

Around the room I saw frozen faces. Lattimer looked as if a hangnail was being pulled out at its root.

"I believe our bountiful society owes much to our stock of residual virtue," I continued. "It is a gift of our forefathers, no less than our factories and schools. Would we squander it, and fail to replenish it?"

A man stood up in the back of the room. "I represent the small shareholders here and frankly, I'm not interested in philosophizing; we're here to make a profit."

"So you should!" I said. "But a business in America does that within the context of disciplining forces. Many other societies have few of the balancing social and institutional structures we take for granted. A more complete model of development would be J–S–L–P—with *justice* a prerequisite, a cornerstone for the reforms in economic efficiency to follow— the stabilizing, liberalizing, and privatizing of markets."

Vice President Jones approached the lectern. "I can assure you, Mr. Burns, as well as the ladies and gentlemen in the audience, that WorldChemm is committed to the highest ethical standards of conduct around the world. It's true, in the past, we've been accused of lapses … we've all made mistakes. But today, for example, we are fully committed to WFCA's monitoring of human rights and environmental standards in all our workplaces worldwide."

A knowing look passed between Vice President Jones and Lattimer, and I recalled the protest banners I saw that morning on the drive in. They didn't mean anything at the time, but now their relevance appeared: "Workplace Fair Rights Association an Industry Smokescreen" and "WFCA a Sham."

Vice President Jones continued, "However, this corporation cannot, and will not, become a global police force. We operate in too many diverse markets, each with separate standards and laws for appropriate business conduct."

The audience was restless. I stepped back to the microphone. "As Vice President Jones says, there is little reason for every country to have the same environmental or labor standards—to think so ignores local preferences for putting food on the table over other values. Equally, it is unfounded to think that wages should be the same in New Delhi as they are in New York, unless the human capital, the physical infra-structure, and other inputs are the same."

There were nods around the room and the audience quieted. I withdrew a card from my pocket. "If I may, let me read something written more than two hundred years ago on the nature of competition. Adam Smith wrote:

> In the race for wealth, and honors...he may run as hard as he can, and strain every nerve and muscle, in order to outstrip all his competitors. But if he should justle, or throw down any of them, the indulgence of the spectators is entirely at an end. It is a violation of fair play, which they cannot admit of...the offender becomes the object of their hatred and indignation.

I braced and went on. "Any multinational company operating solely according to the weakest of standards overseas, may soon discover it has lost that indulgence of spectators—consumers, workers, even shareholders—thus provoking their hatred and indignation. That company could lose profits in two ways."

I wiped my face. The room was completely still. "First, Adam Smith promoted a marketplace in which consumers, not corporations, were king. With improvements in telecommunication, consumers increasingly are able to exercise their moral imaginations—to wonder about the world, to question environmental or labor standards under which products are made—to exercise their power to change the world by what they buy, and what they refuse to buy."

"It's blackmail," muttered the Vice President on the front row. "We only join those NGO certification programs to keep consumer groups off our back."

I continued: "Second, a company with very low labor standards may pass up the chance to earn greater profits through promoting higher productivity." I imagined Smith smiling as I paraphrased *The Wealth of Nations*: "Smith said the liberal reward of labor increases the industry of common people: they are more active, diligent, and expeditious than when their wages are low."

I could also see in my mind's eye Peter's company of dedicated, inventive workers, and the effect of non-monetary rewards—seeing themselves as praiseworthy for their activities on the job. I looked around the room: there were attentive faces, some even nodding approval.

"None of this is new information to those of you involved in WorldChemm's dealings overseas," I said. "While there are always a few bad apples, most large multinationals pay their overseas workers higher wages than do local firms, and pay higher wages than market conditions might dictate. Multinationals provide the potential to improve millions of lives around the world."

There was a hum in the audience and I spoke louder. "However, in carrying out their mission companies endure labor and environmental regulations which they often feel are onerous and unnecessary. We know many such rules exist to benefit only bureaucrats or to provide unfair advantage to a few—and these deserve to be dropped." This drew a smattering of applause.

"But ... it isn't always the case," I said. "Think about this: would America be as dynamic an economy if we still relied upon slave labor? Was that not, in fact, an intolerable burden? What if young children of ten still worked the mines or mills instead of working their school books? What if women were still restricted from certain jobs? Did not the laws outlawing these conditions improve our human capital, and society as a whole? Every generation must fight its own battles for justice, for deciding the rules of competition—the conventions of fair play."

I pressed on. "Some rules thus operate for the long run benefit of society, and make capitalism sustainable and more vital for future generations." I could visualize the sea otters from the Monterey aquarium, saved from near extinction by an international ban on hunting, their survival vital to restoring ocean fish stocks. "It takes moral imagination for change to happen," I declared, "and change is often bitterly opposed by business interests. Yet change is required if the torch of capitalism and freedom is to be passed to the next generation—passed to those very marchers outside this building, and to others around the globe. Each generation has its challenges, and we must think, and act, anew."

From the back of the room the self-appointed spokesman for small shareholders interrupted again. "I still want to know," he asked loudly, "what that Russian aluminum industry is going to be worth in two years."

"All right." I sighed and reached for the computer controls. "Ladies and gentlemen, the formula is here."

The lights dimmed and I clicked the console controls. In ten short slides, I presented the thrust of my dissertation. "You may not understand the math," I said, "but the bottom line is clear." The last slide contained in bold the reduced form equation of the model. There was a hush as the crowd studied it.

"Intriguing," said a woman in the front row who'd been introduced to me as a financial analyst. "It's Tobin's q-theory, with a twist."

"Wonderfully novel," said another.

"Brilliant!" someone else exclaimed.

There was a smattering of applause. "Thank you," I said. "The formula is an interesting mental exercise, perhaps even clever. But it contains little wisdom. It would be foolhardy to base long run projections on these calculations alone."

There was more rumbling in the room.

"The critical parameter, alpha, refers to productivity in the bauxite mines you hope to acquire," I said. "But how can you know about productivity unless you know how workers feel about working for you? Ladies and gentlemen, what is the Russia you would like to see in twenty years? Will you make the investments, not just in plants, but in people? Not just in training people, but in educating them?"

The financial analyst leaned over toward Vice President Jones. "This formula would substantially reduce our risk, which in any market translates into value," she said. "Without this formula, others will be forced to underbid for the Russian industry. That means we can get it for a song. In five years we could recoup our investment and be out with a sweet profit."

There were nods of approval from around the room.

I turned to Vice President Jones. "Is that your plan?"

He replied with a polished eloquence. "WorldChemm must provide proper stewardship of its shareholders' assets. Our long term strategic plans are complicated, but I can assure you we have no plans for disposition at this time."

"Hell, we've got to shut down their smelters," said the "small investor" in the back. "Russian aluminum's been flooding the market. If we owned their source of bauxite and closed their plants, we'd control sixty percent of world aluminum output. Using that formula, our share prices could triple!"

A thought jumped into my mind: Adam Smith on several occasions reviled the "mean rapacity" of merchants and manufacturers, even as he loudly heralded their indispensability to the total system. He'd warned us that seldom do people of the same industry meet together, "but the conversation ends in a conspiracy against the public, or in some contrivance to raise prices." Thus, the statement I'd just heard from the small investor was not all that unusual. It spoke to a common frustration in business—namely, that it is difficult to make a large profit when the market can't be controlled, when prices are forced downward, and the quality of products steadily improve, by unrelenting competition. This tension was the very genius of Smith's system.

Anger toward the small investor seemed out of place, for I occupied no moral high ground. It is the job of business to seek the highest return on its capital, and in so doing, send resources to the areas of greatest benefit to society. That's the role they play in Smith's system, and it would be misguided to ask them to play any other. Moreover, entrepreneurs who overcome innumerable odds and obstacles in bringing products to market deserve our reverence and respect—even as society warily guards against the potential destruction of that market system through cartels and monopolies.

"Our share prices could triple!" the man repeated, searching the room for support.

"With one small problem," I said. "Knowledge is power. Asymmetric or one-sided knowledge—the means by which you hope to gain dominance in this market—can lead to gross inefficiency and grave injustice to consumers and workers alike."

I smiled for the first time. "I won't let that happen ... which is why these equations were posted on the world wide web at eight o'clock this morning."

There was a stunned silence. Leaning on my cane, I limped down the platform stairs out of the room.

26 POSTSCRIPT

Harold Timms entered the vestibule dressed in a tailored blue suit. His face appeared years younger. Gone were the bloodshot eyes, the stooped back, the hesitant stutter. We embraced.

"You're looking great!" I said.

"Amazing what a good night's sleep will do." He smiled widely. "Well, three months of good sleep. My sister's cooking, too."

"No more hallucinations?" I asked.

"Naw. But I'm sorry to hear about your prize."

"It's all right. The Samuelson Committee would have had a hard time selecting me after what I did. I'm not losing sleep over it," I said. "Besides, I've heard it whispered, 'Funeral by funeral, the profession progresses.'"

"Let me fix your collar," Harold said, adjusting the tie strap under my morning coat.

We stood a moment at the entrance. Then we parted the doors and entered the reception hall. The Reverend was waiting and directed us where to stand. Around us were friends and family, among them Lattimer's secretary, Edda McCory, chatting with Peter Chen and Sarah Thompson. A large table dominated the center of the room, and on it rested an open cardboard box that appeared to rock and whimper. It was a gift from our guests: an eight-week-old Sheltie puppy with a green bow tie wrapped around its furry white neck.

The crowd joined their expectant eyes with mine as I looked up the staircase. With little fanfare a slender figure in white descended. It was an angel—my Julia.

As we mouthed our words of betrothal, I heard other words coming silently from inside my mind. Some might call it a chatter or a babble, a voice going non-stop in my head. It didn't bother me. It was just Smith, who had something wise to say about damn near everything.

IV

APPENDICES

*"We are the children of the Enlightenment,
and scarcely any of us would gladly
claim a different patrimony."*

—CHARLES L. GRISWOLD, JR.,
ADAM SMITH AND THE VIRTUES OF ENLIGHTENMENT

A

TIMELINE OF ADAM SMITH'S LIFE

1723   Born at Kirkcaldy, Scotland, a small seaport town oppo-
            site Edinburgh. Day of birth is unknown, but he is bap-
            tized June 5.

1726 (?)   Smith briefly kidnapped by gypsies, according to a con-
            temporary biography by Dugald Stewart.

1737–40   Attends Glasgow University, where he is a student of the
            beloved Frances Hutchinson. Received M.A. degree with
            distinction.

1740–46   Destined for service in the Church of England, he attends
            Oxford University, which turns into a low period of his
            life. He apparently suffers a temporary nervous break-
            down. He is reprimanded by his orthodox tutors for read-
            ing Hume's *Treatise of Human Nature*, and the book is
            seized. During this time, England is thrown into civil war

(1745) by the Jacobite uprising, an attempt to put the Scottish Stuart Pretender, James III on the throne of England and restore the primacy of the pope. Scots are defiled in England, and Smith no doubt experiences some of this prejudice. He rejects the church life.

1746–48   Fresh with a university education but unemployed, Smith lives in Kirkcaldy with his mother and continues his studies privately.

1748–51   Smith becomes an entrepreneur of sorts, becoming a popular freelance lecturer in Edinburgh, where he enters into a deep and lifelong friendship with the most eminent philosopher of the age, David Hume.

1751–64   Elected a professor at Glasgow University, first in the Chair of Logic and Rhetoric, then in 1752 to the Chair in Moral Philosophy. The latter subject covers natural religion, ethics, jurisprudence, and political economy. Smith reports that these years were the "most useful" and "happiest" of his life (Ross, p. xxi). In 1759 he publishes *The Theory of Moral Sentiments*. Smith rises in the university's administration, serving as vice-rector, 1761–63.

1764–66   Smith accompanies Lord Townshend's stepson, the Duke of Buccleuch, on a foreign tour as his tutor. This is a productive period, both financially and intellectually. They live in Toulouse, Geneva, and Paris, where Smith meets with luminaries from the European Enlightenment and the Physiocrats. Among these are Voltaire, Quesnay, and Turgot.

Autumn 1765—Smith and his charge leave Toulouse for Geneva, where he meets Voltaire at Ferney.

January 1766—Hume and Rousseau leave Paris for London, and Smith arrives there soon after. Smith attends the opera season, sees *Tom Jones*, and mixes in the best salons of Paris.

October 1766—The Duke of Buccleuch's brother succumbs to fever and Smith immediately returns to London.

1766–67   Smith stays in London through the winter attending to Lord Townshend's research project on the national debt, which has ballooned during the Seven Years War. Townshend by this time is Chancellor of the Exchequer, an equivalent position to Treasury Secretary in the United States.

1767–73   Living off Townshend's annuity of £300 per year, Smith returns to his birthplace in Kirkcaldy, living in relative isolation with his mother and writing *The Wealth of Nations*.

1773–77   Smith travels for extended stays in London to be near his publisher. Smith hopes, through the publication of *The Wealth of Nations* (long delayed, and finally issued March 9, 1776), to influence Parliament to avoid bloodshed over the colonies in North America. Despite his influence with MP's on both sides of the aisle, Smith fails in his attempt to win them over to the merits of free trade.

Summer, 1776—Smith returns briefly to Scotland where his dear friend Hume is dying.

1777–78   Smith returns briefly to Kirkcaldy, entering temporary retirement, and amuses himself by writing a book on the arts.

1778–90   Moves with his mother to Edinburgh, where he accepts an appointment as Commissioner of Customs for Scotland, a job he fulfills with reasonable zeal. He continues issuing new editions of his books until his death, including a substantial revision of *TMS* published in May 1790. He dies July 17 of that same year.

B SOURCE NOTES

Adam Smith was a master of "one-liners." This is hardly surprising given the fact that he began his illustrious career giving lectures on rhetoric! Readers will be delighted to explore Smith's colorful writings firsthand. For copyright purposes, all quotations from Adam Smith's works (except where noted) come from early editions that are in the public domain, namely:

TMS: *The Theory of Moral Sentiments* (London: H. G. Bohn, 1853).

WN: *An Inquiry into the Nature and Causes of the Wealth of Nations* (London: Strahan and Cadell, 1786).

The organization of these two books differs substantially. In *TMS*, the book is organized by *part*, *section*, *chapter*, and *paragraph*. In *WN*, the work is organized by *book*, *chapter*, *(part)*, and *paragraph*. These reference features are supplied below to help readers locate Smith's passages using other editions of these works. In addition, numbers in brackets [ ] provide a page cross-reference to the Glasgow Editions of these works (see Appendix C, "A Guide to the Literature"). To maintain the flow of dialogue, some of Smith's passages are paraphrased or abbreviated.

If an abbreviated citation is used below, the complete citation is listed in *A Guide to the Literature*.

PREFACE

p. xii   "It is only the teller of Ridiculous Stories...." comes from Smith's *Lectures on Rhetoric and Belles Letters,* J.C. Bryce, ed. (Oxford: Oxford University Press): p. 119. Reprinted with permission of Oxford University Press.

PART I: WEALTH

p. 1   "Every economic act, being the action of a human being..." William Letwin, *The Origins of Scientific Economics* (Methuen and Co., 1964, p. 159). Reprinted with permission.

CHAPTER 1

p. 4   Adam Smith's "harsh" voice and "big" teeth are reported in Ian Simpson Ross' biography, *The Life of Adam Smith* (1995, p. 210). Smith is reported to have been notoriously absentminded, once falling into a tar pit while discoursing on the division of labor (Ross 1995, p. 226). He liked to play with things in his hands, and he spoke at times with a stutter. Physically he was a sickly child, yet had a remarkable memory. His first love was books; his second, strawberries. A delightful biography of Smith by one of his contemporaries is Dugald Stewart's "Account of the Life and Writings of Adam Smith, LL.D." (1793), which accompanies Smith's posthumously published *Essays on Philosophical Subjects* (*EPS*).

_____ Adam Smith is generally regarded as the "father" of modern economics because his treatise, *The Wealth of Nations* (1776) became "the first major, modern theoretical orthodoxy" (Hutchinson 1988, 3). Making such a paternity claim is still a stretch, however, since Smith drew heavily on the works of others going back to Aristotle. It is thus "difficult to accept that any one person alone *could* have founded the subject" (*Ibid.*), and Smith himself never claimed to have done so.

CHAPTER 2

p. 11 The IMF is the International Monetary Fund, based in Washington, D.C. It was created in 1946 to help countries maintain a system of stable currencies so as to promote world trade. After the fixed-exchange rate system collapsed in the 1970s, the IMF became a lender to countries with balance of payments difficulties. Like most banks, the IMF requires that countries receiving loans carry out policy reforms, known here as "S-L-P." For a discussion of its sister institutions, the World Bank and WTO, see the notes to p. 251 in Chapter 25.

_____ "There ain't no such thing as a free lunch," or TANSTAAFL for short, is a famous expression in economics. It conveys the ubiquitous nature of scarcity that imposes opportunity costs on all choices. The on-line *The Jargon Dictionary* lists the originator of this expression as Robert A. Heinlein in his science-fiction classic, *The Moon is a Harsh Mistress* (1966).

p. 14 There are several organizations that present "Samuelson" awards, named for Paul A. Samuelson, the first American to receive a Nobel Prize in Economics (1970). The "Samuelson Prize" described in this book is a fictional devise, and does not refer to any actual award, current or past.

p. 15 Lattimer's professional relationship with Rich illustrates the classic concept of a "moral hazard," in which one party to a transaction has both the incentive *and* the ability to inflict costs onto another party (professors can hold up the progress of experienced graduate students in order to get more research assistance from them). In financial markets we think of "moral hazard" existing because bankers know that the government will pay off depositors if their institution fails, and bankers therefore finance riskier (but potentially higher yielding) investments.

p. 16   The Royal Governor of Virginia, Lord Dunmore, led a British fleet up the Potomac River in July 1776. At Widewater, just below present-day Quantico, they landed and burned Richland, a prominent plantation. The home was rebuilt.

p. 17   "Drambuie" is the brand name of a Scottish liqueur, its secret recipe purportedly brought to the country by Bonnie Prince Charles (Charles Edward Stuart) during the Jacobite uprising of 1745 (see notes to p. 25, Chapter 3). Drambuie was made commercially available only after 1909, so it is unlikely Smith ever tasted it.

CHAPTER 3

p. 20   For an excellent discussion of channeling, see Arthur Hastings, *With the Tongues of Men and Angels: A Study of Channeling* (Fort Worth, TX: Holt, Rinehart, and Winston, 1991).

p. 23   Adam Smith was a humble man who in his lifetime did not flaunt his LL.D. doctorate title (Stewart, *EPS*, p. 350–1n). "Call me simply Adam Smith," is how Smith instructed his publisher (*CORR*, No. 100, p. 122).

That Adam Smith might wish to set the record straight on his views is not too great a stretch. The amount and breadth of research on Adam Smith has surged dramatically in the last decades of the twentieth century (Wight 2002). Modern scholarship reveals a multifaceted Adam Smith greatly enhanced from the one-dimensional view often quoted in principles of economics textbooks. Patricia Werhane (1991, p. 3) notes that many earlier twentieth century views of Smith are "caricatures." Smith's works "display a subtlety and complexity that is at odds with the received image," agrees Vivenne Brown (1997, p. 281).

p. 24   "Economists may honor me with their lips, but not with their hearts..." is a paraphrase of the Gospel of Mark 7: v. 6–7, *The King James Bible*. Smith initially studied for a church calling, and would have known this passage.

p. 25   A discussion of Smith's English accent and the classes in rhetoric he delivered in Edinburgh can be found in J.C. Bryce's introduction to Smith's, *Lectures on Rhetoric and Belles Lettres* (*LRBL*), pp. 7–8.

_____   During the Jacobite uprising of 1745, an attempt was made to put the Scottish Stuart Pretender, James III on the throne of England and restore the primacy of the pope. Ross (1995, pp. 81 and 219) points out that Scots were disliked in England during this time of civil war. See notes to p. 17, Chapter 2.

p. 26   That excessive division of labor could make one stupid is a point Smith developed in *WN*, V.i.f.50 [781–5].

p. 27   Edgar Caye's psychic healings have been carefully catalogued by the Association for Research and Enlightenment (ARE), in Virginia Beach, Virginia (*www.are-cayce.com*).

p. 28   Helen Schucman, an assistant professor of medical psychology at Columbia University, struggled to scribe an insistent inner voice that she would later come to identify as Jesus. Her colleague at Columbia, Bill Thetford, provided support and encouragement for organizing these channelings into a book, which was published anonymously as *A Course in Miracles* in 1976.

CHAPTER 4

p. 33   That Adam Smith valued his *Theory of Moral Sentiments* (*TMS*) over his *Wealth of Nations* (*WN*) is expressed in a contemporaneous third-person account (Ross 1995, p. 408). Circumstantial evidence supports this position by noting the systematic structure of Smith's work, in which *TMS* provides the philosophical foundation, and *WN* and *Lectures on Jurisprudence* (*LJ*) fill in subject details. Smith meticulously revised, expanded, and reissued *TMS* through six editions, a fact consistent with the notion that he regarded the work highly, regardless of whether it was his favorite. Many modern scholars, however, might disagree with Smith's assessment that places *TMS* ahead of *WN*.

p. 34   "Every man is rich or poor according to the degree...." *WN*, I.v.1 [47].

p. 36   The fact that Adam Smith's works are not read routinely in economics graduate programs may come as a shock to some outside the profession. Klamer and Colander in *The Making of an Economist* (Boulder, CO: Westview Press, 1990), note that almost half of economics graduate students surveyed said that the history of economic literature was not important to their education, and over two-thirds said a thorough knowledge of the economy was not even important! The reason for this is the preeminent role of "armchair" deduction in creating highly abstract mathematical models, often devoid of empirical content or testing. While Smith used both deductive and inductive methods, he was thoroughly grounded in philosophy, history, institutions, law, and social science broadly conceived. See the notes to p. 56, Chapter 5 and p. 242, Chapter 23 for additional comments on graduate education.

_____   "Before proceeding to the economics..." This quote comes from R.H. Campbell and A.S. Skinner's introduction to the Glasgow Edition of *An Inquiry into the Nature and Causes of the Wealth of Nations* (Oxford: Oxford University Press, 1996): pp. 4–5. Reprinted with permission of Oxford University Press.

_____   "Wherein does virtue consist..." *TMS*, VII.i.1 [265].

p. 39   "Happiness consists in tranquility..." *TMS*, III.3.30 [149].

_____   "What can be added to the happiness..." *TMS*, I.iii.1.7 [45].

_____ "Do they imagine that their stomach is better..." *TMS*, I.iii.2.1 [50].

p. 42 Many details of Smith's life come from Ross' biography (for example, a discussion of Mme. Riccoboni is found on p. 210).

p. 43 Smith thought the philosopher Jean-Jacques Rousseau (1712–1778) behaved as a "rascal," as indicated in a letter Smith wrote to his best friend, David Hume, published in *Correspondence of Adam Smith* (*CORR*), No. 93, p. 112. In that letter, Smith also joked that Hume was as much a rascal as Rousseau. Hume (1711–1776) was a philosopher, historian, and diplomat, and one of the greatest figures in the Enlightenment.

The account of Smith's kidnapping by gypsies is provided in Stewart, *EPS*, pp. 269–270.

p. 44 The exact day of Adam Smith's birth is unknown, but he was baptized June 5, 1723. Given the high infant mortality rate of that time, one can reasonably surmise that his birth occurred in close proximity to this date. George Stigler and Claire Friedland, in their *Chronicles of Economics Birthday Book* (Chicago: University of Chicago Press, 1989), list Smith's birthday as June 5.

p. 45 John Maynard Keynes (1883–1946) was the twentieth century's nemesis to Adam Smith, in the sense that Keynes advocated a strong role for government policy to counterbalance what Keynes felt was the inherent instability of market forces at the macroeconomic level. Keynesian doctrines have weakened substantially since the 1970s, yet virtually all governments still adhere to Keynes's practical injunction that federal authorities should attempt to expand the economy during times of recession.

_____ "Practical men, who believe themselves to be quite exempt from any intellectual influences...." is from John Maynard Keynes's *The General Theory of Employment, Interest, and Money* (New York: Harcourt, Brace, and World, 1964), p. 383.

CHAPTER 5

p. 51   Smith endorses the temperate use of alcoholic beverages (*WN*, V.ii.K.3 [870]) and notes that abuse of alcohol results from its scarcity, not its abundance. Smith says, "People are seldom guilty of excess in what is their daily fare" *WN*, IV.iii.c.8 [492]. Smith is reported to have occasionally overindulged on wine (Ross 1995, p. 251).

p. 52   Adam Smith's life as a Commissioner of Customs is recounted in all the standard biographies. In a letter, Smith describes burning his own clothes when he discovered that they were contraband (*CORR*, No. 203, pp. 245–6). As Commissioner of Customs, Smith annually earned £500 plus £100 Salt duties, and also received a £300 pension from the Duke of Buccleuch (Ross 1995, p. 306).

——   That Smith secretly gave away much of his income to charities is reported by Stewart (*EPS*, V.4, pp. 325–6). By Stewart's account, Smith lived a modest life: His discretionary spending centered on hosting friends for simple dinners and on maintaining his "small, but excellent" library.

——   Adam Smith's name has frequently been invoked as a mantra by followers of a *laissez-faire* approach to economic policy. Smith's views are far more complex than this term might imply to modern readers. The expression is associated with the French Physiocrats, led by Doctor Francois Quesnay (1694–1774). That Smith had great admiration for Quesnay and his "sect" is indisputable; at one time Smith intended to dedicate the *WN* to him (Stewart, *EPS*, III.12, p. 304). But despite profuse admiration for the man and his system (*WN*, IV.ix.38 [678]), Smith unequivocally distances himself from Quesnay's excessively purist views (*WN*, IV.ix.28 [673–4]). Smith was willing to temper his idealism in order to achieve pragmatic goals. Jacob Viner notes, "Adam Smith was not a doctrinaire advocate of laissez faire. He saw a wide and elastic range of activity for government, and he was prepared to extend it even farther if government, by improving its standards of competence, honesty, and public spirit, showed itself entitled to wider responsibilities" (1928, pp. 153–54). See also the notes to p. 123, Chapter 12 and pp. 170–171, Chapter 16.

_____ "No government promotes the happiness of mankind..." *TMS*, IV.2.1 [187].

p. 53 Adam Smith would never have used the word "capitalism" as this word did not exist in his time. Instead, he referred to the world of "commercial society" *WN*, I.iv.1 [37]. Smith's notion of commerce consisted of small-scale craftsmen consistent with the structure of competitive markets. He was generally not in favor of large joint-stock companies, saying that these companies "scarce ever fail to do more harm than good" *WN*, V.i.e.40 [758].

p. 54 "The violence and injustice of the rulers of mankind..." *WN*, IV.iii.c.9 [493].

_____ "Institutions reflect the circumstances of society," is actually a quote from Montesquieu. Putting these words in Smith's mouth is justified by artistic license, considering Smith copied Montesquieu's plan for lectures on justice (Stewart, *EPS*, I.17, p. 274 and II.50, 294–295). Montesquieu's views on civic virtue are discussed in Gay (1966, p. 58).

p. 55 Smith's belief that society would crumble into nothing without moral precepts comes from *TMS*, III.5.2 [163].

_____ That free markets could be supplanted if they fail to garner the underlying support of society is explored in Viner (1960, p. 68): "[T]he decline of laissez faire in England, and the growth there of systematic state-interference not only with the economy as a whole, but with the free market, came largely as the result of dissatisfaction with the prevailing distribution-of-income pattern.... No modern people will have zeal for the free market unless it operates in a setting of 'distributive justice' with which they are tolerably content." Viner blames the overall decline of free markets in England on the excessive "hostility" of the nineteenth-century laissez-faire idealists to *any* interference with markets. The paradoxical result was the collapse of free markets and the rise of the welfare state.

p. 55   Ronald Coase is said to have coined the term "blackboard economics" to describe formal models having little to do with the real world (Blaug 1998). See additional reference to Ronald Coase in the notes to p. 211, Chapter 20.

p. 56   The reference to Francis Bacon and the bees comes from Gay (1966, p. 16). In terms of methodology, Bacon was an inductive scientist. Modern economists, by contrast, are largely deductive. Smith was certainly a fan of deduction, noting, "It gives us pleasure to see the phenomena which we reckoned the most unaccountable all deduced from some principle...." (*LRBL*, ii.133–4, p. 146). Smith, however, did not ascribe all power to deduction, being aware of the benefits of experimental methods. In *The Wealth of Nations*, for example, Smith mainly uses historical, institutional, and descriptive material in his analysis. It is not too great a stretch, therefore, to suggest that Adam Smith would be wary of much of what passes for modern scholarship in economics. He noted that in rhetorical communication people find "no pleasure in these abstruse deductions" and that the "practicability ... is seldom shewn in a long deduction of arguments" (*Ibid.*). In terms of his work in moral philosophy, Smith is even more clearly opposed to the deductive method: humans cannot deduce moral philosophy, but instead needed to discover it through experience. For a discussion of these issues, see the introduction to the Glasgow Edition of *WN* (p. 3).

CHAPTER 6

p. 57   That a model's prediction is more important than its underlying assumptions is an argument advanced by Milton Friedman (Nobel Prize in 1976) in, "The Methodology of Positive Economics," *Essays in Positive Economics* (Chicago: University of Chicago Press, 1953): pp. 3–43. For a short but powerful critique of this viewpoint, see Daniel M. Hausman, "Why Look Under the Hood?" in *The Philos-*

ophy of Economics: An Anthology, second edition (Cambridge: Cambridge University Press, 1994): pp. 17–21.

"All for themselves and nothing for other people..." *WN,* III.iv.10 [418].

p. 58   Karl Marx, in the 1840s, drew inspiration from Smith's ideas (Ross 1995, p. 418).

Smith's attack on landlords as ignorant and indolent is found in *WN,* I.xi [8]; their "childish vanity" is found in *WN,* III.iv.17 [422].

For Smith's passages on profit, see *WN,* I.xi.p.10 [266] and *WN,* IV.vii.c.61 [612–13].

Smith's famous passage, "People of the same trade seldom meet together..." is from *WN,* I.x.c.27 [145]. That employers collude to sink the wages of workers is discussed in *WN,* I.viii. 13 [84]. For references to the oppression of workers, see *WN* I.viii. [96].

p. 59   "No society can surely be flourishing and happy..." *WN,* I.viii.36 [96].

"...[T]he whole body of the people should share..." *WN,* I.viii.36 [96].

p. 60   Smith's "man of system" creates one of his most enduring and powerful attacks on the arrogance of dictatorship and centralized control; it painfully foreshadows the rise of communism in the twentieth century. See *TMS,* VI.ii.2.17 [233].

p. 61   "It is not from the benevolence of the butcher or the baker..." *WN,* I.ii.2 [26–27].

p. 62   "...led by an invisible hand..." *WN,* IV.ii.9 [456]. Adam Smith uses the "invisible hand" only this once in *WN;* he also uses the term once in *TMS* (IV.1.10 [184]) and once in his "Essay on Astronomy" (*EPS,* III.2, p. 49). Unfortunately, the term acquires a different meaning each time he uses it. For this reason many scholars argue that the "invisible hand" has acquired a far grander metaphorical status than Smith ever intended. For an interesting discussion of the differing interpretations, see Gramp (2000).

——— Smith believed that human nature was rife with "selfishness, stupidity, and prejudice" (Ross 1995, p. 399), but Smith does not endorse or advocate selfishness, even if some good might come of it (Ross 1995, p. xxii). "Selfish" is "sordid" (*TMS*, III.3.5 [137]) and Smith refers to "the violence and injustice of our selfish passions…" (*TMS*, III.4.2 [157]). Amartya Sen, who won the Nobel Prize in Economics in 1998, makes the point that Smith never thought that self-love, or even prudence conceived broadly, would be sufficient to create a good society; rather, he says Smith maintained the opposite view (1987, p. 23). Sen's view is supported by most modern scholarship, which concludes that *TMS* and *WN* present a unified behavioral theory. See also the notes to p. 123, Chapter 12.

——— Bernard Mandeville's famous dictum—that private *vice* creates public *virtue*—comes from his poem, *The Fable of the Bees* (1714). A beehive is kept busy and economically employed tending to each one's lust and vanity: "Thus every part was full of vice/Yet the whole mass a paradise" (2nd edition, London: Bible and Crown, 1723). Mandeville's thesis was roundly denounced by Smith as "fallacy" (*TMS*, VII.ii.4.12–14 [312–313]). Smith notes that, "[T]he notions of this author [Mandeville] are in almost every respect erroneous.…" (*TMS*, VII.ii.4.6 [308]).

——— "Human society is like a great, immense machine…" *TMS*, VII.iii.1.2 [316].

p. 63   "The sentiment of the heart from which any action proceeds…" *TMS*, I.i.3.5 [18].

——— "Every man … is first and principally recommended to his own care…" *TMS*, VI.ii.I.1 [219].

p. 64   "It is the maxim of every prudent master…" *WN*, IV.ii.11 [456].

——— "What is prudence in the conduct of every private family…" *WN*, IV.ii.12 [457].

CHAPTER 8

p. 77　　"...the skill, dexterity, and judgment of workers..." *WN*, I.intro.6 [11]. Smith's emphasis on the division of labor as a means of creating wealth is indicated by the prominent place it earns in *WN*: It is his first chapter. That the "division of labor is limited by the extent of the market" follows shortly in Chapter 3. The role of free trade is covered in many places, but readers can start in *WN*, Book IV, Chapter 2 for a critique of trade barriers.

_____　　"When the division of labor has been thoroughly established..." *WN*, I.iv.1 [37].

p. 80　　"A man's dexterity at his own trade..." *WN*, V.i.f.50 [782]. Education for the poor should be provided to counter the deleterious effects of specialization (*WN*, V.i.f.54 [784–5]).

p. 81　　That goods, not gold or silver, are the true measure of material wealth, is discussed in *WN*, IV.i.1–3 [429–430].

_____　　"The natural advantages which one country has over another..." *WN*, IV.ii.15 [458].

p. 82　　The role of government in national defense is superbly discussed in *WN*, Book V, Chapter 1, and the superiority of standing armies advocated in *WN*, V.i.a.13–23 [696–700].

_____　　In his *Principles of Political Economy and Taxation* (1817), David Ricardo (1772–1823) theorizes that *comparative* advantage in costs of production, rather than *absolute* advantage in costs (à la Adam Smith), can better explain trade. This view predominates today.

_____　　Background material on the Cumberland Highway comes from William R. Newcott, "America's First Highway," *National Geographic*, 193 (3) (March 1998), pp. 82–99. The importance of roads in opening commerce is discussed in *WN*, I.xi.b.5 [163]. That these should be supported with tolls is endorsed in *WN*, V.i.d [724].

p. 85　　For a view of organized crime in Russia, see journalist Stephen Handelman's, *Comrade Criminal: Russia's New Mafiya* (New Haven, CT: Yale University Press, 1995).

That Russian crime figures also operate in the United States is the claim of Robert I. Friedman, *Red Mafiya: How the Russian Mob Has Invaded America* (New York: Little, Brown and Company, 2000).

_____ "Society … cannot subsist among those who are at all times ready to hurt and injure one another" *TMS*, II.ii.3.3 [86].

_____ "The first and chief design of all governments…" *LJ*, i.10, p. 7.

_____ "Justice…is the main pillar that upholds…" *TMS*, II.ii.3.4 [86]. Adam Smith planned to write a book on law that would have completed his trilogy on moral philosophy (*TMS*), commerce (*WN*), and jurisprudence. Not living long enough to do so, Smith had his unfinished papers and manuscripts burned before his death rather than expose his incomplete work to the public (Stewart, *EPS*, pp. 327–8; Ross 1995, p. 404). Nevertheless, scholars have pieced together two sets of student notes that survive from Smith's lectures on jurisprudence at the University of Glasgow, and they have been published as part of the Glasgow Editions (*LJ*). In addition, readers should note that Smith already devotes considerable attention to the issue of justice in *WN* and *TMS*. Scholars find in Smith's work a concern primarily for "commutative" justice—that is, the rules of individual exchange. Having fair rules would allow for a natural system by which an equitable distribution of income and wealth could be achieved. Nevertheless, it would be wrong to think that Smith did not favor certain measures to directly achieve greater "distributive" justice—by which the state might enact laws to help the poor (e.g., fund public schooling, restrict the power of monopolies, and so on). For a discussion of these ideas, see Young and Gordon (1996).

_____ "a wealthy nation is most likely to be attacked…." *WN* V.i.a.15 [698].

_____ "The avarice and ambition of the rich…" *WN*, V.i.b.2 [709].

p. 87   "Every man, as long as he does not violate the laws of justice…" *WN*, IV.ix.51 [687].

_____   "The natural effort of every individual to better his own condition…." *WN*, IV.v.b.43 [540].

Chapter 9

p. 89   E.F. Schumacher's *Small Is Beautiful: Economics As If People Mattered* (New York: Harper and Row, 1974) became an instant classic, arguing for development from the bottom-up, rather than the top-down. The *Genuine Progress Indicator* (*GPI*) is a project of Redefining Progress (*rprogress.org/projects/gpi*).

p. 91   Smith's wonderful parable of the "poor man's son" is found in *TMS*, IV.i.8 [181].

Chapter 10

p. 103   Smith likely attended the opera season in Paris during 1766 (Ross 1995, p. 209). His comments on opera and the attributes of castrati actors are found in *EPS*, II.16, pp. 194–5. Although Smith would surely have been aware of the "Opera Wars" (between King Louis XV and his Queen over the relative merits of French versus Italian opera), this debate actually took place in the 1850s, predating Smith's attendance there (Gay 1966, p. 125, and Wilson 1972, p. 178).

p. 105   Voltaire's comic portrayal of the rich but jaded Senator Pococurante is found in *Candide* (1759). Smith was an ardent admirer of François Marie Arouet, whose pen name was Voltaire (1694–1778). A perusal of *TMS* for Voltaire's name shows the extent to which Smith read, and absorbed, his writings. Curiously, there is also a barbed reference in *Candide* to the manufacturing of pins, which later serves as Smith's now-celebrated example of the division of labor. Whether Smith's use of this example represents a tongue-in-cheek play on Voltaire, whom Smith thought to be century's greatest contemporary writer, is not known (Ross 1995, p. 399). The origin of the pin factory example is commonly attributed to a third source, volume V of Diderot's *Encyclopédie* released in 1755 (Wilson 1972, p. 236). This *Encyclopédie* was a work that Smith held in high esteem (Wilson 1972, p. 7; Ross 1995, pp. 147 and 273), and from which Smith most likely borrowed the pin factory example.

p. 107   "...the misfortunes of the greater part of men..." *TMS*, II.3.32 [150].

_____   The Milton poem on heaven and hell is from *Paradise Lost* (1674), Book 1, Line 253.

CHAPTER 11

p. 110   "The great source of both the misery and disorders..." *TMS*, III.3.31 [149].

_____   "...drives us to violate the rules either of prudence or of justice..." *TMS*, III.3.31 [149].

_____   That "vanity and superiority" are seldom consistent with tranquility is found in *TMS*, III.3.31 [150].

p. 111   The "natural" state of happiness is found in *TMS*, I.iii.1.5 [45].

_____   "Power and riches can not protect you from inclemencies..." *TMS*, IV.I.8 [183].

_____   "This disposition to admire, and almost to worship..." *TMS*, I.iii.3.1 [61].

_____   "...the candidates for fortune too frequently abandon the paths of virtue..." *TMS*, I.iii.3.8 [64].

p. 112   Gary S. Becker won the 1992 Nobel Prize in Economics in part for his work on the economics of crime (see also notes to p. 227, Chapter 22). Becker theorized that economic agents (even criminals) acted rationally to maximize utility: robbers would undertake riskier heists only if the expected payoff increases, which happens when the value of stolen merchandise rises or the probability of getting caught falls.

_____	"It is the vanity, not the ease, or the pleasure..." *TMS*, I.iii.2.I [50].
_____	"The rich man glories in his riches..." *TMS*, I.iii.2.I [50–51].
p. 113	"In what constitutes the real happiness of human life..." *TMS*, IV.1.10 [185].
_____	"The beggar, who suns himself by the side of the highway..." *TMS*, IV.I.11 [185].
_____	"If the chief part of human happiness arises from being beloved..." *TMS*, I.ii.5.2 [41].
_____	"To found a great empire for the sole purpose of raising..." *WN*, IV.vii.c.63 [613].
_____	"How many people ruin themselves by laying out money..." *TMS*, IV.I.5 [180].
_____	"...trifling conveniences which crush their possessor..." *TMS*, IV.I.8 [182–3].
p. 114	"It is this deception which rouses and keeps in continual motion..." *TMS*, IV.I.9 [183].

PART II: TRANSFORMATION

p. 117   "[K]een and earnest attention to the propriety of our own conduct..." *TMS*, VI.iii.18 [244].

CHAPTER 12

p. 122   In a letter written in April 1759, David Hume amusingly reports to Smith the "melancholy" news that *TMS* has been wildly successful in the market, playfully suggesting that such signs of applause must necessarily mean the book is worthless (*CORR*, No. 31, pp. 33–36). The jocular affection between Smith and his best friend makes for delightful reading.

p. 123   Adam Smith was living in Europe during 1764–66, much of this time in France. During this period he met Anne-

Robert-Jacques Turgot (1727–1781), a philosopher-turned-politician who was attempting to advance principles of reform. Smith got along well with him, as testified by a letter Smith wrote to Hume in July 1766 (*CORR*, No. 93, p. 113). Smith also spent time in Paris with Quesnay (see notes to p. 52, Chapter 5 and pp. 170–171, Chapter 16). When King Louis XVI (1754–93) came to power as a young man in 1774, he inherited a daunting feudal economic system of internal monopolies and political control firmly in the hands of the clergy and large landowners. Louis XVI appointed Turgot as Controller-General of Finance in August 1774. Among Turgot's first reforms was the attempt to abolish internal tariffs and guilds that stifled competition. He also proposed granting Protestants full civil rights, and proposed rewriting the tax code to make landowners share the fiscal burden. Vociferous opposition from the nobility and the clergy led to Turgot's dismissal in May 1776 after serving less than 2 years (Gay 1966, p. 167). The French revolution came in 1789, and the King brought to trial. He was beheaded on January 21, 1793.

_____ That Enlightenment tracts were censored in France is a point made by Ross (1995, p. 200).

_____ Most modern assessments of Smith (see "A Guide to the Literature," below) address the issue known as "Das Adam Smith Problem," a theory put forward in Germany in the nineteenth century that said Smith's two books were philosophically incompatible, and reflected different stages of Smith's intellectual development. This theory has been thoroughly debunked (for example, see Brown 1997).

p. 126 "Paradoxes amused Smith…" In Smith's "Essay on Astronomy" *EPS*, IV.34, p. 75, he notes that persons of learning naturally love paradoxes. Smith is also reported to have used paradoxes as a teaching tool (Stewart, *EPS*, p. 275).

_____ Smith's wonderful insights into the "natural" long run price in a market, and the impact on profits and other factors of production, are covered in Chapter VII of the *WN* [72–81].

p. 130   "Before we can feel much for others...." *TMS*, V.2.9 [205].

p. 131   "...if you have no fellow-feeling for the misfortunes I have met with...." *TMS*, I.i.4.5 [21].

CHAPTER 13

p. 134   Thomas Hobbes (1588–1679) wrote that without a strong central authority, a war of man against man would ensue. The result would be "No arts, no letters, no society, and which is worst of all, continual fear and danger of violent death, and the life of man solitary, poor, nasty, brutish, and short." *The Leviathan* (1651), Part i. Chap. xviii. For Smith's reaction, see *TMS*, VII.iii.i.1 [315] and the next note.

p. 135   In contrast to Hobbes, Smith writes that man was born with an "original desire to please" others; going beyond that, humans are born with a desire of becoming what "ought" to be approved of, namely, of becoming worthy of praise (*TMS*, iii.2.6–7 [116–117]. Smith's view would not necessarily conflict with modern evolutionary psychology, since the latter doctrine, unlike *homo economicus*, does not consider humans to be rationally calculating machines. Rather, evolutionary psychology explains current behavior as evolutionarily successful, including innate strategies of benevolence and altruism. My thanks to Erik Craft for making this distinction for me.

_____   That humans are controlled by selfish instincts at the *genetic* level is a case made by Dawkins (1976).

p. 136   "How selfish soever man may be supposed..." *TMS*, I.I.1 [7].

_____   "...the greatest ruffian, the most hardened violator of the laws of society..." *TMS*, I.I.1 [7].

p. 138   "Those who are fond of deducing all our sentiments..." *TMS*, I.i.2.1 [13].

_____ Smith argues that sympathy "enlivens joy and alleviates grief" *TMS*, I.i.2.2 [14].

_____ Affection is nothing other than "habitual sympathy" *TMS*, VI.ii.1.7 [220].

_____ When Smith says love is a "ridiculous" passion of the imagination (*TMS* I.ii.2.1 [31]), he appears to be referring to overidealized romantic love, or even lust—the state of being "in love" in which one's intellectual faculties are impaired. This passion can play an important role in developing other positive passions, however, as indicated in *TMS*, I.ii.2.1 [32].

p. 139 The innocent man in Toulouse that Smith refers to (*TMS*, III.2.11 [120]) is Jean Calas (born 1698), a Protestant merchant whose son converted to Catholicism in order to acquire a position in law. The son subsequently hanged himself. In the religious persecution that followed, Calas was convicted of murder in his son's death, then summarily executed by most painful means in 1762. The apparent judicial prejudice in the case prompted widespread European appeals for justice, led by Voltaire. In 1765, a new panel of judges reviewed the evidence and posthumously exonerated Calas. This episode led to judicial reforms in France and to a movement for religious tolerance.

CHAPTER 14

p. 144 It is doubtful that Adam Smith would agree on the extent to which modern economists maintain the strict division between "normative" and "positive" economics. According to Alasdair MacIntyre in *After Virtue: A Study in Moral Theory* (Notre Dame, IN: University of Notre Dame Press, 1997), such a dichotomy marginalizes meaning and value in the quest for science. I am indebted to Jim Halteman for clarifying this point.

_____ Smith's kind and gentle nature was characterized by bouts of melancholy (Ross 1995, p. 414).

CHAPTER 16

p. 163 Adam Smith did not play poker, but he did play whist, a precursor of modern-day bridge.

p. 165 Rousseau's paranoia and his ingratitude to Hume (and others) is recounted in a letter Hume sent to Smith in 1767 (*CORR*, No. 111, pp. 133–136). Hume befriended Rousseau and found him a financial sponsor in England. However, Rousseau's mental illness apparently caused him to resent his circumstances, and to suggest that Hume had conspired to diminish his status.

p. 168 Rousseau did not aspire to a utopian world in nature. Rather, in *Emile*, Rousseau develops the idea that a child should be allowed to learn from his passions and experiences before being subjected to books and theories; a child's first reading should be of *Robinson Crusoe*. On the whole, the benefits of civilization exceed the costs, according to Rousseau. The attention to Rousseau's "noble savages" may be a misunderstanding of his views (see Gay 1966, p. 62), yet it is a misunderstanding of which Smith may be guilty. Smith says Rousseau paints "the savage life as the happiest of any" (*EPS*, "Letter to the Edinburgh Review, p. 251).

_____ The Rousseau quote, "As soon as one man needs the assistance of others..." is a paraphrase of Smith's view of Rousseau system (*EPS*, "Letter to the Edinburgh Review," p. 252).

_____ "...more capable of feeling strongly than analyzing accurately," is what Smith wrote about Rousseau in his essay on "Imitative Arts," found in his *Essays on Philosophical Subjects*, W.P.D. Wightman and J.C. Bryce, eds. (Oxford: Oxford University Press), p. 198. Reprinted with permission of Oxford University Press. It is unlikely Smith knew Rousseau personally (Ross 1995, 212).

p. 169 David Hume's probable affair with the Contesse de Boufflers is recounted by Ross (1995, p. 212). The line, "My words are virtuous...my actions not so," is a paraphrase of what Ross records the Contesse wrote when contemplating her adultery with Hume.

——————

"Am I beau to no one but my books?" is a paraphrase of what Smith is said to have once told a friend when showing off his library. Adam Smith's romantic attachments have been alluded to at various points, yet very little is actually known of them. Ross' biography (1995, pp. 213–214) discusses the little evidence there is on this subject. Smith apparently had deep affections for a young woman from Fife during Smith's early years there. While Smith traveled as a tutor in France, several French women were smitten with him, including a French Marquise, but Smith apparently avoided these entanglements to fall head-over-heels in love with a married English woman. Given her marital situation, the love was unrequited, and Smith was beside himself, so much so that others in his company amused themselves at Smith's expense. The last mention of any romantic liaison was during Smith's final years, when he was a Custom's Commissioner in Edinburgh. According to his biography, he fell "seriously" in love with a woman known only as "Miss Campbell." She and Smith were reportedly great opposites, which may suggest why nothing ultimately came of this relationship.

p. 170

Quesnay's *Tableau Économique* (1758) is generally credited with providing the first numerical macroeconomic model. Yet, the Physiocratic insistence on a "natural state" that was opposed to manufacturing, and the apparent pomposity and arrogance with which Quesnay's followers presented their views, led many such as Hume, Voltaire, and Rousseau to detest the Physiocrats. Smith was warm in his personal regard for Quesnay, yet clearly aloof from his dogmatism. Smith supports the general view of a harmonious natural order, and the Physiocrat's overzealousness is by inference only a minor error in their system. Its "capital error," according to Smith, lay in representing as "unproductive" the labors of artisans, merchants, and manufacturers (*WN*, IV.ix.28 [674]). See also notes to p. 52, Chapter 5, p. 123, Chapter 12, and p. 171, Chapter 16.

p. 171   That the Physiocratic view is "mysticism masquerading as science" comes from Gay (1966, p. 104).

_____   That Quesnay's system, with all its imperfections, was the "nearest approximation to the truth" is flattery found in *WN*, IV.ix.38 [678]. Yet Smith, in a nod to Quesnay's medical abilities, uses the analogy of the human body to show that Quesnay's insistence on perfection and purity is excessive: Smith says the body preserves "the most perfect state of health under a vast variety of different regimes" and, by analogy, so does the political economy (*WN*, IV.ix.28 [674]).

CHAPTER 17

p. 174   "Better to risk saving a guilty man than to condemn an innocent one" is from Voltaire's *Zadig* (1747), Chapter 6.

_____   Voltaire was jailed at the Bastille twice, once in 1717–18 for 11 months, allegedly for writing a stinging satire of the French Regent, and again briefly in 1726, to keep him from dueling with a nobleman. In the latter case Voltaire was released to exile in England. Life in the Bastille was probably not all that bad: pens and paper, good food and wine, and friends were allowed.

_____   "The greatest good for the greatest number" is the Utilitarian philosophy of Jeremy Bentham (1748–1832).

p. 178   "An innocent man, brought to the scaffold..." *TMS*, III.2.11 [119–120].

p. 179   Smith recounts Rousseau's thesis as, "[W]e have nothing but a deceitful and frivolous exterior; honour without virtue, reason without wisdom, and pleasure without happiness" (*EPS*, "Letter to the Edinburgh Review," pp. 253–4).

_____   "His pride is as hard as the hump of a camel" is a paraphrase of Voltaire's *Letter to Pansophe* (cited in Winwar 1961, p. 309).

CHAPTER 18

p. 181   The ingratitude of Rousseau is expressed in a letter from Hume to Smith in 1767 (*CORR*, No. 111, pp. 133–136) and is also recounted in Ross (1995, p. 211). See also notes to p. 165, Chapter 16.

p. 184   Adam Smith was zealous in attempting to prevent or shorten the "long, expensive, and ruinous war" in the English colonies in America (*CORR*, Appendix B, p. 380, and Ross 1995, p. 295). Smith recoiled at "the madness of modern war" as recounted in his obituary (*LRBL*, Appendix 1, p. 228). Smith's *Wealth of Nations* was certainly read with great interest in the rebellious American colonies. See, for example, the letter Governor Thomas Pownall wrote to Smith from Richmond, Virginia, on September 25, 1776 (*CORR*, Appendix A). George Washington also owned a copy of the book, although in a later edition (Alan Krueger, "Rediscovering 'The Wealth of Nations'," *The New York Times*, August 16, 2001).

_____   "The rulers of Great Britain ... amused the people with the imagination that they possessed a great empire..." (*WN* V.iii.92 [946–947]). Even though Smith may have favored union with America, he was politically astute enough to be aware that Great Britain, for reasons of special interests and pride, would not peacefully give up the colonies, regardless of any net loss they produced (*WN*, IV.vii.c.66 [616–617]).

_____   Smith's support of a constitutional union with America is recorded in a memorandum entitled, "Smith's Thoughts on the State of the Contest with America, February 1778" (*CORR*, Appendix B). For an excellent discussion see Andrew Skinner, "Mercantilist Policy: The American Colonies" in Skinner (1996).

p. 185   For a fascinating account of Virginia's "founding fathers" and their international trade concerns, see Woody Holton, *Forced Founders: Indians, Debtors, Slaves, and the Making of the American Revolution in Virginia* (Chapel Hill: University of North Carolina Press, 1999). For

Smith's discussions on the tobacco trade, see notes to p. 234, Chapter 23.

PART III: VIRTUE

p. 189   "Superior prudence ... is the best head joined to the best heart" (*TMS*, VI.i.15 [216]).

CHAPTER 19

p. 193   Smith's broad definition of "sympathy" is found in *TMS*, I.i.1.5 [10].

p. 195   Smith discusses the "impartial spectator" throughout *TMS*. A good starting place for readers is Part I and especially the beginning to Part III. That humans desire to be praiseworthy is covered extensively in Part III, Chapter II.

p. 196   The "authority" of our internal "judge" is found in *TMS*, III.3.1 [134].

_____   That our eyes deceive us is found in *TMS*, III.3.1–2 [134–135].

_____   "...the selfish and original passions of human nature..." (*TMS*, III.3.3 [135]).

_____   The story of China being swallowed by an earthquake comes from *TMS*, III.3.4 [136–137].

p. 197   "...our passive feelings are almost always sordid and selfish...." (*TMS*, III.3.4 [137]).

p. 200   "...prompts the generous upon all occasions, and the selfish upon many...." (*TMS*, III.3.4 [137]).

_____   "The man of the most perfect virtue...." *TMS*, III.3.35 [152].

_____   "Hardships, dangers, injuries, misfortunes...." *TMS*, III.3.36 [153].

CHAPTER 20

p. 203   The concept of "moral imagination" and its importance for business has become an important avenue of research. Kenneth Boulding (1969), in his Presidential Address to the American Economic Association, discusses the necessity of having "Economics as a Moral Science." See also Werhane (1999).

p. 205   The character Peter Chen is loosely based upon Michael Miller, co-founder and vice president of Evenstar Company. Michael graciously permitted use of some of his story and words here. Other quotes come from the organizational transformation movement in business (see, for example, Hawken 1987). The notion that business is an adventure in human development comes from Österberg (1993).

p. 207   That corporate social responsibility may be good for business is an argument made by the Business for Social Responsibility (*www.bsr.org*), Pfeffer (1998, 1994), and many others. If true, this would not necessarily conflict with Milton Friedman's injunction that the social responsibility of a corporation is to make as much profit for its shareholders as possible—see Friedman's *Capitalism and Freedom* (Chicago: University of Chicago Press, 1962), p. 133.

p. 211   Information on sea otters can be found on the website for the Monterey Aquarium (*montereyaquarium.com*). The phrase "tragedy of the commons" was brought into popular usage by Garrett Hardin's article of that title in *Science* 162 (December 13, 1968): 1243–1248.

_____   Ronald H. Coase won the Nobel Prize in 1991 for his article, "The Problem of Social Cost," *Journal of Law and Economics* 3(1) (1960): pp. 1–44, in which he explains the impact of property rights and transactions costs on externalities like pollution. See also notes to p. 55, Chapter 5.

Chapter 21

p. 214   The staggering rise of Silicon Valley's "dot.com" businesses in a bubble that eventually burst, can to some extent be explained by Adam Smith's ideas. Investors might not behave as rationally as some economic models might predict, as Smith noted when he said that mankind has a great capacity for self-deception, which is the source of "half of the disorders of human life" (*TMS*, III.4.6 [158]). See also Robert J. Shiller's *Irrational Exuberance* (Princeton, NJ: Princeton University Press, 2000).

p. 216   "The customer comes first? Not really. The employee comes first…. There's no way to instill a positive customer service ethic before you embody a positive employee ethic. Responsiveness in, responsiveness out." This quote comes from Paul Hawken, *Growing a Business* (New York: Simon and Schuster, ©1987), p. 197. Reprinted with permission of Simon and Schuster.

p. 220   That a worker would work better in good spirits than disheartened is a paraphrase of *WN*, I.viii.45 [100–101].

p. 221   "Prudence, benevolence, and justice…" *TMS*, IV.iii.1 [237].

Chapter 22

p. 224   "The beggar, who suns himself by the side of the highway…" *TMS*, IV.I.11 [185].

p. 225   Trust arises from shared moral values, and Smith writes that businessmen prefer to keep their business local, since trust lowers transactions costs and reduces risk: "He can know better the character and situation of the persons whom he trusts…" *WN*, IV.ii.6 [454]). For a modern view, see Fukuyama (1993).

p. 227   Gary S. Becker (see also notes to p. 112, Chapter 11) and Theodore W. Schultz (Nobel Prize in Economics in 1979) played important roles in developing and measuring the returns to investments in human capital.

A number of organizations have attempted to broaden the focus of economic research into the social and moral realms. Among the oldest of these is the Association for Social Economics (ASE), which has been in existence since 1941. ASE's constitution identifies social economics as, "...the reciprocal relationship between economic science and broader questions of human dignity, ethical values, and social philosophy" (Elliott 1996, pp. 15–38). A more recently formed organization is the Society for the Advancement of Socio-Economics (SASE), founded in 1989.

_____ See J.S. Coleman, "Social Capital in the Creation of Human Capital," *American Journal of Sociology,* 94 (Suppl.), 1988, pp. S95–S120.

CHAPTER 23

p. 231 Scientific discovery is spurred by "wonder, surprise, and admiration," according to Smith's "Essays on Astronomy," *EPS*, Intro 1, p. 33. Rich's discovery of the "formula" while on a hike would likely not be seen as unusual by Smith.

p. 234 "Before the revolt of our North American colonies..." (*WN* IV.iv.5 [500]). Smith discusses the tobacco trade at various other places in *WN*. For example, Smith notes that Britain annually bought about 96,000 hogsheads (shipping casks) of tobacco from Virginia and Maryland. Domestic consumption in Britain accounted for only 14,000 hogsheads, leaving 82,000 to be reexported to Europe at great profit to merchants and bankers (*WN*, II.v.34 [372–373]). Smuggling in this trade was immense, as recounted by C.R. Fay, *The World of Adam Smith* (New York: Augustus M. Kelley, 1966): pp. 42–47. See also notes to p. 185, Chapter 18.

_____ "...to sell them, man, woman, and child, like so many herds of cattle..." (*TMS*, VII.ii.1.28). Smith discusses slavery at several other places. He notes, paradoxically, that slaves are treated better in authoritarian states than in free republics (*WN*, IV.vii.b.54–55 [586–588]).

_____ "...man the immediate judge of man..." (*TMS*, 3.2.31 [130]).

p. 235 "If God did not exist, it would be necessary to invent him" is from Voltaire's, "Epistle to the author of the book, The Three Imposters" (1768).

_____ "...the humble hope and expectation of a life to come...." *TMS*, 3.2.33 [132]. Despite this flowery rhetoric, most scholars do not think Smith held to the orthodox Christian view of a life hereafter (Ross 1995, p. 406). Smith was critical of organized religion (especially the Church of Rome), arguing that the historical privilege and power of clergy put their private interests in conflict with "liberty, reason, and happiness" (*WN*, V.i.g.24 [803]). Smith, like Voltaire and many others of the Enlightenment, was probably a Deist; Hume was an atheist.

_____ "[B]y acting according to the dictates of our moral faculties..." (*TMS*, III.5.7 [166]).

_____ That we use reason to discern the remote consequences of our actions is found in *TMS*, IV.a.6 [189].

_____ "Prudence ... directed merely to the care of one's own health...." (*TMS*, VI.i.14 [216]).

_____ "...it is not in being rich that truth and justice would rejoice..." (*TMS*, III.5.8 [166]).

p. 236 "[Superior prudence] is the best head joined to the best heart..." (*TMS*, VI.i.14 [216]).

_____ "...perfect wisdom and perfect virtue..." (*TMS*, VI.i.14 [216]).

p. 242 "...mathematicians without a conscience..." Max Hess' criticism of graduate education in economics is supported, to some degree, by the American Economics Association's own Commission on Graduate Education, which warned that programs were producing "too many *idiot savants*, skilled in technique but innocent of real economic issues" (Anne O. Krueger et al., "Report of the

Commission on Graduate Education in Economics," *Journal of Economic Literature* 29(3) 1991, p. 1044–1045). Interested readers may also wish to consult the critiques of several other influential authors: Blaug (1998) and Heilbroner and Milberg (1996). These criticisms are likely having beneficial impacts on the curriculum and methodologies currently taught in economics graduate programs according to Colander (2000). See notes to p. 36, Chapter 4 and p. 56, Chapter 5 for additional comments on graduate education in economics.

_____ For a discussion of Russian organized crime, see notes to p. 85, Chapter 8.

CHAPTER 25

p. 251   The World Trade Organization (WTO) began functioning in 1995 to monitor international trade agreements and to resolve trade disputes. The WTO is a more powerful organization than the one it succeeded, the General Agreement on Tariffs and Trade (GATT). GATT provided a mechanism for multilateral trade negotiations following World War II. The World Bank, with equity provided by member countries, raises funds on world capital markets and makes loans for development projects. The World Bank and the IMF often work together to establish terms of economic restructuring before loans can be made. See also notes to p. 11, Chapter 2).

p. 252   "Blaming the IMF for poverty..." is a paraphrase of Michael Moore, general director of the World Trade Organization, quoted in Martin Crutsinger, "IMF pledges more debt relief for poorest countries" Monday, April 17, 2000 (The Associated Press, *seattlep-i.nwsource.com/national/meet17.shtml* accessed April 14, 2001). Reprinted with permission of The Associated Press.

p. 254   That the nineteenth century was more globalized than the twentieth century is a view held by many economists and backed by numerous statistics. For further discussion, see Streeten (2001).

p. 255 The English Bill of Rights was enacted by Parliament in 1689. It included a Declaration of Rights, which limited the powers of government.

p. 256 In order to forestall consumer criticism, many multinationals are using Non-Governmental Organizations (NGOs) to certify as to the labor and environmental standards in their operations overseas. That this has produced some negative consequences is an idea developed by Ottaway (2001).

p. 257 "In the race for wealth, and honors...he may run as hard as he can...." (*TMS*, II.ii.2.1 [83]), emphasis added.

_____ "The liberal reward of labor..." See *WN*, I.viii.44 [99–101] for Smith's discussion of why paying workers higher wages leads to an increase in productivity.

p. 258 The notion that successful capitalism requires attention to institutional development and to a system of laws and regulations has been widely noted in the academic literature. Adam Smith argues, for example, that employers are far more likely to be able to collude in setting regulations, and that "When the regulation, therefore, is in support of the workman, it is always just and equitable...." (*WN* I.x.c.61 [157–158]).

_____ On the broader issue of how institutions aid market development, see the World Bank's, *World Development Report 2002: Building Institutions for Markets* (NY: Oxford University Press, 2002). For the impact on financial markets, see Alan Greenspan's speech, "The Virtues of Market Economies," June 10, 1997 (available online at the Federal Reserve Board).

p. 259 James Tobin won the Nobel Prize in 1981. His "q-theory" formula is constructed by taking the ratio of the market value of a company to its reproduction costs.

p. 260 "...the mean rapacity ... of merchants and manufacturers..." (*WN*, IV.iii.c.9 [492]).

_____ "but the conversation ends in a conspiracy against the public..." (*WN*, I.x.c.27 [145]).

CHAPTER 26

p. 264   "Science progresses funeral to funeral," is a paraphrase of a quote attributed to Paul Samuelson by Stanley Fischer, "Samuelson's Economics at Fifty: Remarks on the Occasion of the Anniversary of Publication," *Journal of Economic Education, 30*(4) (Fall 1999): 363. The quote may also be a paraphrase of German physicist Max Ernst.

APPENDICES

p. 265   "We are the children of the Enlightenment...." Charles L. Griswald, *Adam Smith and the Virtues of Enlightenment* (Cambridge: Cambridge University Press, 1999): p. 2. Reprinted with permission of Cambridge University Press.

C A GUIDE TO THE LITERATURE

ADAM SMITH'S COLLECTED WORKS

A definitive collection of the works and correspondence of Adam Smith was undertaken by Glasgow University to celebrate the 1976 bicentenary of *The Wealth of Nations*. The "Glasgow Editions" and associated volumes were published in hardcover over the period 1976–83 by Oxford University Press and are the proper starting place for any interested scholar. The six titles were subsequently made accessible in quality paperback editions from the Liberty Fund (Indianapolis, IN) and are highly recommended. Only the first two of these titles were published during Smith's lifetime (as indicated by the dates in brackets). The six Glasgow Edition titles and their abbreviations are:

TMS: *The Theory of Moral Sentiments.* 1976 [1759]. D.D. Raphael and A.L. Macfie, eds. Smith's revised sixth edition of *TMS* was released just a few weeks before his death in 1790.

WN: *An Inquiry into the Nature and Causes of the Wealth of Nations.* 1976 [1776]. Two volumes. R.H. Campbell and A. S. Skinner, eds. The *WN* went through four editions during Smith's lifetime, with the last one appearing in 1786.

EPS: *Essays on Philosophical Subjects.* 1980 [1795]. W.P.D. Wightman and J.C. Bryce, eds. This volume was published posthumously in 1795, and contains a number of Smith's important essays on science, the arts, and metaphysics, the most notable of which is Smith's "Essay on Astronomy." It also contains the interesting contemporaneous biography of Smith by Dugald Stewart, "Account of the Life and Writings of Adam Smith, L.L.D."

LRBL: *Lectures on Rhetoric and Belles Lettres.* 1983 [1963]. R.L. Meek, D.D. Raphael, and P.G. Stein, eds. These are a student's notes of lectures given by Smith at the University of Glagow.

LJ: *Lectures on Jurisprudence.* 1978 [1896/1978]. R.L. Meek, D.D. Raphael, and P.G. Stein, eds. These are two sets of student notes of lectures given by Smith at the University of Glagow.

CORR: *Correspondence of Adam Smith.* 1977. Ernest Campbell Mossner and Ian Simpson Ross, eds. In addition to letters, this volume contains important documents such as Smith's memorandum on the rebellion in the American colonies.

The Liberty Fund maintains an excellent *electronic* library of Smith's *WN* and *TMS*, which makes it easy to search for topics or phrases (*www.econlib.org*). For those who would like just a taste of Smith's writings, there are several other options. First, peruse the Annotations section of this book to locate some of Smith's interesting and controversial passages. Several other books provide annotated excerpts:

Heilbroner, Robert L. 1986. *The Essential Adam Smith* (New York: W.W. Norton and Co.).

Heilbroner, Robert L. 1996. *Teachings from the Worldly Philosophy* (New York: W.W. Norton and Co.).

Ryan, Edward W. 1990. *In the Words of Adam Smith: The First Consumer Advocate* (Sun Lakes, AZ: Thomas Horton and Daughters).

BIOGRAPHIES OF ADAM SMITH

Ross, Ian Simpson. 1995. *The Life of Adam Smith* (Oxford: Clarendon Press, 1995). This is the definitive modern biography.

Rae, John. 1895. *Life of Adam Smith*. This was the standard biography in the field for a hundred years.

Stewart, Dugald. 1795. "Account of the Life and Writings of Adam Smith, LL.D." This short and very readable biography is contained in Smith's posthumously published *Essays on Philosophical Subjects*, which is Volume III of the Glasgow Editions (see above).

Muller, Jerry. 1993. *Adam Smith: In His Time and Ours* (Princeton, NJ: Princeton University Press). This is a fascinating account of the times during which Smith wrote.

Heilbroner, Robert L. 1986. *The Worldly Philosophers: The Lives, Times, and Ideas of the Great Economic Thinkers*, sixth edition (New York: Touchstone Books, 1986). For a short introduction to Smith's life and times, consider this classic.

SELECTED SCHOLARSHIP ON ADAM SMITH

The scholarship on Adam Smith is voluminous and apparently never-ending. Over the period 1981–97 alone, there were almost 3,000 journal articles citing Adam Smith's works. On average, more than 200 new cites to Smith appear every year (Wight, 2002). Recent articles and books on Smith span the academic disciplines—business, economics, law, political science, philosophy, psychology, public policy, and sociology—areas in which Smith possibly continues to illumine pathways.

The items below are useful for exploring Smith the man and his place in economics and the social sciences. Many other fine books and articles deserve mention but unfortunately were precluded due to space limitations. Items with an asterisk (*) indicate literature reviews or assessments of Smith containing additional citation sources.

*Black, R.D. Collison. 1995 [1976]. "Smith's Contribution in Historical Perspective," in Mark Perlman and Mark Blaug, eds., *Economic Theory and Policy in Context: The Selected Essays of R. D. Collison Black* (Aldershot, UK: Edward Elgar).

*Brown, Vivienne. 1997. "'Mere Inventions of the Imagination': A Survey of Recent Literature on Adam Smith," *Economics and Philosophy, 13*(2) (October): 281–312.

Brown, Vivienne. 1994. *Adam Smith's Discourse: Canonicity, Commerce, and Conscience.* (London: Routledge)

Fitzgibbons, Athol. 1995. *Adam Smith System of Liberty, Wealth, and Virtue: The Moral and Political Foundations of the Wealth of Nations* (NY: Oxford University Press).

*Fry, Michael (ed.). 1992. *Adam Smith's Legacy: His Place in the Development of Modern Economics*, (London: Routledge) pp. 1–14.

Gramp, William D. 2000. "What Did Smith Mean by the Invisible Hand?" *Journal of Political Economy, 108*(3), pp. 441–464.

Griswald, Charles L. 1999. *Adam Smith and the Virtues of Enlightenment* (Cambridge: Cambridge University Press).

Hutchinson, Terence. 1988. *Before Adam Smith: The Emergence of Political Economy, 1662–1776* (New York: Basil Blackwell).

Muller, Jerry Z. 1993. *Adam Smith in His Time and Ours: Designing the Decent Society* (New York: The Free Press).

*Recktenwald, Horst Claus. 1978. "An Adam Smith Renaissance anno 1976? The Bicentenary Output—A Reappraisal of His Scholarship," *Journal of Economic Literature 16*(1), 56–83.

Rothschild, Emma. 2001. *Economic Sentiments: Adam Smith, Condorcet and the Enlightenment* (Cambridge, MA: Harvard University Press).

Skinner, Andrew S. 1996. *A System of Social Science: Papers Relating to Adam Smith,* second edition (Oxford: Clarendon Press). This is an outstanding collection of essays by one of the leading experts on Smith.

*Tribe, Keith. 1999. "Adam Smith: Critical Theorist?" *Journal of Economic Literature, 27*(2): 609–32.

Viner, Jacob. 1960. "The Intellectual History of Laissez Faire," *Journal of Law and Economics* 3: pp. 45–69.

Viner, Jacob. 1928. "Adam Smith and Laissez Faire," in J.M. Clark et al., *Adam Smith, 1776–1926* (Chicago: University of Chicago).

Werhane, Patricia H. 1991. *Adam Smith and His Legacy for Modern Capitalism* (New York: Oxford University Press).

West, Edwin G. 1990. *Adam Smith and Modern Economics: From Market Behavior to Public Choice* (Brookfield, VT: Edward Elgar).

*West, Edwin G. 1988. "Developments in the Literature on Adam Smith: An Evaluative Survey," in William O. Thweatt,, ed., *Classical Political Economy: A Survey of Recent Literature* (Kluwer Academic Press, 1988): 13–43.

*West, Edwin G. 1978. "Scotland's Resurgent Economist: A Survey of the New Literature on Adam Smith," *Southern Economic Journal, 45*(2) (October): 343–69.

*Wight, Jonathan B. 2002. "The Rise of Adam Smith: Articles and Citations, 1970–97" *History of Political Economy* (forthcoming, Spring).

Wight, Jonathan B. 1999. "Will the Real Adam Smith Please Stand Up? Teaching Social Economics in the Principles Course," in Edward J. O'Boyle (Ed.), *Teaching the Social Economics Way of Thinking*, Mellen Studies in Economics, Vol. 4 (Lewiston, NY: The Edwin Mellen Press): 117–139.

Young, Jeffrey T. 1997. *Economics As a Moral Science: The Political Economy of Adam Smith* (Cheltenham, UK: Edward Elgar).

Young, Jeffrey T. and Barry Gordon. 1996. "Distributive Justice as a Normative Criterion in Adam Smith's Political Economy," *History of Political Economy, 28*(1): 1–25.

ECONOMICS AS A "SOCIAL," "PHILOSOPHICAL," OR "MORAL" SCIENCE

Below are books and articles dealing broadly with economics as a social, philosophical, or moral science. Also included are critiques of overly formal economics and items relating to psychology and biology.

Ben-Ner, Avner and Louis G. Putterman (Eds.). 1998. *Economics, Values, and Organization* (New York: Cambridge University Press).

Ben-Ner and Louis Putterman. 2000. "Values Matter," *World Economics* 1(1) (January-March): 39–60.

Blaug, Mark. 1998. "Disturbing Currents in Modern Economics," *Challenge* (May–June).

Boulding, Kenneth E. 1969. "Economics as a Moral Science," *American Economic Review, 59*(1): 1–12.

Brittan, Samuel and Alan Hamlin, Eds. 1995. *Market Capitalism and Moral Values* (Brookfield, VT: Edward Elgar).

Brockway, George P. 1991. *The End of Economic Man: Principles of Any Future Economics* (New York: Harper and Row).

Colander, David. 2000. "New Millenium Economics: How Did It Get This Way, and What Way is It?" *Journal of Economic Perspectives, 14*(1) (Winter): 121–132.

Coleman, J. S. (1988). "Social Capital in the Creation of Human Capital," *American Journal of Sociology, 94* (Suppl.), S95–S120.

Coughlin, Richard M. (ed.). 1991. *Morality, Rationality, and Efficiency: New Perspectives on Socio-Economics.* (Armonk, NY: M.E. Sharpe, Inc.)

Dawkins, Richard. 1990. *The Selfish Gene* (Oxford: Oxford University Press).

Ekins, Paul, ed. 1986. *The Living Economy: A New Economics in the Making* (London: Routledge).

Elliott, John E. 1996. "Can Neoclassical Economics Become Social Economics?" *Forum for Social Economics, 26*(1) (Fall): pp. 15–38).

Elster, Jon. 1989. *The Cement of Society: A Study of Social Order* (Cambridge: Cambridge University Press).

Etzioni, Amitai. 1988. *The Moral Dimension: Toward a New Economics* (New York: The Free Press).

Flexnor, Kurt F. 1989. *The Enlightened Society: The Economy with a Human Face* (Lexington).

Frank, Robert H. 1996. "Do Economists Make Bad Citizens?" *Journal of Economic Perspectives, 10*(Winter): 187–192.

Frank, Robert H. 1988. *Passions Within Reason: The Strategic Role of the Emotions* (New York: Norton).

Frank, Robert H. 1987. "If Homo Economicus Could Choose His Own Utility Function, Would He Want One with a Conscience?" *American Economic Review, 77*(4) (September): 593–604.

Frank, Robert H., Thomas D. Gilovich, and Dennis T. Regan. 1993. "Does Studying Economics Inhibit Cooperation?" *Journal of Economic Perspectives, 7*(Spring): 159–171.

Fukuyama, Francis. 1993. *Trust: The Social Virtues & The Creation of Prosperity* (New York: The Free Press).

Goleman, Daniel. 1995. *Emotional Intelligence* (New York: Bantam, 1995).

Hausman, Daniel M. 1992. *The Inexact and Separate Science of Economics* (Cambridge: Cambridge University Press).

Hausman, Daniel M., and Michael S. McPherson. 1996. *Economic Analysis and Moral Philosophy* (Cambridge, Cambridge University Press).

Hausman, Daniel M. and Michael S. McPherson. 1993. "Taking Ethics Seriously: Economics and Contemporary Moral Philosophy," *Journal of Economic Literature, 31*(June): 671–731.

Hayek, Frederick von. 1984. "The Origins and Effects of Our Morals: A Problem for Science," in Chiraki Nishiyama and Kurt R. Leube, eds., *The Essence of Hayek* (Stanford: Hoover Institution Press): 318–30.

Heilbroner, Robert L. 1988. *Behind the Veil of Economics: Essays in the Worldly Philosophers*. (New York: W.W. Norton and Company).

Heilbroner, Robert, and William Milberg. 1996. *The Crisis of Vision in Modern Economic Thought* (Cambridge, UK: Cambridge University Press).

Horgan, John. 1995. "The New Social Darwinists," *Scientific American* (October 1995): 174–181.

Kuttner, Robert. 1996. *Everything for Sale: The Virtues and Limits of Markets*. (New York: Knopf).

Lutz, Mark A. and Kenneth Lux. 1988. *Humanistic Economics: The New Challenge* (Bootstrap Press).

MacIntyre, Alasdair. 1997. *After Virtue: A Study in Moral Theory* (Notre Dame, IN: University of Notre Dame Press).

Mansbridge, Jane J., ed. 1990. *Beyond Self-Interest* (Chicago: University of Chicago Press).

Marwell, G. & R. E. Ames. 1981. "Economists Free Ride, Does Anyone Else?" *Journal of Public Economists, 15*: 295–310.

McCloskey, Donald. 1994. "Bourgeoise Virtue," *American Scholar,* 63(2) (Spring): 177–191.

McKee, Arnold F. 1987. *Economics and the Christian Mind* (New York: Vantage Press).

Myers, Milton. 1983. *The Soul of Modern Economic Man: Ideas of Self-Interest* (Chicago: Chicago University Press).

Nelson, Robert H. 1991. *Reaching for Heaven on Earth: The Theological Meaning of Economics* (Savage, MD: Roman and Littlefield).

Phelps, E. S. 1973. Introduction to *Altruism, Morality, and Economic Theory* (New York: Russel Sage Foundation).

Piore, Michael. 1995. *Beyond Individualism* (Cambridge: Harvard University Press).

Powelson, John P. 1998. *The Moral Economy* (Ann Arbor: University of Michigan Press).

Putnam, R. D. (1993). "The Prosperous Community: Social Capital and Public Life," *American Prospect*, *13* (Spring): 35–42.

Putnam, R. D. (1995). "Bowling Alone: America's Declining Social Capital," *Journal of Democracy,* 6(1): 65–78.

Rabin, Matthew. 1998. "Psychology and Economics," *Journal of Economic Literature,* 36(1): 11–46.

Sen, Amartya. 1987. *On Ethics and Economics.* (Oxford: Blackwell).

Swedberg, Richard. 1987. *Economic Sociology* (London: Sage).

Wilson, James Q. 1993. *The Moral Sense* (NY: The Free Press).

THE NEW PARADIGM TRANSFORMATION IN BUSINESS

The items below address social and ethical concerns in business. Most (but not all) are by writers and business leaders who support the new organizational transformation paradigm view, but it would be a mistake to categorize these writings. They entail a broad spectrum of views, many of which could be contradictory.

Adams, John D., ed. 1984. *Transforming Work: A Collection of Organizational Transformation Readings* (Alexandria, VA: Miles River Press).

Arrow, K. J., (1993). "Social Responsibility and Economic Efficiency," in T. Donaldson & P. H. Werhane, eds., *Ethical Issues in Business* (Englewood Cliffs, NJ: Prentice Hall): pp. 255–266.

Blanchard, Kenneth, et al. 1997. *Managing by Values* (San Francisco: Berrett-Koehler).

Block, Peter. 1993. *Stewardship: Choosing Service over Self-Interest* (San Francisco: Berrett-Koehler).

Bolman, Lee G., and Terrence E. Deal. 1995. *Leading with Soul: An Uncommon Journey of Spirit* (New York: Jossey-Bass).

Bracey, Hyler, et al. 1993. *Managing from the Heart* (Atlanta, GA: Heart Enterprise).

Chappel, Tom. 1994. *The Soul of a Business: Managing for Profit and the Common Good* (New York: Bantam).

Dehler, Gordon E. and M. Ann Welsh. 1994. "Spirituality and Organizational Transformation," *Journal of Managerial Psychology,* 9(6): 17–26.

Gioia, Joyce L., and Roger E. Herman. 1998. *Lean and Meaningful: A New Culture for Corporate America.* (Oakhill Press).

Harman, Willis, and Maya Porter, eds. 1997. *The New Business of Business: Sharing Responsibility for a Positive Global Future* (San Francisco: Berrett-Koehler).

Hawken, Paul. 1987. *Growing a Business* (New York: Simon and Schuster).

McCormick, Donald W. 1994. "Spirituality and Management," *Journal of Managerial Psychology,* 9(6): 5–8.

Morris, Tom. 1997. *If Aristotle Ran General Motors: The New Soul of Business* (Henry Holt and Company).

Österberg, Rolf. 1993. *Corporate Renaissance: Business as an Adventure in Human Development* (Mill Valley, CA: Nataraj Publishing).

Peale, Norman Vincent, Kenneth Blanchard, and Norman Peale. 1996. *The Power of Ethical Management* (New York: Ballantine).

Pfeffer, Jeffrey. 1998. *The Human Equation: Building Profits by Putting People First* (Cambridge, MA: Harvard University Press).

Pfeffer, Jeffrey. 1994. *Competitive Advantage through People* (Cambridge, MA: Harvard University Press).

Ray, Michael and John Renesch. 1994. *The New Entrepreneurs: Business Visionaries for the 21st Century* (San Francisco: Sterling and Stone).

Ray, Michael and Alan Rinzler, eds. 1993. *The New Paradigm in Business: Emerging Strategies for Leadership and Organizational Change* (New York: Tarcher/Perigee).

Werhane, Patricia. 1999. *Moral Imagination and Management Decision-Making* (New York: Oxford University Press).

INTERNATIONAL ECONOMIC ISSUES AND INSTITUTIONS

The following items are helpful for providing a context for the backlash against globalization that manifests itself in peaceful protests and in violent acts. They are listed topically, starting with general overviews first. Both sides of the issue are presented.

Micklethwait, John, and Adrian Wooldridge. 2000. *A Future Perfect: The Essentials of Globalization* (New York: Crown). This is an excellent overview of globalization by two journalist for *The Economist* magazine.

Streeten, Paul. 2001. "Integration, Interdependence, and Globalization," *Finance and Development, 38*(2) (June): 34–37. This article explains the relative level of globalization today as compared to 100 years ago.

Roberts, Russell. 2001. *The Choice: A Fable of Free Trade and Protectionism*, 2nd edition, (Upper Saddle River, NJ: Prentice-Hall). This provides an excellent overview of David Ricardo's theory of comparative advantage in the format of an academic novel.

Krueger, Anne O. 1998. "Whither the World Bank and the IMF?" *Journal of Economic Literature, 36*(4): 1983–2020. An insider's view of the role of two major multilateral financial institutions, the World Bank and the International Monetary Fund (IMF).

Stiglitz, Joseph. 2000. "The Insider: What I Learned at the World Economic Crisis," *The New Republic* (April 17): 56–60.

Fischer, Stanley. 1998. "The Asian Crisis and the Changing Role of the IMF," *Finance and Development, 35*(2) (June).

Danaher, Kevin, ed. 2001. *Democratizing the Global Economy: The Battle Against the World Bank and the International Monetary Fund* (Monroe, ME: Common Courage Press). For views strongly opposed to the World Bank and IMF, see this book and the Web site "50 Years Is Enough: U.S. Network for Global Economic Justice," (*www.50years.org/*) which is a coalition of some two-hundred organizations working to transform or eliminate the World Bank and the IMF.

Ottaway, Marina. 2001. "Reluctant Missionaries," *Foreign Policy* (July/August 2001): 44–54. This article argues that imposing on multinationals to advance environmental or human rights agendas creates its own set of problems.

THE ENLIGHTENMENT

The articles and books below proved helpful in placing Adam Smith within the intellectual history of his times.

Commager, Henry Steele. 1977. *The Empire of Reason* (New York: Anchor Press).

Gay, Peter. 1966. *Age of Enlightenment* (New York: Time Incorporated).

Lukes, Steven. 1995. *The Curious Enlightenment of Professor Caritat* (London: Verso).

Tarnas, Richard. 1991. *The Passion of the Western Mind: Understanding the Ideas that have Shaped Our World View* (New York: Ballantine).

Wheelwright, Philip. 1959. *A Critical Introduction to Ethics* (New York: Odyssey Press).

Wilson, Arthur M. 1972. *Diderot* (New York: Oxford University Press).

Winwar, Frances. 1961. *Jean-Jacques Rousseau: Conscience of An Era* (New York: Random House).

D

A GUIDE FOR INSTRUCTORS

Saving Adam Smith speaks to contemporary topics covered in a variety of courses in economics, business, philosophy, and related disciplines. Specifically, the book addresses economic theories and business ethics within the context of practical examples and applications, suitable for both principles and advanced courses, in the following topics:

Wealth creation and trade:

- Opportunity cost
- Specialization of labor
- The gains to trade
- Diminishing returns
- The role of prices and profits in allocating resources
- The "invisible hand"
- Human capital formation

- Savings and capital accumulation

Market failure and the role of the state:

- Monopoly
- Public goods, for example, public education, highways
- Moral hazards
- Government failure
- Tragedy of the commons

Structural reform in emerging markets:

- Stabilization, liberalization, and privatization of markets
- Inequality in structural reform
- The rise of oligarchies in Latin America, Russia, and elsewhere
- Sustainable development
- Corruption

Moral foundations of capitalism:

- Is wealth the source of happiness?
- The Enlightenment as a foundation for democracy and capitalism
- The role of justice as a prerequisite for sustainable development
- Distinction between self-interest and selfishness
- How a moral conscience develops: Smith's "impartial spectator"
- Role of the "invisible hand" in markets *and* morals

Business management and ethics:

- The role of values in business management
- Adam Smith and human resource development
- Organizational transformation
- The role of social capital and trust in production
- Labor and environmental certification programs in international trade

E ACKNOWLEDGMENTS

Adam Smith stands at the forefront of this effort, towering over any other person with a claim to this book. Were it not for the wit, wisdom, and unending insights that flowed from his scribe's pen 200 years ago, I would have no book. My growing affection for Smith, stirred by his profound works, made the writing of *Saving Adam Smith* a joyful labor of love. A second major debt is owed to the legion of modern scholars who over the past thirty years profoundly transformed our knowledge of, and appreciation for, Adam Smith, and made his writings both accessible and understandable to a modern audience (see *A Guide to the Literature*).

The production of this novel was a thoroughly collaborative effort: literally hundreds of students, and scores of colleagues, friends, and family members read early drafts and made large and small suggestions for improvements. Any errors remain solely mine. Drafts of the book were used in Principles of Economics, Economic Development, and MBA International Economics classes. My deep thanks to all those students who participated, among which I particularly thank Rodrigo Pinto, Jason Savedoff, Jason Farrelly, Dan Gertsacov, Brandt Portugal, Matias Sacerdote, and Andrew Olson.

Numerous colleagues at the University of Richmond and elsewhere took a turn at educating me on subjects ranging from the Enlightenment to the New Business Paradigm. Especially helpful were Clarence Jung, Erik Craft, Ted Luellen, John Treadway, Scott Davis, Tom Bonfiglio, and Richard Coughlan. Andrea Maneschi provided helpful encouragement and contacts in the field of History of Thought, and Bill Thweatt, my first teacher in the field, inspired me on how exciting it could be. Maria Merritt provided insights on David Hume. Joanne Ciulla gave helpful advice on publishing, and Deans Randolph New and David Leary funded a faculty reading group on Adam Smith. Dean Karen Newman supported the effort in various ways, including covering research expenses for copying, travel, and other overhead items. Sue Hopfensperger, who manages departmental matters, provided cheerful assistance at all stages of manuscript preparation.

Scholars of Adam Smith played a critical role as outside reviewers. These included Jeffrey Young, Jerry Muller, and Patricia Werhane. Andrew Skinner generously served as an unofficial reviewer, providing several helpful suggestions, as did James Halteman in that same role. John (Mort) Morton and Peter Dougherty likewise provided strong encouragement. To all of these I owe a great debt. From the business community, Rolf Osterberg and Michael Miller (see also the notes for p. 205, Chapter 20) provided valuable insights for the business paradigm explored. Darby Williams and Robin Nakamura gave excellent feedback on management issues in a Silicon Valley start-up business. My thanks and appreciation to these generous folks. Friends and family members also provided abundant moral support as well as excellent editorial suggestions. These readers included JoJo Wight, Jody Wight, Pickett and Tom Viall, Rod and Allison McNall, Tom Davey, and Jack and Renee

Fiedler. Dan Davis helped scout locations on a cross-country trip across America; it is unlikely that a more congenial and interesting companion could be found for such a trip!

Bill Beville, Regional Acquisition Editor for Prentice Hall, showed immediate enthusiasm for the project and was very helpful getting it reviewed by others up the chain of command. Timothy Moore, Vice President of Prentice Hall PTR, wins my eternal gratitude for seeing the book's potential and for providing outstanding material and moral support for its completion. Gretchen Comba provided helpful editorial assistance early on, and Joe La Zizza provided excellent final editing. Scott Suckling and Anne Garcia were patient and able project managers. Russ Hall and Russell Roberts both played the valuable role of fiction editors, and I am greatly indebted to them for suggestions that strengthened the novel's argument, its scope, its plot, and its characterizations. Russell Roberts deserves a special, additional thanks. A few years ago he wrote a wonderful novel about international trade (*The Choice: A Fable of Free Trade and Protectionism*) which served as an inspiration. Before *Saving Adam Smith* was more than just an outline, Russ willingly shared his time, ideas, and encouragement, for which I remain deeply grateful.

Early research and writing of this book took place while I was on sabbatical during 1997–98; gracious acknowledgment is made to the University of Richmond for that release time. Bill and Nancy Rhodenhiser assisted with my sabbatical transition to California, and Randy and Bonnie Linde graciously provided a home away from home. During my sabbatical, office support and a stimulating environment were provided by the Institute of Transpersonal Psychology (ITP) in Palo Alto, California, a graduate school of psychology (including moral psychology). There is much in that setting that I think Adam Smith would find congenial, and I am grateful for the support of the outstanding faculty and students. In particular, I would like to thank Jim Fadiman, Arthur Hastings, Michael Hutton, and Steve Sulmeyer for their contributions to this project.

Finally, it is no surprise that the greatest help has come from my wife, Jean McNall Wight, who lived with me and the book for 4 years. She assiduously read the manuscript in its entirety several times, making copious suggestions. The book would not be what it is without her touch on nearly every page. The book is dedicated to her. Thank you.

ABOUT THE AUTHOR

Jonathan B. Wight was born in Washington, D.C., and grew up in Africa and Latin America. He teaches economics and international studies in the Robins School of Business at the University of Richmond.